Marketing in Tourism, Hospitality, Events and Food

A Critical Approach

Second Edition

Craig Hirst and Richard Tresidder

(G) Goodfellow Publishers Ltd

 Published by Goodfellow Publishers Limited,
Woodeaton, Oxford, OX3 9TJ
http://www.goodfellowpublishers.com

British Library Cataloguing in Publication Data: a catalogue record for this title is available from the British Library.

Library of Congress Catalog Card Number: on file.

ISBN: 978-1-910158-30-2

 Design and typesetting by P.K. McBride, www.macbride.org.uk

Cover design by Cylinder

Printed byBaker & Taylor, www.baker-taylor.com

Contents

About the authors

Dr Craig Hirst is Senior Lecturer in Food Marketing at the Sheffield Business School, Sheffield Hallam University. He is interested in the socio-cultural aspects of food marketing and consumer behaviour, and particularly how meaning is attributed in the marketplace.

Dr Richard Tresidder is a Lecturer in Marketing at Keele University. Richard Holds a Doctorate in the semiotics of tourism and is particularly interested in the socio-anthropology of tourism, hospitality, events and food and how these experiences are represented in marketing texts.

Acknowledgements

I would like to thank Emmie for all support and understanding during the production of this book.

RT

Faye, Ralph and Felix, thanks for allowing me the time to work on this project. Once again your patience has been immeasurable.

CH

Additionally we would like to thank Tim and Sally at Goodfellow Publishers for their continued support in producing this second edition.

1 Introduction

On the theme of marketing in tourism, hospitality, events and food

■ Introduction

The first edition of this book was motivated by a lecture series presented by the two authors at the Sheffield Business School. These lectures aimed to provide a critical framework for students to apply their previous marketing knowledge to the marketing of tourism, hospitality, events and food (THEF). During this time, although there was a large body of critical and conceptual marketing literature being produced outside of the sector, there wasn't a definitive text that reflected these debates and brought together a critical framework in which to surround the study of marketing of THEF experiences that could be recommended to students; we therefore took the opportunity to write one ourselves. This second edition continues our quest to introduce a critical consumer-orientated approach to the study of marketing and practice in our sectors, and as a result updates the ideas and examples introduced in the original. The book also adopts a new structure through the addition of three new chapters (2,3 and 4) which, with the inclusion of Chapter 5, introduce and position its critical approach.

■ Why this book is needed

The study of tourism, hospitality, events and food (THEF) has a long tradition of academic development, which has mixed together management theory and concepts with theories from the social sciences. This multi-disciplinary approach is reflected in the majority of THEF university courses and has given rise to many special interest groups that have produced knowledge in these areas. This has created a critical approach to the contemporary study and analysis of THEF. However, the theoretical development of marketing in the subject area has not kept pace, and has largely developed around marketing practice and general marketing concepts and theory, rather than developing a critical understanding of the marketing process within these sectors more specifically. The sectors covered by this book form both a significant element of the service economy and a critically important role in the lives of consumers. Consumers use tourism, hospitality, events and food as markers of their lives; they save hard to escape for a couple of weeks and justify working hard to engage in what is fundamentally a significant component of their lived experience. While we introduce a diversity of ideas about marketing in this second addition, and hope to stimulate a debate about the nature of marketing and consumption in our sectors in general, the ideas in this publication are not to be considered as a replacement for traditional approaches. Therefore this work should be seen and treated as a complementary text, to be used alongside the more management-orientated texts that constitute the recommended reading on most courses in our field. Ultimately the purpose of this book is to provide critical insight into many of the perspectives and theories that inform aspects of marketing practice such as segmentation, targeting and positioning, and specifically the role of THEF marketing in creating meaning and value for consumers.

Due to the critical nature of this text, this book doesn't simply draw inspiration and ideas from the academic debates that surround and inform contemporary marketing theory and practice, it also plumbs a wide range of other academic disciplines for insight and understanding. So while traditional and emerging theories of marketing feature heavily in the arguments developed in this book, the areas of consumer research, sociology, social theory, anthropology, and cultural studies, also play a major part. This multi-disciplinary approach enables the marketer to adopt a holistic understanding of their role and practice, linking together business studies and the social sciences; the result is to create an inclusive, creative and rigorous approach to the field of study. The ability to understand the world we live in, in respect of the wants, needs, desires and aspirations of the consumer, and their relationship to tourism, hospitality, events and food, is fundamental to being a successful practitioner in these sectors. That is to say, the adoption of a reflexive approach to marketing which is informed by a critical understanding of the marketing process and the nature of customers and consumption will provide the THEF marketer with a set of theoretical and conceptual tools that will enhance their practice and operational effectiveness.

The dominant approach to marketing that you see duplicated in nearly all generic marketing texts and marketing programmes serve to reproduce the marketing paradigm that is embedded in notions of economic and psychological exchange. There is much value in these texts and this general approach as they ground our understanding of marketing on the whole, as well as provide industry-relevant data and case studies. In addition, and perhaps most importantly, they also focus attention on the key function of *value*, which is central to the marketing process and practice in general. This being the case, as you will see as you delve into this book, these approaches have limitations, and we feel that they work to obscure what is really in play and at stake in THEF marketplace transactions. There are a few exceptions to this exchange approach of course. Of particular note, is:

1   The work of Consumer Culture Theory (CCT) researchers (see Arnould & Thompson, 2005; Thompson, Arnould & Gielsr, 2013) who collectively acknowledge that marketing and consumption are located within a broader framework of socio-cultural practices; and

2   The work developing from the Service Dominant Logic (SDL) school of thought (e.g. Vargo & Lusch, 2004), which amongst

other things acknowledges that markets and value are co-created through the interactions between various marketplace actors.

However these alternative approaches are in the minority and often sit on the margins of the discipline; infrequently taught in marketing and THEF programmes. Accordingly, in recognition of this, this book aligns with the philosophy and themes identified by the CCT and SDL traditions, and their ideas are explored throughout this text. As you may come to appreciate in reading through the chapters, the benefits of adopting a more socially and culturally aware approach, alongside ideas that consumers are active agents in the marketing process enables the marketer to understand that other factors and agents come into play in creating the meaning, value and experiences that are central to the consumption of their products.

■ How to use this book

This book provides a critical analysis of the marketing process and as such should be used alongside more traditionally orientated marketing texts. The theory developed here does not supersede the work of these traditional theories and approaches, but complements them by offering a number of alternative perspectives which collectively provide greater understanding of the marketing process. Additionally, the book provides insight into the particular and unique nature of tourism, hospitality, events and food marketing in the form of experience marketing. This is of particular importance, as the consumption of THEF is extraordinarily rich in social, cultural and individual significance. In order to effectively market, or promote, such experiences it is important to understand how this significance is both embedded and created in contemporary consumer society. As such, there are certain themes that run throughout the book that inform the agenda for the critical marketing of THEF and understanding its consumption, these include:

- Value creation
- Culture and the production of socio-cultural meaning
- Consumer motivations and value

- Market place meanings and values
- Market place resources and practices
- Ethics and morality

Structure and outline of chapters

This book provides a critical introduction to customer-based marketing within the sector, and the structure and content of the chapters will take you on an academic journey that builds towards a manifesto for the effective marketing of tourism, hospitality, events and food. As such the remainder of the book is organised as follows:

Chapter 2 (*THEF Marketing and the Exchange of Value*) locates the concept of THEF marketing within current mainstream marketing theory and practice. Although this book offers an alternative or complementary approach to contemporary marketing practice, it is important to recognise that much of the literature has been motivated or has emerged from these central and traditional marketing debates. In this respect this chapter, documents and explains the central concepts and processes integral to traditional theories of THEF marketing, which are premised upon the idea that marketing is transaction orientated and built around exchange relationships. It is important that we understand this dominant approach and philosophy of marketing, if only to use it has a backdrop to compare and contrast the other approaches that we introduce and explore later in this text.

Chapter 3 (*Marketing as Interaction and Service*) introduces a philosophy and approach to THEF marketing that significantly challenges the assumptions and logic of the exchange perspective and offers a broadened view of the marketing process. Fundamentally it shows that consumers are recast as active players in value creation rather than being mere targets of marketing activity, and documents the ways in which they engage in complex forms of consumption to co-create personalised forms of value. As a result of this switch in thinking, this chapter argues that marketing practitioners are being de-centred from their privileged role as value creators, to a role that is more in tune with being facilitators of value creation processes. In explaining this conceptual shift, this chapter outlines many of the constructs and assumptions that support this turn in thinking. In particular it examines the constructs of co-creation and multi-dimensional consumer value, and shows how important the concept of interaction is to value creation. We close by arguing that while the exchange perspective provides an important foundation for thinking about THEF marketing, in essence it obscures the true relationship between consumers and producers, and in order to improve practice, marketers must understand the important and varied roles that consumers play in the marketing process.

Chapter 4 (*Marketing and THEF Consumption as a Socio-Cultural Process*) introduces the reader to the socio-cultural perspective of marketing and demonstrates how important meanings and values are to THEF marketing and consumption, and how these underlie a range of consumer goals and projects. This chapter also explores the ways in which the meanings of products and experiences are co-created and produced between the actions and activities of a range of actors in the THEF marketplace. In addition, in our review of this approach we draw further attention to the creative and productive roles of consumers by examining how they achieve their own peculiar and unique goals through their interactions with the symbolic properties of the THEF marketplace.

Chapter 5 (*Putting the Experiences into Experience Marketing*) explores how experience marketing must differ from the norm. It achieves this by examining how tourism, events, hospitality and food fulfil such a significant role in contemporary society, culture and the economy in general. This chapter also explores the sociological and cultural foundations of the experiences provided by these sectors, and how consumers relate to, and engage with them as part of their everyday lived experience. Concepts that are central to THEF experiences are defined and described and we argue that in relation to these, their marketing requires special attention. Just as tourism, hospitality, events and food reflect social and cultural movements, so should its marketing.

1

Chapter 6 (*Consumer Resources and THEF Experiences*) acknowledges both the service dominant and cultural perspectives of marketing, which together recognise that marketplace meanings, value and experiences are created through the consumption process rather than through the actions of the marketer per se. This deviates from the dominant view that expresses that value and meaning is exchanged through transactions, and at the point and moment of purchase. Accordingly the focus of understanding consumers from the point of being discrete market segments that display a set of characteristics which together will constitute their consumption preferences and patterns, switches to one in which we analyse the consumer resources that are brought to bear and integrated with market place resources in the creation and production of valuable and meaningful THEF experiences. This is essential knowledge in the THEF sectors, where consumers are seen to engage in protracted and complex interactions and relationships with the marketplace.

Chapter 7 (*Marketing and Identity*) examines how consumption patterns are used by consumers to define their position within society and to locate them in relation to differentiated social groups. The choices consumers make about the products they consume are central to this process, as the food we eat, the destinations we visit, the events we attend and how we consume them become social markers of who we are, or want to be. The significance of this is manifold as our tastes and consumption practices locate us within consumption groups or tribes, and conversely exclude us from others. Understanding group membership and the dynamics integral to these, provide an alternative means of segmenting or targeting potential markets, thereby offering a more nuanced approach to this critical marketing function. This compliments more traditional approaches such as demographic, socio-economic and psychographic traditions.

Chapter 8 (*The Semiotics of THEF Marketing*) demonstrates how THEF marketing draws upon a range of signs, images and themes to convey and produce products that resonate meaningfully with the consumer. This process creates a language of experience that can be defined as a semiotic convention or approach. By examining various aspects of marketing across our sectors it is possible to identify a semiotic language that is utilised by marketers and the various conventions and meaning systems that they draw upon. As marketers it is important that we understand these conventions and semiotics more generally, as by doing so we will be able to tailor and construct products and marketing materials that consumers find more appealing and valuable. The chapter closes with an examination of the power implications of meaning-based approaches to marketing practice.

Chapter 9 (*Interpreting Marketing*) charts how individuals interpret and make sense of marketing and the marketplace more generally. It recognises how the life-world and personal biographies of individual consumers and their experiences and consumption inform how they find meaning within marketing. By understanding how consumers approach the interpretation process, marketers will be able to shape and construct more meaningful and relevant marketing strategies that resonate more effectively with their audiences.

Chapter 10 (*Ethics, Sustainable Marketing and The Green Consumer*) analyses how the politics of sustainability and the green agenda influence and impact the marketing of THEF. There is a growing acknowledgment within THEF marketing that it is mutually beneficial to work towards a sustainable agenda. The ethics of the production, dissemination and consumption of THEF experiences is becoming increasingly questioned across a number of dimensions. These include concerns about cultural, social and environmental sustainability. There is a long traditional of sustainable tourism experiences that range from trekking in undeveloped areas, to visiting Centre Parcs, while food production has developed clear links with the 'Fairtrade', organic and slow food movements. Organisations such as Marriott Hotels have invested heavily in their green credentials and large events such as Glastonbury Music Festival have their foundations in raising money for charities. As such the notion of sustainability has become one of the central themes to experiences marketing and has seen the emergence of the green consumer. The theme of sustainability within experiences marketing can thus be seen to fulfill a number of objectives that can be broadly divided into three elements.

- The first is where sustainability is used as a means of product differentiation, which seeks to add value to the brand. The aim of this approach is to reinforce the market's perception of the organisation in the hope of influencing buyer choice and market place behaviour; in other words it adds an economic value to the company's or organisation's products and bottom line.

- The second is related to meeting consumer requirements for sustainability. Many consumers demand sustainable products and solutions for their consumption, and will actively seek out products that meet these demands, while purposely avoiding those that don't. In this respect sustainability has an experiential dimension that adds meaning and value to a consumer's life and THEF organisations ignore these concerns at their peril.

- Finally, is the view that organisations pursue these agendas as ends in themselves; simply for altruistic reasons and a belief that it is the right thing to do. This perspective thus aligns with the philosophy that we wish to promote through this text, which is that THEF marketing should be an inclusive practice that takes consideration of a broad range of stakeholder interests and sustainability concerns.

In summarising this publication, Chapter 11 (*Conclusion*) presents a manifesto for the development of a critical customer-orientated approach to the marketing of tourism, hospitality, events and food, which offers an inclusive and holistic framework through which to analyse and appreciate contemporary marketing practice within the field, and across the sectors more generally.

■ Conclusion

Although this book is broken into chapters and many of the debates are interwoven with each other, the book has been constructed to enable the reader to dip into the specific subject themes developed within each chapter. If you read it in its entirety, the book will take you on a journey that will introduce the major critical themes that have emerged within the field of marketing over the past decade or so. Although, this work presents an approach that is often critical of traditional approaches, it must be re-iterated that these remain and will always remain the cornerstone of management practice. Although this may be the case, it is important that as students, academics and practitioners we question and analyse our approaches, if only to reflect on our practice.

2 THEF Marketing and the Exchange of Value

■ Introduction

The following four chapters locate the concept of THEF marketing within current marketing debates. Although this book offers an alternative or complementary approach to contemporary marketing theory and practice it is important to recognise that much of the literature has been motivated or has emerged from these debates. Numerous perspectives of marketing exist, and these frame the way in which we think about the nature of marketing and ultimately provide the logic and frameworks that govern practice. Each of these perspectives offers different ideas about the nature of markets and marketing, as well as the roles of marketers and consumers. In this respect it is our contention that a broadened view of marketing that is informed by an understanding of each of these perspectives will strengthen practice and afford a more nuanced and penetrating analytical framework through which to interpret the marketplace. As such, these four chapters set out to explore and define these perspectives, starting with the view that THEF marketing is based around exchange relationships.

■ Marketing and the exchange of value

Since its birth as a discipline, marketing has arguably been grounded in what is known as the exchange paradigm, or more lately what has been coined goods dominant logic (Vargo and Lusch, 2004, 2008). Up until recently this has been the case for both theory and practice. From the point of view of the literature, this is the most common perspective and the one that most marketing frameworks and theories originate from. The underlying feature of this perspective, which distinguishes it from those that will be discussed in the next few chapters, is how it conceives of the roles and differences between marketers and customers. Following the general logic of economic theory and how this presents the differences between producers and consumers, the exchange perspective holds that customers seek out and purchase products to experience the *value* that is built and stored in them, for either immediate or future use. In this respect marketers are instrumental in producing, communicating and delivering the value that is perceived and ultimately consumed. To complete the exchange, the customer supplies money to the company and/or advocacy about the product or brand in return. Broadly speaking, this view simply holds that marketing operates at the intersection of production and consumption and serves the marketplace by mediating supply and demand.

In effect, the key issue in play here is the concept of value, broadly defined (see Chapter 3 for a thorough examination), and how it is experienced. Accordingly, this perspective of marketing embraces the view that marketing centres on the production and exchange of value, and it is the differences between who is active in its production and consumption that is central to its logic. To summarise, in the words of Schau, Muñiz Jr., & Arnould (2009, p.30):

> "Modern marketing logic, as derived from economics, advance[s] a view of the firm and the customer as separate and discrete; the customer is exogenous to the firm and is the passive recipient of the firm's active value creation efforts."

As such, the exchange perspective is the closest approximation to the essence of marketing as defined by both the CIM (Chartered Institute of

Marketing) and AMA (American Marketing Association) and mostly underlies the definitions found in most general marketing text books. This perspective thus structures most thinking around the marketing process whereby marketers are tasked with:

1　Analysing and segmenting markets to identify opportunities for value creation;

2　Profiling customers based upon need states and personal characteristics and their potential to provide reciprocal value;

3　Efficiently allocating marketing resources in a competitive marketing context to position their products and meet the identified needs of their potential customers; and

4　Engaging in review activity to determine the success of their efforts and activity as well as the value that they have created for both themselves and their audience.

Accordingly the exchange perspective places the marketer in the privileged role of value creator and experience manager, and we will now examine this thinking to offer a more detailed view of this marketing tradition and its implications for practice

■ The basic idea of exchange

As inferred above, the central idea of exchange is that two or more parties come together in a transaction-orientated relationship to derive some form of sought value from the other entity. This suggests that markets are mobilised and sustained by a scarcity of goods and other resources which are deemed valuable to members of society, and that marketing relationships are constituted on the one hand by agents who are able and willing to produce and supply these goods or resources, and on the other, by people or institutions who both need or want them and are able to allocate their own resources to acquire their benefit (Kotler, 1972) So, in a very basic sense in seeking to satisfy hunger a person will exchange their money with a food producer for a form of nourishment such as a sandwich. In this example the customer may also be gaining the benefit of being able to manage the scarcity of time over a busy working day and short lunch break by buying this sandwich from a local convenience store or supermarket. This is an important element of practice within THEF marketing, and the theory underlying it accounts for many types of transactions in the sectors covered in this book, as many associated products and activities carry the immediate benefits that are exchanged with customers for payment and investments of time, such as: the efficient sustenance from a snack or ready meal; the enjoyment from attending an event, or; the psychoactive effects experienced from consuming an alcoholic drink.

◼ From restricted to complex exchange

The examples described above reflect what Bagozzi (1975) terms *restricted exchange*, which is essentially the exchange of value between two parties. This is the simplest and most basic form of exchange which is easy to understand, and does indeed represent some incidences of exchange in the THEF sectors, such as when an organisation is solely responsible for all of the resources and skills that are combined to produce and take a product to market that is then acquired by a customer for their sole use, however the nature of exchange is often more nuanced and fragmented. In these cases more than two parties are involved in the exchange process, and can be seen to sit in both the demand and supply side spheres of the relationship. These are what Bagozzi (1975) terms *complex patterns of exchange*.

◼ Complex exchange and the demand side

In many market transactions, the customer who is directly involved will not be the final recipient of the product or service that is exchanged, and therefore the evaluator of its value. This is often the case with the products and activities that constitute the THEF sector. For example, when a purchasing officer representing a company (the customer) purchases the accommodation of a travelling executive (the consumer), or when a parent (the customer) buys an ice cream for an infant (the consumer). In both these cases it will be the consumer (the executive or the infant) who will directly benefit from the value in the product or service that has been purchased from the market

2

on their behalf. However in making this distinction it is worth noting that the customer may also receive some form of indirect benefit from these transactions. In the first example for instance, the employer of the executive may indirectly benefit from increased productivity and performance due to the rest and recuperation that is enabled by the accommodation whilst the executive is in the field. In the second, the parent may benefit from the respite and momentary freedom from the demands placed on their attention.

These illustrations also allow us to neatly differentiate between customers and consumers. The above discussion demonstrates that while sometimes the customer and consumer is the same person, often they are not. However as also shown, even though the consumer is the direct beneficiary of the exchanged entity and its value (effects), the customer may also benefit from indirect effects. In the case of the parent and infant for example, if we remove the company who produced and sold the ice-cream from the equation for the moment, we have a classic example of social exchange whereby the confectionery is being offered as amongst other things a symbol of love and affection in exchange for reciprocated affection or good behaviour. If we reinsert the company at this point we can build another picture that further demonstrates the complex nature of exchange. Rather than solely being purchased for the product attributes of flavour and sweetness that provide a combination of hedonic benefits, refreshment and sustenance for the child, the ice-cream is being put into service for behaviour modification by being appropriated as a treat, for incentive or reward. Thus we see the parent receiving direct benefits and value from the purchase of the ice-cream that may be far removed from those intended by the producing company who offered it for exchange. These latter points raise interesting questions about the nature of value (what it is that is actually exchanged), in terms of its character or form, and how, when and by whom it is produced or created, which are currently central concerns of the marketing academy. Together these have important implications for both marketing theory and practice going forward. Significantly, they bring the notion of exchange as a foundational concept of marketing into question (for example see Grönroos, 2008, p.309). Resultantly we will return to these important issues later in the book, however for the time being we will continue our focus on this perspective by examining further forms of complex exchange, but this time on the supply side of an exchange relationship.

■ Complex exchange and the supply side

In the above examples of exchange, we have focused our attention on the producing company and their relationship to customers and consumers. Our attention will now shift to examine examples of complex exchange that exist in the production and supply side sphere, whereby a producing company utilises the products, services or activities from other companies to improve their performance in creating value and satisfying their customers' requirements. In these instances, activity is often performed by organisations that:

1   Have a specialisation for producing and adding further value to a product or service than would otherwise be possible by the producing company conducting these activities alone; and

2   Are able to facilitate smoother transactions with end users and customers to better meet their needs.

For example, travel agents act as valuable intermediaries for travel companies when they broker complex forms of exchange with the tourist, adding real value to the experience, and advertising agencies perform an important role in stimulating consumer behaviour for companies across the THEF sector.

The logic underlying these types of relationships is manifold, but in general terms organisations are inclined to engage in these configurations when they are unable to achieve their goals through their own skills, resources or knowledge. On the other hand companies may enter into these arrangements when there is greater potential for creating value and/or incurring less cost from performing the value creation function independently. Accordingly, amongst other types of arrangements and relationships, we see THEF organisations:

1   Outsource marketing communications activity to specialist businesses such as social media marketing and creative production companies;

2   Contract with cleaning companies for related services such as the maintenance and care of hotel rooms or, facilities management companies who may supply air-conditioning and building maintenance activities;

3   Use marketing research companies to provide insight into consumer requirements and the structure and conduct of markets. Kantar Worldpanel are a good example of this as they offer real-time insight to companies in the food industry through their consumer panels and research into buyer behavior and category/brand performance;

4   Form relationships with manufacturers to produce 'own label' products for retail, such as Farmers Boy who produce meat and dairy products for Morrisons.

Moreover, an organisation could also contract *in* supporting activities, such as payroll or Human Resource operations to allow them to concentrate on the things they are good at doing, or wish to prioritise; that is, to focus on their core competence and distinctive capabilities (Prahalad & Hamel, 1990). In most of these cases, a reciprocal relationship will be evident as the contracting company will be receiving the provided and sought benefits in exchange for one or more bundles of value such as payment, an extended or exclusivity contract, or the exchange of knowledge, information and skills. In this sense, using the lens of the exchange paradigm as a conceptual frame we can see that producing organisations can engage in combinations of downstream supply, upstream distribution, as well as supporting activities (see Porter's 'value chain', 1980) in seeking to add value and exploit their own distinctive set of skills, resources and competencies through exchange relationships.

Bearing in mind that in this book we are predominantly focusing on consumer marketing and therefore do not wish to get drawn into too much discussion of business to business marketing, the above points are worth indicating and illustrating due to their role in the value creation process for the end user.

■ Hybrid exchange relationships

While it is recognised that the satisfaction of needs are not always conditional upon some form of exchange with the marketplace, such as when a consumer acts to become self-sufficient, in contemporary market-based societies most needs are satisfied through either total or some form of hybridised exchange (Houston & Gassenheimer, 1987). For example, although an individual or family may elect to grow their own food rather than purchasing it from a supermarket, or an independently minded traveler constructs an itinerary for a vacation without utilising the services of a travel agent, the market must feature somewhere to facilitate engagement in these practices, and in some way be key to their outcomes. So in the case of the former, to grow their own food the individual or family may be reliant on a garden centre for the seeds required to start the process, and then further down the chain become dependent on either the gas or electricity suppliers and producers and retailers of the cooking appliances and dining utensils that will be required for preparing and consuming the produce as a meal (Houston & Gassenheimer, 1987). Equally, the knowledge and skills required for growing food may have origins in market provided resources such as books or a college course and so on (ibid, 1987). This logic will also hold true in the case of the independent traveler who will be reliant on the outfitter market for maps, guidebooks, tents, backpacks and other related resources.

This being the case, it is prudent to note that not all exchanges are necessarily and always market transactions. The guidebooks or cookbooks could have been acquired as a gift (e.g. Giesler, 2006; Sherry, 1983) for example, or they could have been exchanged through swapping (Sherry, 1990), loaned and borrowed or, accessed through donation as part of a ritual of voluntary disposition (Cherrier, 2009). Interestingly, these forms of exchange that by implication, extend the life and ultimately the value of a product are being explored as a means to a more sustainable future. Such practices, it is argued result in less waste, more efficient use of scare material resources, and mitigate against environmental degradation (e.g. Cooper, 2010).

■ The problems for marketing within the exchange perspective

According to Bagozzi (1975), within the exchange perspective marketing has two central and significant problems and these by implication must govern practice. The first is that marketers have to understand the factors that influence and bring about the need or potential for exchange in any given market, that is "...why *and under what conditions* do people and organizations engage in exchange relationships *or not?*" (ibid, p.38, italics added). Second, marketers must be cognizant with how to:

■   *Create* the conditions to stimulate exchange;

■   *Resolve* or *satisfy* those needs for exchange that presently exist; or

■   *Reverse* existing needs or consumer behaviours.

Or put more simply, marketers must understand how to: create valuable marketing propositions to stimulate consumer behaviour; deliver value to those who presently require it; or devalue or lessen the appeal of certain goods, activities or market place behaviours, for social, sustainable, or other market benefits.

In accepting Bagozzi's (1975) first problem, and in order to construct a suitable and relevant marketing proposition and offer, the marketer must be tasked and focused upon the mechanics of his or her marketplace. They must be aware of the competitive conditions and dynamics of the market, its infrastructure, and perhaps most importantly the behaviours and requirements of consumers (which we return to this later in the chapter). Equally marketers also have to understand and appreciate how changes in the macro environment that surrounds their market, may influence each of these former elements and which in turn might present possible opportunities for creating value for consumers in ways and areas that may be unexploited or underdeveloped.

In recognition of Bagozzi's second and third problems, marketers must on the one hand, know how to produce and disseminate value, and on the other, mitigate against it. In respect of this we can usefully draw upon the work of Kotler (1972) who has outlined the four basic tasks and functions of marketing to illustrate how value can be created or dissipated, these are: *configuration, valuation, symbolisation* and *facilitation*. We will examine each of these in turn and follow up by relating these to more contemporary articulations of the marketing mix.

■ Constructing the marketing offer to produce or reduce value

■ Configuration

To build or reduce value the marketer must develop an offer that is deemed either desirable or undesirable by the consumer and then work to competitively position this in the market. In respect of this, a marketer is firstly tasked with developing and designing the *social object*, which is the term used by Kotler to classify the product, such as a physical good, service, idea, initiative, destination, place, person, personality, behaviour or other marketable entity. This process and set of activities is called *configuration*. Here, to be effective the marketer must take account of trends in the market, and the features and benefits that will be desirable to the customer, as well as those that are most likely to stimulate a preferred response from the intended audience. The social object should also be differentiated from competing products and configured in a manner that is considered to be of superior value by consumers (Armstrong & Kotler, 2012).

In relation to this it is worth bearing in mind that the concept of configuration more generally captures the theory and nature of a number of useful allied concepts from the marketing literature. The most obvious of these is the product concept from the 4Ps, but it equally embraces the additional 3Ps of the widened services marketing mix, and the theory underlying the SER-VUCTION model (Eiglier & Langeard, 1975) as well as that of the Servicescape (Bitner, 1992). So in this respect and taking into account that THEF organisations in general can be broadly classified as companies that deliver services (Solomon et al, 1985), this literature and its associated theory is useful as it posits that perceived and realised consumer value can be enhanced through:

1   The configuration of optimal *processes* both front stage (visible) and backstage (invisible) of the service context;

2   Planning and managing to get the most from the participants involved in the delivery and performance of the service including the behaviours and interactions of staff and customers; and

3   The planned and active management of the physical evidence including those elements that constitute the servicescape such as the ambience, décor and signage etc., (Bitner, 1992).

In some cases however, a marketer may be compelled to make a product less desirable to an identified target audience to stem or moderate its use. For example a marketer may attempt to positively influence and change a deleterious behaviour such as the frequent overconsumption of high calorific foods and beverages to improve the health of an at-risk audience. Or in the case of tourism, a destination manager may seek to protect a destination from environmental damage that is being caused by large and excessive flows of tourists. In these cases the undesirable features and caveats would be the foremost consideration in the configuration process. This practice and process of de-valuation in the market has been coined 'de-marketing' (e.g. Kotler and Levy, 1971) and, as explained below, is a process that may draw upon the full complement of mix variables as well as much other marketing theory to achieve its goals and purposes (see Kotler and Levy, 1969 for an early but seminal explication of the scope of marketing from the exchange perspective). More recently the process of de-marketing has become more widely known and theorised as Social Marketing (e.g. Grier & Bryant, 2005)

■ Valuation

Second, the marketer must construct and apportion a *valuation* and set a price for the product. Logically this must be attractive to the target audience and sufficient to generate the expected demand effects against a range of changeable market conditions. Indeed in relation to theories of price elasticity, the valuation can be a key variable in stimulating or stultifying demand. Essentially the monetary expenditure expected from the target audience must be considered from their point of view and evaluated in relation to their own perceptions of value. And this is also the case for any other costs that a customer may incur or perceive as relevant when making decisions about purchasing and engaging with a THEF product or activity, such as their time, or mental and physical effort. Equally, marketers ought to consider the range of opportunity costs that may be factored into an evaluation of value by a customer, be they economic or otherwise. The valuation must also be sufficient to generate a suitable return on investment. In this respect the marketer must be mindful that whilst endeavouring to produce the optimal (positive or negative) value for the target audience vis-à-vis competitors, this must be achieved at a sensible cost or within a minimum cost structure to maintain competitive advantage. Likewise the valuation must be perceived by customers to be favourable against those of directly or indirectly competing products or substitutes, and in respect of de-marketing this must also include the competing behaviours or products that may hinder a public health marketing or sustainable tourism campaign, etc., from achieving their behavioural goals.

■ Symbolisation

THEF marketing utilizes a specific language of marketing which draws from a wide range of historically embedded words and images that are used to underpin the marketing and advertising of food, tourism, events and hospitality. This area of interest is often overlooked and, arguably, has not been academically developed at the same pace as other areas of marketing. In respect of this, this book has dedicated a chapter to the semiotics of experiences (see Chapter 8) so we will not elaborate much here. However, to save diverting the reader's focus and attention, we will simply offer the explanation that symbolization refers to two key aspects of marketing practice. First of all it relates to the process of communicating and sharing product-related information with a target audience, and second it refers to the process of producing meaning and symbolic value. In this respect symbolisation refers to the processes and methods involved in transferring significant and relevant meanings to the product through its design and configuration, as well as advertising, and other communicative activities (McCracken, 1986 & 1989). Continuing the thread of argument about de-marketing, it is worth bearing in mind that the meanings which marketers produce can be desirable or otherwise, depending upon their specific intentions and marketing goals. By implication, this process will also incorporate decisions about the selection of the best forms of media to deliver messages as well as choices about the frequency and places in which they are delivered.

■ Facilitation

Fourth and finally the marketer can add value by making the acquisition or location for the performance and delivery of the product more convenient and accessible for the target audience, Kotler (1972) terms this *facilitation*. Here, marketers must consider how the location or means through which a product is delivered or accessed by the customer impacts upon their perceptions of value. Factors that may come in to play in these calculations may relate to the effort, time and money that a consumer expends in achieving access or acquiring the good. However it is worth noting that ease of access is not always positively correlated with value, and in some cases the reverse is often true. For instance, products and experiences that are perceived as luxury, rare or scarce are examples of this. In these cases often the effort, time, money and uncertainty of whether one will ultimately gain access to an activity or performance, or ownership of the desired object adds value in itself, by enhancing the product's perceived or actual scarcity. In some cases a marketer may also be acting to remove a social object from the market or impede access to it. In these instances, the employed tactic could be to devalue the product by making it difficult to access or acquire in some manner, or by being selective of who, or when one has access, and the conditions by which they are granted access.

■ Kotler's framework and its relationship to the marketing mix

Despite its age, Kotler's (1972) four part exchange framework fruitfully resonates with both the elementary building blocks of marketer created value – the marketing mix – and many other forms of contemporary value creating activity and processes related to transactional exchange. In fact, we favour this to the more familiar 4Ps framework as it allows the range of marketing applications such as services marketing, place marketing, social marketing, cause related marketing, and public health marketing, to be reflected rather than just merely those purely of a commercial and manufactured good based nature. This is essential when this book is directed at students and practitioners that cut across each of these categories of marketing and industry sectors. However to aid understanding, and to familiarise the reader with how this framework relates to the more familiar models such as the 4Ps (McCarthy, 1964), the 4Cs (Lauterborm, 1990), or the 7Ps of Booms and Bitner's (1982) services marketing mix, we have included a table that maps the respective concepts in relation to their operational and conceptual similarity (Figure 2.1).

Organising Framework			
Configuration	Customer/Client Needs	Product	Product Process Physical Evidence Participants
Valuation	Costs	Price	Price
Symbolisation	Communication	Promotion	Promotion
Facilitation	Convenience (Lauterborn 1990)	Place (Borden 1964) (McCarthy 1964)	Place (Booms & Bitner 1981)

Figure 2.1: Frameworks of marketing practice

■ Market segmentation and targeting

Having examined the elementary frameworks utilised by marketers to produce value for their audiences, we will now briefly explore the basic theoretical concepts and practical activities that are deployed by marketers to segment the market and understand their customers. This is essential to show how marketers who act in accordance with the exchange logic attempt to improve marketing performance by aligning their marketing offer and programmes around customer needs and insight. This section will also provide a useful starting point for later arguments which highlight the differences in thinking that exist about consumers between the exchange logic and the emerging perspectives of marketing that will be examined in the following chapter and later in the book. In particular this section will reveal some of the assumptions about the nature of consumers and consumption in respect of their role and involvement in value creation.

The received wisdom within the exchange perspective is that markets are characterised by divergent demand and customer heterogeneity which essentially implies that basic differences in user needs and preferences exist in the marketplace (e.g. Dickson & Ginter, 1987; Wendell & Smith, 1956). That is to say: customers differ in their requirements and seek a range of different value propositions from the market. Therefore in order to create meaningful and valuable relationships with customers and increase marketing performance, marketers must concentrate their efforts on identifying subsets of customers who are homogeneous in their requirements. In the words of Christopher (1969, p.99):

> "It is no longer sufficient, or indeed practicable, to appeal to the global market; there has been a recognition that a product market is not homogeneous but rather is composed of several or many sub-markets. Each of these sub-markets or 'segments' represents a distinct and different grouping of consumers... [therefore]... the search for marketing strategies which will enable the firm to identify and capture discrete segments of the overall market is becoming increasingly important."

2

These ideas are intrinsically tied to the philosophy of the market orientation which suggests that it is futile trying to serve a mass market or bend demand to align with your existing offer, instead, marketers should produce products and build their marketing mix around what consumers want, rather than trying to sell what they currently produce (Moore and Hussey, 1965). Moreover, from a theoretical point of view, the basic idea of market segmentation is also premised upon the assumptions that:

1   Consumers are mere recipients of value;

2   Products are bundles of benefits, or containers of value and experiences, that customers simply access through consumption (Holt, 1995); and

3   The objective of marketing is to locate and create the right fit between an identified need in the market and the organisation's/ product's value proposition. Or visa-versa.

Crucially, in relation to these assumptions and the logic of exchange more generally, the customer is treated as a target belonging to a larger cohort of customers who seek similar forms of value or experiences from the THEF marketplace.

Segmentation variable	Basic assumption	Typical characteristics used to build profile and create market segment
Demographics	Needs and wants vary in relation to differences in demographic markers	Age, gender, family size, stage in the family lifecycle, ethnicity, religion, generation (e.g. Baby boomers or millennials etc.)
Geographics	Needs and wants vary geographically	Country, region, neighbourhood, postcode, Population density, climate
Psychographics	Needs and wants are shaped by differences in psychological traits or lifestyles	Activities, interests and opinions, Values, attitudes and lifestyles, Personality and beliefs
Socio-economic	Needs and wants are structured by differences in status and socio-economic resources	Income, occupation, educational attainment, social class
Behavioural	Present or anticipated behaviour is an indicator of future product use	Use occasions, benefits sought, user status, loyalty status, buyer readiness stage

Figure 2.2: Variables for market segmentation and consumer profiling (Adapted from Armstrong & Kotler, 2011)

2

Over time, these central ideas about the nature of consumers and consumption have led to the creation of a range of arbitrary and scientific profiling techniques (see Beane & Ennis, 1987) as well as a plethora of variables that are used to break down the total market into meaningful and clearly defined segments of consumers who share similar levels of interest in a marketer's value proposition (McDonald & Dunbar, 2010). These are mostly related to either the personal characteristics of the segment or location and behavioural information. The most notable and widely used of these are (1) demographic, (2) socio-economic, (3) geographic, (4) psychographic and (5) behavioural variables (see Figure 2.2 for details) and research shows that companies may use both single variables and combinations thereof to segment their markets. What is more, while it has been suggested that there isn't any one correct way to segment the market, there is a strong argument to suggest that multivariate market segmentation offers greater precision in targeting and securing opportunities for creating value (Beane & Ennis, 1987). This implies that companies who draw upon a range of variables are able to build a more complete picture of the consumer than those that merely rely on one or a couple of variables alone; which in turn may lead to competitive advantage through the creation and realisation of marketing efficiencies. Simply put, the more marketers know about their customers, the more successful they will be in designing and delivering the marketing offer. This being the case, Armstrong & Kotler (2012) strongly suggests that any market segment should always be assessed and selected in relation to its measurability, accessibility, differentiability, and substantiality. Whereby a company:

1   Is able to make a meaningful and relatively accurate measurement of the segment in terms of its characteristics, size and scope;

2   Has the capacity and capability to access and serve the market with a degree of ease;

3   Ensures that the segment is clearly and conceptually differentiated from others in relation to how they respond to marketing stimuli and the benefits and value they seek; and

4   Believes that the market is substantial and affords the opportunity to deliver relatively long term value or high returns on
investment.

▪ Conclusion: the production and supply of value

To draw the discussion of this perspective to a close, it is evident
that within this tradition the fundamental purpose of marketing is
to produce value, through the creation and facilitation of exchange
relationships. Broadly construed this means that THEF marketers are
tasked with identifying the needs and wants of a social unit – be they
individuals or organisations – in order to deliver value through the
creation, communication and distribution of a product that is attractive
and beneficial to them. This is done to generate a form of reciprocated
value for the marketing organisation, whereby in the case of a private
enterprise this value will amongst other things take the shape of a
healthy financial return or advocacy in the form of positive word of
mouth. Or on the other hand, in the case of cause-related organisations
and initiatives etc., the value may be realised in relation to achieving a
positive behaviour change in a market, such has influencing healthier
food choices or encouraging environmentally sensitive tourist behaviours. In producing these desired outcomes, marketers must by implication understand the competitive dynamics of their market as well as
the mechanisms and tools through which they can create and deliver
the optimum level of value. That is to say:

> Marketing is the social process by which individuals and groups
> obtain what they need and want through creating and exchang-
> ing products and value with others (Kotler, 2008).

or

> Marketing is the management process responsible for identify-
> ing, anticipating and satisfying customer requirements profit-
> ably (CIM, 2010).

As such the focus and activity of marketers from this perspective
ultimately resides around three core themes and concerns, these are;

1   Purchasing or acquisition and the stages and processes leading to this;

2   The satisfaction of consumers by delivering the expected value to them through providing an appropriate product or experience, at a time, location, price, and in the case of services within an environment and time-frame that is agreeable; and

3   In the instance of apparent dissatisfaction, recovery of the situation through service guarantee, product recalls or returns policy.

Accordingly, the logic of exchange positions the marketer in an ordinate role in the value creation process and the customer as simply a recipient. However, as this book progresses over the following chapters we will see that this perspective and its associated theory is starting to run into conceptual problems from both an academic and practical point of view. This is precisely because this perspective:

1   Broadly over-emphasizes the importance of the marketer's role in value creation;

2   Misjudges the nature of products by simply assuming that they are containers of value; and

3   Underestimates the nature of consumers and consumption, in the sense that consumers simply seek out and experience the value that is assumed to reside in a product during consumption.

In contrast to this, a growing body of evidence from a number of schools of marketing thought are identifying and mapping out a different point of view (e.g. Vargo & Lusch, 2004 & 2008a; Arnould & Thompson, 2005; Holt, 1995), which when combined, suggest that it is the consumer who creates their experiences of value through their interactions with the marketplace and products etc., rather than the other way around. Instead of being central to the process of value creation, marketers are now placed in a lesser but no less important role as practitioners who shape the context through which valuable experiences can be created and realised. Accordingly we are simultaneously seeing the balance of power shift from the marketer to the user, but not a diminished role or set of responsibilities for the marketer themselves. In fact in view of the new perspectives of THEF marketing that we are about to discuss, we are arguably witnessing the opposite; that is to say the marketer's role becomes more nuanced, interactive and involving. To explore this thinking in more detail and what it means for practice, the next chapter will examine the perspective which is broadly based upon the premise that THEF marketing is an interactive process that is facilitated though the exchange of service rather than value, and that customers are active participants in value creation rather than mere recipients.

3 Marketing as Interaction and Service

■ Introduction

This chapter introduces a perspective for marketing that is profoundly different from that which was described in the previous chapter, yet is critical to both the process of marketing and our understanding of the role of the consumer. Essentially this perspective moves marketing on from a discipline underscored by exchange of value towards one that can be better explained by the concepts of interaction and the exchange of service. Or as Vargo and Lusch (2004, 2008a, 2008b) posit, a switch from a *goods dominant* logic to a *service dominant* logic. Broadly construed, this perspective sees a reorientation of the nature and roles of market actors and recasts value creation from being an unequivocal management practice to a co-constitutive process between consumers, organisations and their stakeholders. In particular, this orientation de-centres marketing practitioners from their privileged role as value creators to a role that is more in tune with being the facilitator of a value creation process. In relation to this, this perspective privileges the marketing audience who switch from being mere targets of marketer-created value to active players and co-creators of personalised value.

In making this conceptual shift we will demonstrate that many of the foundational constructs and assumptions underlying the exchange paradigm have been recast and will follow by arguing that as a result so should the way in which we think about marketing. The impact of this is that it challenges and reformulates practice across our sectors, which must also align with this re-orientation and shift in logic. Importantly to aid this shift, the language of marketing needs to be changed to accommodate the essence and underlying characteristics and features of these changes. In this sense we will argue at the end of the chapter that standard marketing concepts such as 'consumer' or 'audience' may need revision so as not to obscure and limit thinking. Importantly we will demonstrate the central role that consumption plays in value creation and as a result will explain the key concepts and process integral to it. In this respect we follow the argument of Vargo & Lusch (2004, p.12) that the service-centred view of marketing "is inherently… consumer-centric and relational".

From goods logic to a logic of service

Over the last decade a new direction in marketing has arisen that challenges the underlying logic of the exchange perspective. This emerging perspective similarly holds the concept of value as central to its thinking, however it is its focus around who creates value where it fundamentally differs. Rather than holding the assumption that marketers produce, and customers use value, this view suggests that value creation is a shared and fluid process, and that value is dynamically produced through the activities and interactions between THEF marketers and their audiences.

While there is a lot of debate about the origin of this perspective (e.g. Levy, 2006), most literature cites a paper by Vargo and Lusch (2004) as a key moment in this 'turn' in marketing thought. While this and later papers flesh out the orientating propositions of this perspective, which number between 8 and 10 in total (see Vargo and Lusch, 2004 & 2008a), the key concepts and ideas through which we ground our arguments in this chapter are:

1   Service and interaction;

2   Consumer resources and consumption practices;

3   Co-creation and co-production;

4   The consumption cycle; and

5   Multi-dimensional consumer value.

We will discuss each of these in turn, but must point out at the start that there is significant overlap and co-dependency between these concepts.

3

■ Service and interaction

This first of these concepts simply acknowledges the fact that consumers put products into *service* to meet their own specific goals. In this respect, an acknowledgment of the fact that different consumers may pursue different goals from other consumers, or that a consumer may pursue different goals when consuming the same product on different occasions or in different contexts, implies that the experience and outcome of consumption is determined by the individual (Holbrook, 1999; Vargo & Lusch, 2007). Accordingly, while a group of consumers may be sharing in the same basic experience during the consumption of a THEF product such as a music festival, they could each be using the occasion for different reasons and in turn creating unique experiences and forms of value. So, for example, one attendee could be there purely to see their favourite bands perform while another may attend to revel in the atmosphere or enjoy a convivial social experience with their friends. In respect of practice, this implies that THEF marketers must begin to account for the multi-dimensional nature of their products and the experiences that they potentially provide, and to not become fixated on one particular form of value or set of experiences. On the contrary they need to understand that consumers produce the experience of their products on their own terms. We deal with these issues later in the chapter when we discuss the nature of consumer value and the concept of co-creation in more detail.

In light of this discussion we can see that unlike the exchange perspective, which infers that value is stored within a product itself, the service logic posits that value is only experienced and realised in use. In this respect rather than being entities that contain value, THEF products are better conceived as marketplace resources which hold the potential for value and which allow for significant variation in interpretation and use (Holt, 1997). Furthermore, following Holbrook's (1999, p.5) assertion that consumer value is best conceived as an "interactive relativistic preference experience", we concur that the experiences derived by consumers of THEF products are dependent upon *interaction*. To be precise, it is only when a consumer interacts with a product and its marketing that perceptions and evaluations of value are brought into being.

Importantly, in relation to the temporal range of many THEF experiences, interaction becomes more significant, and this is because consumer interactions of such products can vary in scale and scope. That is to say, people can spend a lot of time in a restaurant, hotel, or visiting a heritage tourism site or farmers market etc., or on the other hand quickly nip into a supermarket to grab a few grocery items or pick up a pint of milk. Additionally, during their consumption of THEF products a consumer may interact with the natural environment, other consumers and service delivery staff, and a range of marketing materials and messages, as well as other experiential touch points during their experience. Therefore the potential for directing or curating the experience of consumers and the value that they perceive and create during consumption becomes increasingly complex and problematic. The difference that a seasonally busy supermarket may make on the experiences of customers at Christmastime, or a rude and arrogant maître d' on the diners of a restaurant, are but two examples of the many factors that THEF marketers have to consider during the design and delivery of their offer. This is because the nature of the services offered by the THEF industries generally means that consumption is inseparable form the process of producing them which bring into play a whole range of operational issues that marketers of manufactured products never have to think about (Shostack, 1977).

■ Consumer resources and consumption practices

The service logic of marketing also illuminates a different but complementary way of thinking about consumers from that of the exchange perspective. Rather than solely profiling the market in terms of broad customer characteristics as market segmentation theory suggests (e.g. McDonald & Dunbar, 2010), that is by demographic, socio-economic, or psychographic variables etc., service logic requires a shift in orientation to a focus on *consumer resources*, (e.g. Arnould, Price & Malshe, 2006) and *consumption practices* (Holt, 1995). This switch is based upon the changing nature of value creation and debates about who is involved in its production. On the one hand, if we accept that value is produced purely by marketers as per exchange theory, then it is reasonable to accept that we can make valuable use of market segmentation principles and practice. This is the case because we would be subscribing to a view that we can match the value embedded in THEF products with a group of consumers whose needs, wants and financial resources etc. match our value propositions and positioning in the market. On the other hand, when we begin to think about THEF consumers as value creators themselves, we need a refreshed way of thinking.

Put simply, this argument suggests that value is created only when consumers integrate their own resources with those offered by the marketer during the process of consuming the product itself. This line of thinking is obviously at odds with market segmentation theory which broadly accepts the assumptions about value drawn from the exchange perspective, in the sense that a product can be conceived as a bundle of benefits or container of value that a person can access simply through consumption (Holt, 1995). Given this shift in thought, rather than merely profiling our customers prior to consumption as we would when engaging segmentation studies, this approach calls for greater consideration of the process of consumption itself, which we discuss later in this chapter. To be precise, in addition to segmenting their audiences, THEF marketers must also study the resources and consumption practices that consumers deploy when shaping their experiences, and creating value, and this in turn will supply rich consumer insight that can be leveraged to improve the THEF marketing offer as well as any related marketing activity.

So let's consider what we mean by resources and practices. On the one hand, following Arnould, Price & Malshe (2006) we define consumer resources as the range of personal assets and capabilities that people utilise when interacting with products and the marketplace, such as their time, effort, knowledge, skills, imagination, creativity and money etc., (see Chapter 6 for detailed review) and on the other, following Holt, (1995: 1) we simply define consumption practices as "what people do when they consume". In this respect, it is what consumers do, and the resources they deploy during their consumption of THEF products that creates the value they desire and which in turn allows them to achieve their goals. In Kozinets' (2002) study of the Burning Man festival for example, we are shown how festival participants who, in spite of paying between $390 and $1200 per ticket (2016 prices), engage in a range of de-commodification *practices* to facilitate their goals of escaping the market and consumerism. In particular they:

1   Employ gift giving and barter to sidestep monetary exchange and economic transactions;

2   Attempt to subvert their everyday roles as customers by engaging in performance art and making offers to the wider Burning Man community in the form of artworks and installations; and

3   Mask or disguise any significant markers of the marketplace such as brand logos and trademarks etc.

In performing these *practices*, 'burners' engage a range of *resources* such as their creative imaginations, interpersonal skills and resourcefulness. Moreover, in order to survive the harsh conditions of the Nevada Desert where the festival takes place, burners take along sufficient supplies and draw upon a range of material *resources*, such as water, sunglasses and suncream etc. In advance of embarking on their journey to the desert, burners may also seek to develop their knowledge and survival skills by reading books or consulting websites or magazines. In fact the Burning Man website itself offers a range of *resources* and guidelines for this specific purpose.

This insight, which shows how value is crafted through consumption, demonstrates how vitally important it is for THEF marketers to account for the resources that consumers bring to bear when interacting with their marketing materials and the experiences they offer. Or as Vargo and Lusch (2004), Holt, (1995), and Arnould Price and Malshe (2006) suggest, we need to think about the resources and practices that our customers integrate with those that we supply through our products and other marketing materials as they produce their experiences. Importantly this means that the marketer needs to focus much more on what takes place through a customer's journey during selection, acquisition, consumption and withdrawal from our products; and not only on figuring out who our customers are prior to their purchase of our goods and services.

Co-creation and co-production

In view of the discussion above, it should be clear that the most significant departure from the exchange perspective of marketing is the keen focus upon how value is created. Rather than the creation of value being seen as the sole preserve of marketers, we now see that consumers play a fundamental, if not central role. In this respect the literature now acknowledges the notion of value co-creation or co-production, whereby both organisations and consumers are viewed has value creators with shared roles in the value creation process. This perspective therefore has significant implications for how THEF experiences are created and the ways in which we practice marketing more specifically. To draw upon the lexicon of consumer resource theory (Arnould, Price and Malshe, 2006) we now see that THEF organisations offer but one resource amongst the gamut of resources that customers and consumers bring to bear in their value creating activities. While THEF marketers still play a key role in defining their unique selling points and value propositions through their marketing and product configuration activities etc., and providing the objects and spaces central to value creation, they must now be flexible and comfortable in the fact that their consumers perform a similarly active role. Consequently, by embracing the ideas of co-creation and co-production, THEF marketers have a much better opportunity for facilitating the value creation of their customers.

This being the case however, our sectors allow for different levels and types of consumer engagement in the value creation/production function. Vargo and Lusch (2008a) and Grönroos (2011) for example, distinguish between co-creation and co-production making the argument that these are different concepts. Specifically they maintain that while co-creation always takes place, co-production is optional. We will address this important distinction by dealing with each of these important concepts in turn.

■ Co-creation

Co-creation on the one hand, can be understood through dealing with each entity of the consumer/company dyad separately. First and foremost value is created in use, and can only be realised by the consumer during the process of consumption. For example, tourists who stay at resorts such as One&Only find different meaning and value through consumption, and their experiences could range from the purely romantic and spiritual, to simply rejuvenating themselves and recharging their batteries, through to more ambitious attempts to escape the mundane reality of everyday life. This is the case because consumers are motivated through seeking to accomplish a range of goals and projects that vary and marketers only create space in which they can co-create value. However as argued earlier, for value to be created, there must be some resource or combination of resources offered by the THEF marketer to be acted on by the consumer. These resources include all aspects of the marketing offer and mix, such as promotional materials and communication media as well as the features, and attributes of the product or servicescape itself. So to return to the examples outlined above:

1   To facilitate romance a consumer may draw upon the provision of candlelit shoreside dining facilities;

2   To escape their quotidian experience a consumer could make use of the bars and social opportunities; and

3   The spa facilities and beaches may help the consumer in their efforts of rejuvenation.

These then are what, in many cases, the marketer offers in the form of a *value proposition* or *marketplace resource* but it is only through the activation of these by consumers that value is realised. The implication of this for THEF companies is that all they can aim for in their activity is to offer attractive propositions or resources for consumers that may prove meaningful or valuable, and to then facilitate the value creation process through acts and processes of co-creation (Vargo and Lusch, 2004).

■ Co-production

Co-production on the other hand involves the customer engaging directly in the configuration and design of the marketing offer itself (Vargo and Lusch 2008a, Grönroos 2011). In these cases, the customer may be invited to partake in the production process by assisting in the development of a new product or marketing campaign, or to evaluate the existing marketing offer. In these instances amongst other things they may be:

1   Recruited into a sensory or tasting panel to evaluate a new food product;

2   Be involved in a focus group to assess the effectiveness of a company's advertising; or

3   Be used as a mystery shopper to evaluate and feedback upon the customer's journey and experience in a supermarket

In other cases however, the consumer may be inseparable from the actual production and delivery of the product itself. Indeed this will be the case for many of the products delivered by the THEF sectors, such as a restaurant meal, or a staged packaged holiday experience like those offered by the Sunsail brand. These issues have been widely discussed in the literature concerning services marketing, which led to Booms and Bitner (1981) extending the 4Ps framework to 7Ps. This was undertaken to reflect the nature of many service encounters that bring about the direct and interpersonal interactions between customers and service delivery staff. Being part of an audience at an event or having a meal in a restaurant is an illustration of this, as in each of these cases a consumer is integral to the ambience of the experience, and resultantly are a fundamental component of the value production process. According to this thinking, the process and extent of value co-production that is evident across the experiences offered by the THEF sector can range from extensive and wide ranging to very little or none at all (Vargo and Lusch, 2008a). So, on the one hand a customer may conduct much of the value producing activity themselves, as is the case for the grocery shopper who navigates the supermarket aisles to fill their basket and uses the self-service tills to check out. On the other hand, in cases such as formalised fine dining the consumer may have little room to produce value. In these cases the balance of value is arguably mostly created and delivered by the restaurant. This was especially the case with Chef Ferran Adrià's infamous elBulli restaurant concept, where a customer's only real choice was whether to join the waiting list to get a table or not. If successful in this lottery, consumers got to "enjoy a five-hour meal of thirty-some completely original, whimsical dishes prepared by Adrià and his team of thirty to forty cooks" (Hannah, 2009). In witnessing this mult-isensory spectacle however, diners were expected to sacrifice their sovereignty and agency of choice to the creative freedom and expression of Adrià and his team. That is to say, they ate what they were served.

The consumption cycle

Having established in the first half of this chapter that value is created and uniquely experienced by consumers as they integrate their own resources with those of the THEF marketplace during consumption, it is crucial that we have a good understanding of this process so that we can identify the key areas where value can be created. Therefore the following section briefly reviews this process and the concepts that are central to it, to clearly show the key areas of the *consumption cycle* where consumers have the potential to create valuable experiences through their interactions with the marketplace.

■ Selection

The consumption cycle (see Figure 3.1) cuts across the process orientated categories of selection, acquisition, consumption and disposition (Soloman, 2006; Arnould & Thompson, 2005) and arguably commences at the initial research stage as consumers review the marketplace to identify and select the products that are most likely to meet their requirements and which are accessible within the limits of their present stock of resources. Therefore, *selection* refers to the means by which consumers seek out product related information and knowledge about THEF products and user experiences to inform their purchase choices.

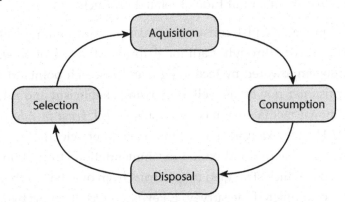

Figure 3.1: The consumption cycle

Consumers are continually making choices yet, historically, the information available to them was greatly influenced by marketers and was mostly generated by organisations through their communications and advertising. In this respect brand information was heavily weighted in an organisation's favour and marketers could exercise a high degree of control over their value propositions and messages. Under these conditions the consumer would typically appraise competing offers in the market based upon the claims made by an organisation or through other visible aspects of the marketing mix such as the product itself. However, the media scape has changed and fragmented over time, fundamentally changing and broadening the communication and media channels to which consumers now have access, as well as the ways in which they interact with the marketplace. This, it is argued has democratised the marketplace, and consumers are increasing in power and influence as they flock to interactive social media platforms such as Twitter, Instagram, Tripadviser and Snapchat to share their views and experiences (Kozinets, 2015 & 2016; Dahl, 2014; de Langhe, Fernbach, & Lichtenstein, 2016). Kozinets (2002b) for example, has demonstrated the ways in which coffee aficionados create and share value between themselves on the <altcoffee> online user group. By providing reviews, recommendations and critiques of products and methods of preparation and consumption of coffee, this community provides an active and dynamic resource for its members, which not only enhances the experience of consuming coffee, but also aids selection and purchasing through providing an informational source about a multitude of related products.

Indeed, whilst consumers have always communicated between themselves through traditional forms of word of mouth, they are now empowered by technology, and research points to a new era of consumer power, as well as growing skepticism and mistrust in traditional media channels. Nielson's *Global Trust in Advertising Survey* (2011), for example, shows that consumers clearly favour in person word of mouth and online recommendations to traditional forms of media, which struggled to gain trust from over half of the respondents who completed the survey. Likewise, a recent report by Mintel (2014) shows that Tripadviser is becoming the preferred medium for seeking recommendations in the travel and hospitality market and presently secures 260 million unique visitors a month. Amongst other things, the reasons reported for why this is the case include:

1   Its perceived reliability;

2   The diversity of information that is shared about personal experiences with the service providers under review; and

3   The fact that it gives personal recommendations and opinions.

Moreover consumers report that the option to select reviews for families, couples, solo and business travelers etc., allows them to tailor and personalise recommendations to their own specific requirements during the selection process.

These examples clearly show that consumers are more than willing to integrate these social and technological resources (see Chapter 5) into their information searches to co-create personalised forms of information value, to either achieve their own goals or to help others achieve theirs. Accordingly consumers now have the potential to link into a range of relatively unlimited networks of communication that allow unmediated flows of product-related and consumption experience information and user-generated content. These are significant changes in marketplace behaviour and communication, and clearly tip the balance of influence towards the consumer rather than the marketer.

What is more, research shows that selection can be a hedonic and emotional activity, and offer numerous forms of value in its own right. Arnold & Reynolds (2003) for example have developed a scale from their research into shopper behavior that portrays a range of motivations for consumers engaging in this activity. In particular this study shows that shopping can be experienced as amongst other things:

1   An adventure;

2   A means to unwind and relax;

3   A way to bond with others and show love; or

4   An exciting value enhancing game of bargain hunting.

As such these findings cast doubt on previous conceptualisations of shopping which suggest that it is a mundane, utilitarian and instrumental activity rooted to product selection and the exchange paradigm. On the contrary, shopping is an idiosyncratic consumption practice with numerous valuable and meaningful ends which can be flexed in relation to a consumer's goals and resources, and in light of this, this process is more attuned to the logic of the arguments about service and co-creation presented in this chapter.

■ Acquisition

Acquisition is the next stage of the consumption process and generally refers to the means by which people acquire or come to possess a product, or gain access to a service or experience that is offered in the marketplace. Ultimately, this involves some form of marketing exchange, and arguably approximates the logic of the exchange perspective most closely. That is, the consumer exchanges a unit of value such as money or their time for the benefit of acquiring a product. However, if we are to accept the argument of Grönroos (2011, p.298) that "value is accumulating throughout the customer's value-creating process" including acquisition, then we cannot simply remove this stage of the consumption process from theories of co-creation. That is to say, purchasing and other forms of acquisition are fundamental to a consumer taking ownership of a product for their use; which is where consumers are most likely to be active in value creation. What is more, a transaction may not always simply imply a customer handing over money to a cashier or entering their debit card details into on online payment form; on the contrary they may in many cases be involved in a complex negotiation over the price of a product or other forms of incentive, as well as the terms and conditions of its use. They may also barter with an organisation to seek an upgrade or add additional features and benefits to a product before agreeing on a sale. In the words of Prahalad & Ramaswamy (2004, p. 6-7):

> "Armed with knowledge drawn from today's increasingly transparent business environment, customers are much more willing than in the past to negotiate prices and other transaction terms with companies. We are moving toward a world in which value is the result of an implicit negotiation between the individual consumer and the firm… Informed, connected, empowered, and active, consumers are increasingly learning that they too can extract value at the traditional point of exchange".

Consumers are also increasingly turning to comparison sites and utilising other resources to locate the best deals and prices in their efforts to more efficiently allocate their financial resources, and in this sense we cannot neatly separate out acquisition from a consumer's value creating capabilities and capacity.

Consumption

Consumption refers to the actual use of a product or engagement with an activity or service, and is arguably the point in the consumption cycle where the most value is either realised or created, as argued throughout this chapter. Having dealt with these arguments in detail we will not elaborate further here, instead we will simply acknowledge that we follow Holt's (1995) view of consumption in the respect that:

> "consuming is a varied and effortful accomplishment under-determined by the characteristics of the object. A given consumption object (e.g., a food, a sports activity, a television program, or an art object) is typically consumed in a variety of ways by different groups of consumers."…

…and in relation to this, that the value accrued through consumption is shaped by:

1   the context, time or situation in which it unfolds;

2   the manifold consumer goals that frame and direct it (Holbrook, 1999); and

3   the resources (Arnould, Price & Malshe, 2006) and consumption practices (Holt, 1995; 2007) that individual or groups of consumers bring to bear during the process.

Dispossession

The final process of the consumption cycle, dispossession, includes the numerous ways in which a consumer withdraws or removes themselves from a consumption experience or disposes of a product once it has served its primary purpose. As with all the previous elements of the cycle, this can be anything from a simple unconsidered act that may diminish value, to a drawn out immersive process that extends the value creation process, and may incur the integration of a range of consumer resources. So for example, having peeled an orange or eaten the contents of a bag of crisps, one could merely throw the peel or packet in the bin, bringing the life of the product to an abrupt end, or alternatively a consumer may place the peel in a compost heap for future consumption in the form of fertiliser, or seek to recycle the crisp packet to placate their ethical values. Likewise in returning home from a holiday or festival the consumer will be left with memories or collected artifacts in the form of souvenirs or photographs that will serve to extend the temporal range of their experiences. In these cases, the consumer continues to accrue and create value in some form or other. For example, each time a consumer sits down with a friend or family member to share these memories they are bringing their experience back to life. What is more, these memories and mementoes may be brought to bear as resources to inform future purchase decisions, thus closing the loop of the consumption cycle. Importantly, marketers of service-orientated businesses, who do not fully benefit from the tangible reminders of physical products, should take great care in the memories that are left with consumers.

In summary, the consumption cycle is an individual journey for the consumer, whereby each person finds different meanings, means of choosing, acquiring, consuming and disposing of the experiences within the consumption of tourism, hospitality, events and food, and in doing so produce unique and personally relevant forms of value. This relationship, it can be argued, is partly formed by the fact that each consumer is an individual with a different life biography that will inform and direct the process, but is equally shaped by the resources that they bring to bear throughout consumption. As each consumer will relate to the consumption process differently, it is important that we have the ability to define and locate the forms of value they seek to create. Therefore the next section explores this area of interest in some depth.

◼ Multi-dimensional consumer value

As argued in this chapter, one of the central ideas of the service and interaction perspective of marketing is that consumer value is uniquely experienced and determined by the beneficiary (Vargo & Lusch, 2007), which implies that each and every consumer has the potential to experience the consumption of a THEF product in a very different way. This suggests that consumer value is multi-dimensional and idiosyncratic, and that various forms of value exist and may present themselves at different times based upon changes in consumer goals and intentions. To aid thinking here, and to flesh out what we mean by consumer value, we can usefully draw upon a typology presented by Holbrook (1996, 1999) that offers insight into the multidimensional nature of consumer value from the point of view of the service and interaction perspective. Specifically this typology reveals the different types of value that consumers may seek to experience through their consumption of the THEF marketplace and the ways in which different goals may manifest themselves in the form of consumer value. Specifically this model contains eight dimensions of value (see Figure 3.2) which we will now discuss in turn.

		Extrinsic	Intrinsic
Self orientated	Active	EFFICIENCY	PLAY
	Reactive	EXCELLENCE	AESTHETICS
Other orientated	Active	STATUS	ETHICS
	Reactive	ESTEEM	SPIRITUALITY

Figure 3.2: Holbrook's framework of consumer value (Holbrook 1996, 1999)

■ Efficiency

The nature of value here is premised upon the efficient use of scarce consumer resources, and is experienced and judged in relation to how well a product meets these specific needs. In this respect consumers create this form of value by using products that save money, time, space or cognitive effort. Quick service restaurants and drive thru's as well as convenience stores and 'on the go' food are good examples here, as are budget hotels and airlines. As well as this, marketplace resources that save consumers cognitive effort and speed up the purchase decision making process also hold the potential to offer the value of efficiency, and examples include, amongst other things, all-inclusive holiday packages, and the services provided by travel agents and tour operators. Marketing communications that are effectively targeted may also fit here if they prevent a consumer from expending effort and time in locating and evaluating them.

Excellence

Excellence relates to a product's ability to provide a quality experience or perform its function in an excellent way. There is a huge literature on product and service quality (see Parasuraman, Zeithaml & Berry, 1988; Buttle, 1996, Lages & Fernandes, 2005; McCabe et al., 2007) which will not be reviewed here, but it is worth noting that quality is itself a multi-dimensional construct and is understood and evaluated by consumers in a variety of ways. For the sake of brevity, we will simply state that perceptions of quality are evaluated subjectively by consumers, based upon an assessment of the relative superiority of a product or service across a single or combination of its feature/s and attributes as well as its ability to meet or exceed their requirements. In hospitality for example, a consumer's preference judgment could be based upon an evaluation of their experiences of service quality as measured by the friendliness, attentiveness and responsiveness of staff (Booms & Bitner, 1980). Consumer judgments and expectations will also often be shaped by a product's market positioning, in the sense that excellence will be expected from those, brands that promise to deliver it. So where a company claims that 'This is not just food' (M&S), or that their role and responsibility to consumers is 'To fly. To serve' (BA), they are by implication signposting customer expectations about the experience they offer, and as a result will be evaluated in relation to these claims.

Status

Holbrook (1999) broadly defines status-orientated consumption as the set of consumer behaviours premised upon the goal of achieving favourable responses from others, in terms of securing their respect or admiration. We develop this concept further, alongside that of esteem (see below) in Chapter 7, where we re-frame it as cultural capital endowments and resources. Through this lens, this form of consumption is on the one hand, predicated by a purposeful attempt to achieve distinction and advance one's social position, or on the other, to seek acceptance and membership within social groups though the acquisition and use of THEF products or services. So, for example, the socially visible purchase and use of scarce and high value items like a bottle of Domaine de la Romanee-Conti Romanee-Conti Grand Cru, or attendance at elite sporting events like the Cartier Queen's Cup may be directed at realising this value. In this way, this form of consumption is a demonstration of a consumer's material resources or economic mastery. In a similar manner the demonstration of a consumer's knowledge of real ale or micro-brewery beer through public lectures or invited talks may be undertaken to build status within this particular field, while eating at the chef's table in a Michelin starred restaurant is an illustration of how this value may be realised, in the field of fine dining. Accordingly, status consumption can be operative in a range of distinct consumption fields and spaces, from allotments where people compete for recognition through growing their own food, through to expeditionary travel pursuits such as commercially organised climbing experiences to Mount Everest (Tumbat and Belk, 2011).

■ Esteem

For Holbrook (1996, p.4) esteem is "the reactive counterpart to status", as it is similar in its reputational effects, but rather than actively pursuing these effects, a consumer merely experiences these passively by consequence of ownership of a good or engagement in an activity or service. Although esteem is passive, it is important and valuable to consumers nonetheless. This is because esteem is often related to belonging, and 'fitting in', or marking out what lifestyle/s or role/s one aligns with (Holbrook, 1999). In this respect, while a specific consumer's motivation may not be focused on building esteem, because of the social nature of consumption it will possibly have these effects. So while a backpacker may be pursuing an ulterior motive such as play or a spiritual experience, they will be generating social capital through their pursuits, which by implication will mark them out as belonging to a specific lifestyle or social group. This logic holds for the connoisseur of exotic or local foods who will, as a consequence of their consumption and taste, be classified socially as a 'foodie'.

Play

Holbrook (1996), argues that play is about having fun and engaging in ludic activity. In this respect a broad range of consumer experiences and products from all of the sectors covered in this book fit into this category. For example, many food products draw upon the repertoire of play and fun in their market positioning. Pringles snacks, for instance, endorse the value of play through the strap-line "once you pop you can't stop" and the imagery of sharing and parties used in their advertising. Many supermarkets also produce packaged 'finger' and 'bite-sized' foods that are designed with parties and celebrations in mind, and food itself is often the centrepiece of celebration and related rituals such as weddings, birthdays and Christmas. On top of this we find tourism concepts such as Thomas Cooks Club 18-30 package holidays wedded to the idea of play, and Ibiza is well known as a party island. Other destinations also have their reputations and brands rooted in this concept. Monaco, for example, has a global reputation for being the playground of the rich and famous, while Las Vegas has built its economy on the back of adult play and entertainment. Moreover, Glastonbury is arguably an event designed for the ludically inclined and spirited, and at the extreme, concepts such as Hedonism resorts are positioned to satisfy the liberally minded adult consumer. To this end we can reflect upon a range of contemporary expressions that relate to the experiences sought from interacting with these products, such as "blowing off steam", or "letting your hair down". As such, it is clear to see that play is central to the experience of many products that are marketed and consumed within the THEF sectors, and hedonism is a fundamental element of the consumer experience.

Aesthetics

Aesthetic consumption is an autotelic experience whereby a consumer interacts with a product for personal enjoyment and pleasure, or to extract its fine and idiosyncratic qualities. To this end, aesthetic consumption is appreciative, and is often, but not always, accompanied by connoisseurship. Accordingly, a product is appreciated as an end in itself, and is evaluated through a range of aesthetic criteria that an individual consumer supplies during consumption. Thus the motivation to attend a cultural event, such as the Royal Academy of Arts annual exhibition, or Glyndebourne Opera Festival may be based around the aesthetic experience and its value. Likewise a consumer may immerse themselves into some wilderness or landscape to experience its beauty, while fine wine or food can be consumed to appreciate their organoleptic qualities. With regard to each of these examples, a consumer arguably needs to be equipped with the requisite knowledge and skills (or cultural capital endowments) to inform their evaluations and shape their experience (see Holt, 1998), which supplies further evidence to the argument that value is uniquely and phenomenologically experienced in relation to the resources consumers bring to bear in their consumption (Vargo & Lusch, 2007).

■ Ethics

Experiences that allow consumers to express moral duty or obligation can be classified as ethical ones. Here a consumer is drawn to, or repelled by, those products and services that align to a consumer's ethical criteria or which allow them to make a difference through their consumption. As such, individuals are consuming ethically and creating experiences of this value when they purchase fair trade and organic food, or when they select products that use less intensive methods in their production, such as free range eggs or Chipotle Mexican Grill burritos. The consumption practices related to recycling, repurposing or reusing products also fit into an ethical consumer framework but will demand the resources that facilitate these goals. What is more, brands that subscribe to strict ethical guidelines or are sensitive to the wider socio-cultural and ecological environment and have business policies related to these may be rewarded by consumers who seek these values and commitments. On the other hand, companies that don't adopt these frameworks and practices may be vilified and treated accordingly through boycotts or consumer activism (Neilson,

2010; Klien, Smith & John, 2004). In light of this, and with regard to the many ways in which ethical and sustainable consumption and activism may manifest itself and be practised, it can be characterized as a "highly complex form of consumer behaviour, both intellectually and morally as well as in practice" ((Moisander, 2007:1), and connected to this, it may be argued that the experience and practice of ethical consumption will vary in relation to the consumer resources that come to play in these instances of consumption. In view of this we return to a more thorough discussion of ethics and sustainable marketing in Chapter 10.

■ Spirituality

The last consumer value in Holbrook's (1999) framework, spirituality, relates to the sacred and humanistic aspects of consumption and encompasses experiences that:

1   Produce feelings of ecstasy, transcendence, or rapture;

2   Are in themselves magical; or

3   Allow the portrayal and demonstration of one's adoration, alignment or appreciation of faith.

As such, we can easily classify and align certain foods, food practices, and religious rituals that have food at their centre, with the latter of these definitional constructs. Within the Hindu faith for example, food is literally a gift from god and is treated accordingly, with great respect. In the commercial sphere we have food that is related to religious events like Easter eggs or Christmas cake. We also have food related to religious practices such as the bread and wine of Holy Communion, or the fasting associated with Ramadan. Pilgrimage is an aspect of faith and spiritual experience that would also feature in accordance with our sectors, and people from all faiths make great journeys that span the globe to pay respect and homage to their spiritual leaders and theological values, and a tourism industry has been built around these rituals. Likewise, both small and large-scale events are organised and attended for the purpose of worship and celebration of deities and religious belief systems.

With regards to the former of Holbrook's aspects of spirituality, a review finds that the literature is full of examples of marketplace activities and consumer behaviours that produce magical and extraordinary experiences. These are often predicated on Belk, Walendorf, and Sherry's (1989) seminal paper concerning the sacred and profane aspects of consumer behaviour. Thus we have studies that catalogue, but are not limited to the ways in which consumers:

1   Are rewarded with transcendental, transformative and magical experiences, while finding communion with nature through participating in guided white water rafting excursions (Arnould and Price, 1993; Arnould, Price and Otnes, 1999, Price, Arnould, and Tierny, 1995);

2   Find communitas and momentarily experience utopia through Star Trek conventions (Kozinets, 2001) and anti-market events like the Burning Man Festival (Kozinets, 2002a);

3   Extract peak experiences and ecstasy through raving and clubbing (Goulding, Shankar, Elliott and Canniford, 2009) and the consumption of music and art (Panzarella, 1980); and

4   Experience combinations of these phenomena through embarking upon extraordinary journeys and engaging in frontier travel (Laing, 2006).

In closing, having reviewed Holbrook's typology of consumer value, we can see that THEF products can indeed be experienced in many different ways. So taking a bottle of wine as an example, we can suggest that amongst other things this product could be consumed:

1   In a social context to impress others (Status);

2   To appreciate its organoleptic qualities through connoisseurship (Aesthetics);

3   In celebration of somebody's birthday or to toast a bride and groom at a wedding (Play);

4   During holy communion (Spirituality) ;

5   As a quick way to become intoxicated before going out to a city's bars for the night with a group of friends (Efficiency); or

6   As an enjoyable way to unwind and relax at home following a
hard week at work (Excellence).

■ Conclusion

To close, this chapter has examined an approach to marketing that
significantly challenges the logic and assumptions of the exchange
perspective and re-orientates the focus of marketing from purchasing
to consumption, and this in turn has allowed us to evaluate and locate
the critical approach adopted within the remainder of the text. While
the exchange perspective provides an important foundation for thinking about THEF marketing, it arguably obscures the true relationship
between consumers and producers, as well as the roles that they
perform in value creation.

Following Vargo and Lusch (2004, 2006, 2008a, 2008b) this chapter
broadly sets out an approach for THEF marketing that is built around
a number of precepts, which are in obvious contrast to the exchange
perspective. Our approach assumes that consumption is the process
through which value is extracted from the product by the consumer
and that the nature and attributes of products broadly structure what
is experienced by consumers during consumption. These are:

1   Service is the fundamental basis of exchange; marketers supply
knowledge, skills and resources to consumers for their use and
appropriation;

2   Service is exchanged for service; consumers integrate their
own knowledge, skills and resources with those offered by the
market to create valuable experiences;

3   The customer is always a co-creator of value; and

4   Consumption, including each of the activities and processes of
selection acquisition, consumption and disposal, is the site of
value creation.

Accordingly, in line with the rest of the argument we have presented in
this chapter, we are making the claim that consumption is a dynamic

interactive process of value creation that offers the opportunity to create numerous forms of value and that the resulting experience is determined through the process of consumption rather than by the attributes and configuration of the product itself. In this respect consumer value is neither universal in nature and never static, nor finalised and complete. Resultantly, the definitions and terminology that traditionally delineate the terms *consumer* and *consumption* are now being re-thought and re-labelled, and we agree that these seem more fitting. Having adopted and integrated producerly and creative behaviours into their theories of consumption, a range of theorists are now utilizing portmanteau terms to describe both the actor involved in the process of value creation and the process itself, leaving us with labels such as *pro-sumer* and *pro-sumption* (e.g. Ritzer, Dean & Jorgenson, 2012), and *co-producer* and *co-production* (Vargo & Lusch, 2008a).

Of course in this chapter we have solely focused on a dyadic company/customer relationship, which is justified through the main thrust of this text. However as Vargo and Lusch (2008a) correctly point out, this reorientation of marketing to interaction and exchange of service extends across the range of marketing actors who may enter into some form of marketing relationship, such as a network or co-service agreement, and thus spans the value chain (Porter, 1980). For example, the relationship between a restaurant and their suppliers who provide locally sourced food etc. are both mutually supportive and generate various forms of value, by sharing and co-creating a value chain.

However this being the case, the ideas and assumptions of the service and interaction perspective are sometimes limited because they do not fully recognise or capture the cultural significance of marketing per se. Nor do those of the exchange perspective. Consumers do not merely go to market to satisfy latent needs and wants, nor solely to create value. Often amongst other things, they are there to engage in a complex consumption process that informs and (re)produces their identity. Marketers too are not merely agents who propose or facilitate valuable experiences for their audiences; they are also intermediaries who broker and circulate cultural meaning in the marketplace;

meanings that have become very valuable for both consumers and the organisation alike (Arvidsson, 2005). As will be discussed in the next few chapters, THEF fulfills a significant role in contemporary society, and in order to understand, locate and effectively market such products and experiences, marketing practice has to be located and theorised within a culturally orientated framework. It must be stressed that in developing an holistic approach to THEF marketing, we do not discount the traditional exchange perspective or the more recent service dominant logic, but incorporate and enhance these within the cultural and social context of the marketplace and consumption more generally. Therefore to explore these important ideas in detail the next chapter introduces our next perspective that broadly positions marketing as a cultural process and practice.

4 Marketing and THEF Consumption as a Socio-Cultural Process

■ Introduction

This chapter introduces a perspective of THEF marketing that builds upon the preceding two by introducing the important idea that both marketing and consumption are fundamentally cultural activities. By this we mean that the marketing and consumption of THEF products and services not only create value but also mediate and (re)-produce socio-cultural meaning and values. Additionally this chapter further locates the consumer by examining their motivations and more fully explains the reasons for interacting with the THEF marketplace as well as the outcomes of their consumption. When taken together, this forms a culturally orientated definition and view of the marketing audience. In doing this we will demonstrate that this perspective also reinforces the view of consumers that is advocated by the service perspective of marketing, as much of the theory that supports this turn in thought highlights the central role that consumers play in both meaning production and in creating cultural and social value. Put simply, as will be evidenced in this chapter, consumers integrate their own resources with the *cultural resources* supplied by the THEF marketplace, to construct their own meanings and create their own forms of socio-cultural value (Arnould, Prices & Malshie, 2006). Or to utilise the language of the service perspective: THEF products in their broadest sense "provide the service of identity provision and communication" (Arnould, 2007, p.58). Finally, in embracing the view of meaning co-creation more generally, we will show how symbolism in the THEF marketplace is shaped in relation to the activities and stories that are shared by a range of agents who have an interest or stake in an organisation's products or services.

In this respect, to explore these important ideas more fully we draw upon a broad body of theory and research to illustrate:

1   The symbolic nature of THEF products and services and the manifold goals consumers pursue through interacting with the symbolism afforded by the THEF marketplace

2   The roles that THEF consumption plays in community formation and sociality;

3   The ways in which consumers extend the cultural and symbolic value of THEF experiences beyond the immediate service encounter; and

4   How the meanings of THEF products are co-created by multiple *authors* in the marketplace.

■ The symbolic nature of THEF products and the goals consumers pursue

The notion that THEF marketing and consumption can be broadly understood as a socio-cultural practice is based upon the idea that marketers are fundamentally engaged in a process of selecting and circulating systems and units of meaning through their marketing activities and products. To draw on the ideas of McCracken (1986), in effect, marketing is a conduit through which meanings in the 'culturally constituted world' pass through the THEF marketplace to consumers. Accordingly a key theme of this approach is the idea that THEF products and services have the potential to hold and carry meanings which in turn become valuable resources for consumers. Or as McCracken (1986:71) puts it "consumer goods have a significance that goes beyond their utilitarian character and commercial value. This significance rests largely in their ability to carry and communicate cultural meaning".

Central to this view, is the idea that THEF consumption is not a purely instrumental or autotelic act, in the respect that a consumer takes a vacation to relax, shops at a discount grocery store to save money, or consumes a bottle of fine wine to appreciate its idiosyncratic character. On the contrary, it is also an expressive process whereby consumers utilise the meanings from the marketplace to communicate things about themselves or to find solidarity with others. Or, in the words of a pioneer of this approach, Sydney Levy (1959, p.118), *"people buy things not only for what they can do, but also for what they mean"*. Consider, for example how Waitrose or Marks and Spencer's Simply Food both differ from each other and also differ in relation to Tesco or ALDI, in terms of their symbolic meaning and social significance. These and other food retailers and brands, as well as other products that cut across the THEF sectors more broadly, clearly carry and denote deep socio-cultural associations that have developed dynamically over time, and in so doing serve the market in a variety of ways. That is to say THEF products take shape as *cultural resources* to be deployed in consumption. In support of this argument, a sweeping review of the literature quickly reveals the numerous ways in which consumers appropriate the symbolism afforded by THEF products and servicescapes to accomplish a range of goals and projects which amongst other things, include;

1   The construction and realisation of independent and collective identities (e.g. Arsel & Thompson, 2011), for instance that of the foodie (Getz et al., 2014), independent traveler (Caruana, Crane & Fitchett, 2008), or skier and snowboarder (Edensor & Richards, 2007). Consumers also use the cultural resources provided by the THEF marketplace to perform and realise age (Goulding & Shankar, 2004) gender (Goulding and Saren, 2009) and sexual identities (Kates and Belk, 2001), and some of these ideas will be discussed later in this chapter.

2   The attainment and construction of specific lifestyles (Holt, 1997), e.g. the health lifestyle (Cockerham, 2005) or the bohemian or hipster lifestyle (Holt & Cameron, 2010).

3   The accomplishment of specific life projects and themes such as, to follow a morally responsible and ethical life, to act globally whilst thinking locally, or to be a caring mother and successful executive and wealth creator simultaneously (Thompson, 1996).

4   The use of brands to help reconcile and therapeutically redress significant cultural contradictions and anxieties that threaten their identity and sense of existential security (Holt and Thompson, 2004; Holt, 2004b; Humphreys & Thompson, 2014) by participating in brand sponsored self organising events like HOG (Harley Davidson Group) meets, drinking Jack Daniels, (Holt, 2006), or eating Ben & Jerry's ice-cream (Holt & Cameron, 2010). The significance here being that these activities or brands are fabricated around cultural templates or myths that act as alternatives or salves to dominant ideologies or lived experiences of consumers. For example Ben & Jerry's draws on a challenger code and expression of back to the land and anti-corporation, that is appealing to US liberal consumers who feel alienated by corporate structures, ideology and relationships (Holt, 2004a). The former examples collectively reflect the outlaw, gunfighter or frontier myth of the US which offer more comfortable templates of masculinity for some male consumers who wish to (re) assert themselves and experience freedom, against the backdrop of forces that are perceived to be emasculating them.

In respect of practice, the significance of these goals imply that THEF marketers must purposefully select symbols, images, and materials, as well as use language that convey meanings that are considered important to their customers when designing their products and producing marketing materials. So to return to the example of the Burning Man Festival that was discussed in the previous chapter; in order to reconcile their contempt of brands and achieve their goals of escaping the logic of the market burners would value communications that revoke the primary status of the marketplace and devalue the role of brands and commercial activity more generally (Kozinets, 2002a). Additionally, following widespread media reports about unsavoury behaviour at Ascot (Kupfermann, 2014) most attendees would welcome a return to the traditional and prestigious values and symbolism that underscored this event in the past, and as such appreciate the dress code that the organisers now supply for attendees and the ways in which they ensure that it is followed (see http://www.ascot.co.uk/dress-code).

In light of this insight and the arguments presented thus far, it is vital that THEF marketers fully understand the relationship between what their products stand for and mean to a range of stakeholders, and in what ways these meanings hold value for their customers. As argued by Levy (1959:122):

"Most goods say something about the social world of the people who consume them. The things they buy are chosen partly to attest to their social positions".

And Ho and O'Donohoe (2014:859):

"Thus, we prefer products and consumption practices with positive symbolic meanings aligned with our desired selves, and we avoid those with negative symbolic meanings related to undesired selves"

Marketers *must* therefore become accustomed to the cultural scripts and symbols that give life to these meanings and be conscious of how marketing can be used to transfer them to their offer. To be precise, THEF marketers must think carefully about the meanings that resonate with their consumers and how they can assist in creating them, and in acknowledgement of these critically important issues for THEF marketing practice, we have dedicated a whole chapter to their discussion later in the book (see Chapter 8).

■ THEF consumption and community interaction

Another significant aspect of the socio-cultural approach to THEF marketing is how it illuminates the social aspects of THEF experiences and how consumers are impelled to seek out community ties and experiences through their consumption. According to Arnould & Thompon, (2005: 873) the research that investigates these phenomena draw heavily from the seminal work of Michel Maffesoli which shows that:

> "The forces of globalization and postindustrial socioeconomic transformation have significantly eroded the traditional bases of sociality and encouraged instead a dominant ethos of radical individualism oriented around a ceaseless quest for personal distinctiveness and autonomy in lifestyle choices. In response to these potentially alienating and isolating conditions, consumers forge more ephemeral collective identifications and participate in rituals of solidarity that are grounded in common lifestyle interests and leisure avocations".

In respect of this, this field of study reveals that consumption in general, and the consumption of THEF products in particular, are primary vehicles through which to realise goals of sociality and community (McAlexander, Schouten & Koenig, 2002).

Many THEF products are profoundly communal and offer a way in which to link with others and engage in shared experiences, such as a Thanksgiving meal, taking a vacation with friends, or attending a music festival; they thereby offer significant social value (Belk & Costa, 1998). A growing body of research has thus started to map the ways in which brands and products link people together (Cova, 1997; Cova & Cova, 2002) and help them to forge community (Muñiz Jr., O'Guinn & Thomas, 2001), and communal identity (Wallendorf & Arnould, 1991) as well as providing insight into the nature and anatomy of consumption practices within these communities, and how these in turn create value and meaning for their members (Schau, Muñiz Jr., & Arnould, 2009). Moreover, much of this work has strong ties to THEF products, such as food and drink (Cova & Pace, 2006; Kozinets, 1999), brandfests (McCalexander, &Schouten, 1998), and tourism (Wang, Yu & Fesenmaier, 2001).

Importantly, research has also demonstrated that these communities are often made up of relatively heterogeneous groups of people who bear little in common other than an interest or passion for the product or experience (Thomas, Price & Schau, 2012; Cova, 1997). For THEF marketers, the learning here is obvious, as this finding alone significantly challenges market segmentation theory which is broadly dependent upon consumers sharing one or more personal characteristics with each other, such as their age, income, or values etc. Instead the criterion of commonality through which we may be able to successfully define a valuable segment from this perspective is based upon commonality of interest in a THEF product, service, or activity. In their study of 'thirty something' ravers, for instance, Goulding and Shankar (2004) provide ample evidence of chronological age being a problematic if not largely unsuitable basis for segmentation in the Dance Club and Rave market, inferring instead that it is a consumer's interest in this specific lifestyle pursuit which locates them as a meaningful group. Drawing extensively on the work of Barak (e.g. 1985) this research shows that age is both a cognitive and behavioural manifestation as well as a multi-dimensional construct which is experienced in relation to what a consumer does and the interests they hold. Thus, rather than being a concept that reflects a range of differentiated periods of time that are uniformly shared across the lifecycle of people in relation to common life projects and activities, such as finding a job, settling down and getting married etc., age is *socially constructed* and something that is deeply entwined with culture and with the individual lived experience and activities of consumers.

As such, in this research dance clubs and raving seemingly provide consumers in their thirties and above, with an experiential escape hatch from other normative structures and expectations that frame their lived experience of age, such has doing 'grown up' work or having serious responsibilities that are linked to chronological age and accumulated work experience and knowledge. Therefore clubs and raving are a reflection of shared interests rather than something that can be defined on the basis of the age profile of its users. In this respect the rave and clubbing lifestyle provides:

■   the platform and context for older consumers to experience youth and construct their identities in relation to *doing* the activities of the young and performing youth; and

■   'the *link*' that brings a group of heterogeneous people together as a meaningful market segment.

Another valuable 'take-away' for THEF marketers from these ideas is that "work on…consumption communities emphasises that part of what companies…[really]…end-up selling is access to like-minded consumers" (Arnould, 2007:63). Indeed, this is the case for Goulding & Shankar (2004:649), who claim that "the club setting provides many contemporary consumers with an environment which links them with others who share something that is mutually valued". The upshot of this is that THEF marketers ultimately become relational partners and facilitators of community experiences, rather than the purveyors of valuable and meaningful experiences per se. In accordance with this argument, THEF marketers must have the capacity to develop the tools, skills and competencies for community service and maintenance. Marketers must seek ways in which they can facilitate and enhance their customers' peer-to-peer interactions and communications, as this will not only augment their experiences, but also allow them to offer more value in general and over time by helping to keep their products and experiences alive in the minds of their customers long after they have exited the encounter or disposed of the good they have consumed.

New technology, for example, in the form of Web 2.0 and mobile etc., is providing new ways for consumers of THEF products to come together, and share their experiences over protracted periods of time. Nutribullet, for instance, which is a food blending product designed to extract nutrients from whole foods to make them more amenable to absorption by the body, encourages community interaction and long term engagement through a wide range of social media platforms. For example, at the time of writing its sponsored Instagram account has

72,000 followers and shares frequent posts related to recipes and other brand related content, as well as photographic and textual content from their users, which display and relay their own creations and recipes. Likewise, the organisers of the Burning Man festival offer a number of platforms for 'burners' and prospects to interact both on and offline. Their online forum 'ePLaya' for example, has over 52,000 members and presently carries 951,631 individual posts around 48,260 topic themes (see https://eplaya.burningman.com). Their website also hosts thousands of images, from 'participant photographers' that document the experience of the festival over time. In the off-line context, the Burning Man project also supports a Global Regional Network made up of affiliates who co-ordinate and facilitate community activity. According to their website, these actors organise mini events and activities and use technology to leverage 'dialog, collaboration and inspiration' to keep the Burning Man spirit alive (see http://regionals. burningman.com/main/about-the-regional-network).

This insight is crucial for THEF marketers because it demonstrates how consumers are sharing their experiences of the marketplace in rich detail with others in a multitude of online and offline mediated environments, both pre-, during, and post-consumption. And this is happening whether it takes place through the sponsored platforms that are owned and managed by the marketing organisation or otherwise. In this sense THEF experiences transcend both time and space, and are increasingly self-organising and directed, whereby the emphasis shifts to the consumer who does much of the work involved. On the one hand, space is transcended as consumer experiences and interactions, in the form of photos, videos and the written word, are moving beyond the confines of the actual physical consumption of the product itself, into virtual spaces and mobile platforms such as Instagram, Twitter, Facebook, YouTube and Trip Advisor. In this respect, these experiences also transcend time, as these communications leave virtual footprints between consumers which evidence their experiences in virtual space for others to view or comment upon at their leisure. Not only does this show how experiences can be improved by community interaction, it also provides a cautionary note, along with a number of marketing opportunities for THEF marketers more generally.

In terms of the opportunities for THEF marketers, these behaviours and the platforms and contexts in which they unfold provide new places and media through which to interact with their audiences, and to facilitate peer to peer communications. As for the caution, marketers need to engage with these communities in order to monitor how these interactions either enhance or devalue their value propositions and marketing programmes and the meaning and significance they provide. In this respect, marketplace social media and consumption communities in general offer a platform for marketing research, whereby marketers can account for their customers' preferences and record their gripes, as well as map the ways in which their customers create their own experiences, meaning and value (see Kozinets, 2010). These communities thus afford opportunities for both product development and service recovery in equal measure, along with a chance to augment the experience of consumers by bringing them closer together.

◼ How consumers extend the cultural and symbolic values of THEF experiences

Although the cultural approach to marketing suggests that consumption of the THEF marketplace is central to consumers' collective and individual identities, it is important to note that there are significant differences between the ways in which identity is enacted or performed in relation to physical goods and intangible experiences such as those which are offered in our sector. Holt (1995) for example argues that much theorising and research which investigates the relationship between identity and consumption focuses predominantly on person-object relations and how consumers use material goods in an instrumental manner to communicate their identity or mark out group affiliation. These studies, he claims, simply show that consumers can reap a product's identity value purely through its use and display, such as by wearing a branded item of clothing or parking a certain model of car on the drive in front of their house. However, these accounts are limited in explaining how consumers accrue these meanings from the consumption of intangible ephemeral experiences that don't result in ownership or possession, like those that are offered in the THEF marketplace. So while a consumer may accrue the meanings and status from attending a prestigious event, flying business class on vacation, or making a guided climb of Everest for example, this is only short lived, and may not be recognised by those whom a consumer really wants to influence. In these instances, Holt's (1995) research shows that consumers mitigate this problem by drawing upon a range of resources and practices which increase the chances of being associated with their symbolism over time and across social contexts and situations. Thus consumers of THEF may extend the temporal boundaries of a product's symbolic and identity value, though amongst other things:

- The purchase and wear of clothing related to the experience, such as a concert t-shirt, branded trucker cap or team jersey. Holt's research, for instance, focused on baseball spectatorship and an obvious means of associating with the team and the game was to wear clothing adorned with the team's insignia and colours;

- The collection of souvenirs, postcards, photographs and videos which are both displayed or shared with acquaintances and used as prompts in conversations about their travels or experiences. Schwartz & Halegoua (2015:1647) for example explain how "postcards with photographs of distant locales or familiar places, annotated by the sender, articulate something social and spatial about presence at particular moments in time"; and

- Storytelling, which for Holt is the primary vehicle through which consumers "specify their relationship" and ties with a product or activity, and which allow them to fill in the details and elaborate on their experience. That is to say, stories allow consumers to richly describe their experiences and demonstrate that they have indeed 'been there and done that'. In this sense stories about consumption or which relay information about encounters and experiences with the THEF marketplace can be classified as *cultural resources* that are brought to bear in identity performances.

In Richardson's and Turely's (2007) work into football fandom, for example, we are shown how stories and a range of other consumer resources and practices are used both at football matches and through other peer to peer interactions outside of attending a game to maintain social distinctions between 'real fans' and 'day-trippers', and as a means by which in-group membership is achieved and awarded to others. In this respect, it is what fans do, and the resources they deploy in their interactions with others both during and following games that creates the value they desire and which in turn allows them to achieve their goals of being identified as 'proper supporters' and to accrue elite status. In this context, identity value is produced in a number of ways. On the one hand fans accrue status through practices related to frugality and service (ibid) whereby they are expected to attend all matches including European games no matter what, and in doing so, are forced into allocating their scarce economic and temporal resources efficiently. However, in doing so *their frugality is socially rewarded in terms of the cultural capital gained from going on these 'European away trips'. Supporters can join in the storytelling and mutual recounting of these experiences, the effect of which is to reaffirm the group of their distinctive identity as 'real fans'.* (2008:35). Furthermore, by virtue of their status, 'real fans' are classified by their encyclopedic knowledge of their team's history, players and current form, as well as the knowledge about the detail of each game, and are able to relay this through further stories and the display of collected artefacts such as photographs and match programmes.

Of course while this example and the concepts outlined beforehand offer a rich picture into the classificatory practices consumers of ephemeral products perform in constructing or embellishing their identities and affiliations, and the resources that they bring to bear in these practices, they do not capture the socio-cultural context of today's technology enabled marketplace and the channels through which people communicate and place themselves on display. Therefore, following Belk (2013) we cannot ignore the role that technology plays in identity construction and as a result we must assume that a consumer's social media applications now become a primary site through which they channel their experiences and classify themselves with these products as they stream their lives and experiences online (Sheth & Solomon, 2014). Thus to return to the example of football fans, armed with a range of mobile devices these supporters may then leverage social networks, such as Facebook, Twitter or YouTube to share their stories and experiences on a broader scale. What is more, location-based social media such as Foursquare, Instagram and Facebook etc., which provide geo-coded information in real time to reveal the destinations to which a consumer travels and the myriad places and social contexts they inhabit, enhance these practices. Thus we are seeing the emergence of the spatial self whereby *"millions of people...[are using]... these tools to annotate their physical locations and instantly...[sharing]... them with various social groups such as...[their]... 'friends' and 'followers"* and in relation to this *""the spatial self is becoming a prominent part of our daily life".* (Schwartz & Halegoua, 2014:1647). As a result, THEF marketers would be wise to augment their customers' experiences and consumption of their products by equipping them with the resources and technologies to continue reaping the benefits of their meanings long after they have withdrawn from their physical encounters. That is to say, to support their consumers' socio-cultural work and identity performances producers and marketers of ephemeral and transitory experiences need to pay attention to the symbolic 'half-life' of their products and their effects. By not taking ownership of these types of experiences, consumers may require other forms of physical evidence and collected artefacts and memories that they can share with their social networks and friends both during consumption and into the future.

■ Co-creating meanings in the THEF marketplace

While we advocate a cultural approach to marketing which promotes the view that marketing practice intermediates culture and produces valuable symbols, it is not to say that we are reasserting an exchange perspective of marketing, whereby marketers are solely responsible for imbuing their products with meaning. Nor are we advocating that marketers are the only agents who transfer meaning to their products and services, or that consumers interpret THEF products and servicescapes in the same way. Rather, the cultural approach we adopt within this book dovetails with the service logic of marketing in the respect that the meaning of goods and service are co-created and produced by a range of actors in the marketplace through their interactions, albeit with the addition that these are mediated by the socio-cultural contexts in which they are situated. Doug Holt (2004) has made great strides in developing this line of thinking in his work and theories about cultural branding. This approach which asserts that brands *"function as conduits for the expression of ideological meanings"* (Humphreys & Thompson, (2014:879), suggests that most new products start off in life as empty vessels which acquire meaning over time as they interact with different agents in culture. These agents, or as Holt calls them, *authors,* imbue the product with meaning as they share their stories and experiences, and bring their own interpretive logic into their representations. This view is shared by Humphreys & Thompson, (2014:879) who concur that the cultural meanings of a brand *"are often established not through the strategic actions of marketing management per se but, rather, through the representations of these brands in popular culture via television shows, movies, political discourse, and news media coverage".*

This insight is crucial for THEF marketers as it illustrates that it is not just consumers who co-create the value and meanings of their products, and a gamut of case studies and academic research that cut across the THEF sectors supports this view (see Holt, 2004a; Holt & Cameron, 2010). In his examination of Jack Daniels for example, Holt (2006) demonstrates through a genealogical analysis of the brand that its meanings and market value have been co-created and shaped over time as the product has diffused through culture. In particular this brand has garnered value and success as it as ridden the coat-tails of popular culture, absorbing meanings from how it has been represented in the movies and popular fiction as well as from authentic celebrity endorsements. In the post war years, for example, Jack Daniels absorbed meanings from Hollywood icons such as John

Huston, a famous American film director and film, actor Humphrey Bogart, who were both renowned Jack Daniels fans and "unabashedly championed an old-school view of manhood, aligned with the western frontier" myth through both their work and lifestyles, and the media celebrated them in equal measure, widely reporting on their tastes and lives (ibid, p.366). Holt goes on to detail how the whisky brand then gained further cultural traction from being a central theme and prop in the movie HUD, soaking up the film's tough guy modern cowboy narrative in the process. What is more, the association with Paul Newman, the film's lead actor, who at the time was a rising Hollywood star renowned for portraying cowboy roles added additional cultural bolster. Thus, *"HUD's popularity, and Paul Newman's rise to fame… served to cement Jack Daniel's iconicity as the drink for those American men who identified with these values in the face of a rapidly evolving society"*, which at the time, seemed to be turning its back on these ideas of masculinity in favour of those aligned with the white collar worker and organisational man (Holt, 2006:372). In this way, according to the findings from this research, *"Jack Daniel's cultural power stems from its role in sustaining a particular ideal of masculinity in American society"* and that these expressions were constructed through amongst other things, the brands portrayal in popular culture and the media, and only retrospectively embellished by the marketing programmes and activity of the company itself (Holt, 2006: 373).

In a similar manner, recent research by Beresford (2016) demonstrates how the ALDI supermarket brand has managed to grow and capture significant market share from incumbents in the UK at a time when the overall grocery market was contracting. Through a systematic longitudinal analysis of UK news articles reporting the brand from 2007 to 2015, this research shows how the media gave the brand a helping hand by re-shaping its brand meanings from that of a down market discounter to a legitimate place to shop for consumers with middle class taste and sensibilities. In particular, the findings reveal significant changes in the quantity and qualitative content of the news articles over time, and these can be mapped in relation to its growth and changes in its appeal and customer base. At the starting point of the analysis, the articles typically repeat narratives associated with supermarket carrier bag snobbery but this changes over time through to articles applauding the products and reporting on new store openings being flooded by middle class consumers, who fill the car parks with expensive executive German cars and Land Rovers, etc. This research also shows how middle class consumers themselves became central authors in the realignment of the ALDI brand and in doing so helped to popularise the brand with their cohort as they shared their positive experiences of the retailer and its products with their friends around dinner tables and at the school gates.

In addition to being key authors in the meanings of THEF products and brands, research in the cultural tradition also shows how consumers themselves produce or embellish the meaning of marketing materials and products as they interact with them throughout the consumption cycle. In general this body of work investigates the numerous ways "in which commercial narratives are shaped, consumed, and transformed during marketplace interactions between producers.... consumers" (Chronis, 2008: 7) and the cultural contexts in which they are situated (Askegaard & Linnet, 2011). In this respect, following Penaloza (2000) this perspective draws our attention to the important idea that both the marketplace and marketing objects and materials are in effect cultural mediations that are produced through the actions and interactions between marketers and their audiences.

In their study of the Whitby Goth Festival, for instance, Goulding and Saren (2009) describe in detail how many of the attendees of this event draw upon a range of *media representations* related to vampire mythology to achieve their consumption goals of subverting mass-marketed representations of the female body and beauty ideals, in their consumption performances to "put the curves back into the feminine", "blur the boundaries" between the genders, and pursue "gender as fantasy" (ibid, 2009:27). This, the authors argue, is because the mythology of the vampire itself subverts 'traditional' notions of sexuality, with vampires being represented as androgynous and sexually ambiguous in much of the literature and media. Thus, knowledge of the myth and the media which disseminates it, such as Bram

Stoker's Dracula, act as essential *cultural resources* through which the consumption at the festival is practiced and experienced.

In a similar way, research that investigates the consumption of Gettysburg demonstrate how visitor experiences of this historic battle field site are shaped in relation to their prior knowledge which is in itself informed by a range of cultural texts and associated life experiences (Chronis, 2008). By explicitly drawing on the work of Stern (e.g. 1989) who, similar to Holt (2002; 1998) surmises that products and marketing materials are cultural texts and narratives that are open to multiple readings and meanings, this research shows that:

> "...consumers bring their prior knowledge to their experience of... Gettysburg. The movies they have seen, the books they have read, and the oral histories they have listened to are welded together through their... experience. Mass media, travel literature, history books, and popular novels (i.e. *The Killer Angels*) suffuse their present experience.... [Thus consumer experiences of]... Gettysburg... [are]... always mediatized and constructed intertextually". (Chronis, Arnould & Hampton. 2012: 278).

Finally, in their four year multi-site ethnographic study of five Lesbian and Gay Pride Day Festivals, Kates and Belk (2001) demonstrate how these events are symbolically consumed and experienced in relation to a multitude of complex and multi-layered meanings and motivations. On the one hand the festival is a carnivalesque space for experiencing "spontaneous fun and extraordinary" emotion "that transcends the everyday", while on the other, it marks a "symbolic protest of the dominant culture" (2001:403) which stands in "defiance of conservative sexual norms" (2001:420). In contrast, the festival also stands as a symbol of "pride in self, concern for other human beings, emotional support, and acceptance of others" (2001:411). Additionally the festival provides a context to express a range of identities from the excessive and extreme through to the more sober; indeed for some who align with "more conventional norms of propriety usually associated with mainstream middle-class sensibilities"the excesses of the festival conflicts with "their personal constructions of sexual identity"(2001:407). Thus, in agreement with Holt (1997: 334) these events can be conceived as "polysemic symbolic resources… that allow for significant variation in consumer interpretation and use", and importantly, this is a characteristic of product experiences that is arguably shared across the THEF sector.

What is more, the findings from each of these studies parallel many others in this genre, which collectively detail:

1   The ways in which consumers negotiate their own meanings from their experiences;

2   How cultural representations including those from the media pattern the experiences of THEF;

3   The numerous ways cultural narratives and historical context become *cultural resources* that are selectively used in consumption (See Belk & Costa, 1998; Peñaloza, 2000; Thompson & Tian, 2008), and how these in turn are integral to the consumption practices and interpretive strategies of consumers more generally (Kozinets, 2001); and

4   How consumers integrate and use their knowledge, life experiences, cultural capital resources (Holt; 1998; Moisio, Arnould & Gentry, 2013) and values (Thompson & Troester, 2002) in their consumption to shape their experiences, which is something we evaluate in more depth in Chapters 7 and 9.

Thus, in light of these arguments, following Thompson & Troester (2002: 550) we advocate an approach to THEF marketing that includes an analysis and appreciation of the *"imbricated layers of cultural meaning that structure consumer actions in a given social context…[and which]… shape consumers' interpretations of their experiences"*. That is to say, to improve the outcome of marketing practice and research, THEF marketers should concentrate on the culture and context in which their consumers create their experiences and identities, not only on the individual needs, personal characteristics, and resources of consumers more generally. In addition, having demonstrated how the meanings of products are often co-created through the cultural work and narratives of a range of authors that sit outside of the organisation's control and influence, THEF marketers need to accept the idea that they are but one mediator amongst a range of cultural intermediaries who shape the culture (Holt 2004a) and value of their brands. By embracing this view, THEF marketers may find that they can allocate their scarce marketing resources more efficiently and effectively. That is to say, they may be able to leverage the cultural work of these 'other' authors through their own practice and media channels. This is indeed the case with many brands across the sectors that presently encourage and share their customers' branded content and celebrity endorsements through their own social media platforms and communication channels.

4

■ Conclusion

This chapter has introduced the reader to the socio-cultural perspective of marketing and represents a third approach through which to consider the THEF marketplace and the experiences it affords. In drawing attention to the cultural approach, we show how important meanings and values, and notions of identity and community are to THEF marketing and consumption, as well as to product symbolism more generally. This chapter has also drawn attention to the numerous ways in which the meanings of products and experiences are co-created and produced by a range of actors in the marketplace through their interactions and cultural work. We can see from this perspective how important the stories that these authors relay in the marketplace are to both meaning creation and product symbolism over time. Thus like Hall (1997), Holt, (2004), Thompson & Haytko (1997), and Arnould & Thompson (2005) before us, we offer a view that marketplace meanings, which include the meanings of adverts, products, servicescapes and so on, are negotiated and mediated between marketers, consumers and other authors who have a stake in an organisation's success or demise. In addition, this approach draws further attention to the productive and creative roles of consumers and the ways in which they interact with the symbolic properties of THEF products through their resources to achieve their own peculiar and unique goals. People do not just consume products from the THEF marketplace to create value and seek entertainment etc., they engage these as *cultural resources* in the hope of, amongst other things, shaping and realising identities and forging community and kinship. Accordingly, THEF marketers must begin to accept their role as cultural intermediaries and guardians and facilitators of community practices. In so doing they will realise the significant value and potential that these roles offer to practice. Not only will they be able to design more compelling and meaningful products and experiences, and create more expressive marketing materials, they will also be able to develop more lasting and durable relationships with their audiences.

5 Putting the Experiences into Experiences Marketing

■ Introduction

In order to understand how experiences marketing needs to differ from other forms of marketing, we first need to identify why THEF plays such a significant role in contemporary society and so, as a consequence, why its marketing requires special attention. Just as THEF reflect social and cultural movements, so does its marketing. As the western world has moved from what may be defined as the era of modernity into the era of post-industrialisation/modernity, this shift has been accompanied by certain social, cultural and economic traits that have resulted in a restructuring of society (Harvey, 1989, Lash and Urry, 1994). It is argued that this has led to a period of 'social (dis)-organization' (Franklin and Crang, 2001:7). This 'social (dis)-organization' can be seen to be the result of an alleged fragmentation of society and culture (Harvey, 1989). We now live in a society that is dominated by the media, traditional communities have broken up, trends are fleeting, our lives change very quickly, and this has resulted in feelings of uncertainty. As a result of these feelings we have turned to activities that provide comfort and meaning. Contemporary experiences marketing frames these activities within the marketing language and processes of food, tourism, hospitality and food.

Additionally, experiences marketing reflects the social and cultural movements that circulate contemporary society, and draws on discourses, rituals and trends to create a complex form of marketing practice that offers the entry into dreamscapes and marketingscapes, in which emotions and the needs of the consumer are met by utilising a range of marketing strategies, conventions and representations. This is what differentiates experiences marketing from other forms of marketing. Before the significance and meaning of experiences marketing can be charted, it is important to identify themes that have emerged from the shift to the post-industrial/modern era as experiences marketing can be perceived as both the result of these themes, and as a reaction to them. For authors such as Eco (1990) and Foucault (1987), the contemporary world is dominated by signs, to the point that the individual's social and cultural location is governed by 'simulational' (Foucault, 1987) and 'hyperreal' (Eco, 1990) relations. As Baudrillard asserts:

> The era of simulation is everywhere initiated by the interchange-ability of previously contradictory and dialectical terms...the inter-changeability of the beautiful and the ugly in fashion; of the right and the left in politics; of the true and false in every media message; of the useful and useless at the level of objects; and of nature and culture at every level of meaning. All the great humanist criteria of value, all the values of a civilisation of moral, civic and practical judgement, vanish in our system of images and signs. Everything becomes undecidable. (1993:128)

The result of this for the individual is that the relationship between the signified and signifier becomes blurred, for example, as a reaction to the economic downturn that followed the credit crunch of 2008, food retailers in the UK introduced 'basic' ranges that included smoked salmon and extra virgin olive oil etc., thus blurring the boundaries between luxury and utilitarian categories of food. The Venetian Hotel in Las Vegas offers you the opportunity to sit down outside the Coliseum drinking a cappuccino while the Roman sunset romantically sets every twenty minutes. This version of the world becomes central to the discourse that creates the foundations of experiences marketing.

The continued globalisation and preoccupation with signs, brands and the media within contemporary society has led to a type of spatial dislocation. For Jameson:

> this latest mutation in space – post-modern hyperspace – has finally succeeded in transcending the capacities of the individual human body to locate itself, to organise its immediate surroundings perceptually, and cognitively to map its position in a mappable external world. (1991:44)

According to Jameson people no longer know where they are; they are lost both socially and spatially in the processes of the de-differentiation that surrounds culture and society. Experiences marketing is a consequence of this de-differentiation, as it plays representations of time, place, emotions, relationships, destinations and experiences by creating a dreamscape in which the consumer can escape everyday life. Mike Featherstone comments that:

> If we examine the definitions of postmodernism, we find an emphasis on the effacement of the boundary between art and everyday life, the collapse of the distinction between high art and mass/popular culture, a general stylistic promiscuity and playful mixing of codes. (1991:65)

The outcome of this de-differentiation is a breakdown in the distinctiveness of each area of social and cultural activity; each area implodes into one another bringing at every opportunity, spectacle or play. The impact of this on the consumer is that the relationship between the world represented in experiences marketing and the real world become blurred. A good example of this is where tourism marketing presents images of destinations, beaches or attractions that are completely devoid of signs of modernity such as cars or telegraph poles. This emptying of markers of development, people or technology has the effect of providing the consumer with greater freedom to find individual meaning within the interpretation process. This is achieved in experiences marketing by utilising a collage of words and images that creates a very specific language of experiences (This will be further discussed in Chapter 8).

The impact of collage and the blurring of boundaries in cultural production, media and THEF marketing directly influences the individual's consumer personality and their relationship to marketing communications by shifting reference points. For example, there has been a trend for fusion food, whereby food styles and traditions become blurred creating a distinctive gastronomic style. However, food reflects both culture and geography, and its grounding means something to people. Fusion food no longer relates food to geography, but it does relate to a more global definition of culture (Tresidder 2015). Marketers, designers and editors draw from global cultures creating global trends, however this makes it difficult for us to think about how the things we buy, eat or drink link us to notions of home. For Jameson (1985) this creates a form of schizophrenia as we draw from a range of influences, cultures and styles that do not link together and we lose links to foundations that defined our culture and identity. Harvey states:

> If personal identity is forged through "a certain temporal unification of the past and future with the present before me", and if sentences move through the same trajectory, then an inability to unify past, present, and future in the sentence betokens a similar inability to "unify the past, present and future of our own biographical experience..." (1993:53).

What this means for practice in experiences marketing is that the use of timeless images removes an element of meaning or signposting of experience, so that the individual consumer will be able to mediate their own THEF experiences, values and worldview, to create their own understanding or interpretation of the represented experience. (see Chapter 9). In practice, this creates a problem for the marketer as they have to accept that the marketing process will be understood in multiple ways by consumers, as the above process frees or separates them from their established cultural foundations. For example, when we visit an iconic destination such as the Tower of London, we arrive with a set of temporal knowledges that draw from sources such as films, television, news, advertisements, literature and personal experiences. Consequently, a collage of historical and cultural influences informs the consumer's understanding of destinations and other THEF experiences.

Contemporary marketing practice's preoccupation with the signi-fier (the image) rather than the signified (meaning) and with surface, rather than roots, reduces marketing to "a series of pure and unrelated presents in time" (Jameson, 1985). As such, postmodernism creates a form of social and cultural fragmentation (Jameson, 1984) that leads to a lack of coherence within the production of signs and images and as such impacts upon the individual's perception of the world by dislocating reference points. Experiences marketing is located within two interrelated debates: first, that the signs and images contained within adverts and THEF servicescapes reflect the postmodern traits of de-differentiation etc.; and second, that the consumer may find some sense of comfort or belonging within experience marketing by entering into the dreamscapes created within campaigns and offered in the manifold products that constitute the THEF marketplace.

The previous sections are important in understanding the signifi-cance of experiences marketing, as they argue that the shift to post-industrialisation has led to consumers possessing feelings of 'being rootless' (Lane and Waitt, 2001) and of 'alienation' (Gabriel, 1993), additionally it has created new sets of media-influenced wants and desires (to have the ideal body, partner, car, holiday meal etc.), that can never be achieved (Rojek, 1995). It is within this environment that the marketing and consumption of THEF plays a stabilising role for both society and the consumer. Experiences marketing offers what Uzzell (1984) refers to as 'escape hatches' from the pressures and uncertainty of modern society. This is achieved by experiences marketing utilis-ing a set of marketing practices and conventions that draw from a range of discourses and traditions that enable the consumer to find roots in a rootless society, to escape and make sense of everyday life. Experiences marketing creates a time and space that is different from everyday lived experience and is central to the message contained within marketing communications. The first way in which experiences marketing creates escape hatches is through the creation of a notion of time that reflects the entry into a world where experiences and prod-ucts are elevated to a higher level than their actual experiential status.

■ Experiences marketing and the sacred

As stated above, experiences marketing utilises a set of conventions and approaches that represent events, tourism, hospitality and food in a particular way, so that they are seen to possess a heightened significance within the rootlessness of the post-industrial/modern world. Experiences marketing both utilises and creates a discourse of THEF that differentiates representations of time and space by elevating the represented experience to that of the 'extraordinary' and is in direct opposition to everyday reality. This process is best demonstrated in food marketing: for example, we see a ready meal being presented in a fine dining or aesthetically constructed frame, and this breaks the link to the mundane nature of ready meals, elevating it to extraordinary or even the sacred (see Tresidder, 2010a, 2011). The configuration of time and space utilised within experiences marketing is specific to the promotion of THEF, and this practice reinforces the binary relationship between the profane/everyday and the sacred/extraordinary nature of the experience. For example tourist advertisements will often show the tourist at work and then on holiday, and the convention will often make work dark and rainy, while holiday is light and sunny. We can understand this differentiation of time and space by developing Durkheim's (1995) conception of the 'sacred and profane' within food, hospitality, events and tourism marketing.

THEF marketing becomes just one of the means by which the consumer frames their experiences of the social, and as such, constitutes an important role in their life. Just as Silverstone (1988) envisages television as a 'ritual frame', a cognitive, imaginative and practical space in which everyone can access the things that mark off the social from the private (Couldry, 2001:158), it can be argued that experiences marketing constructs a ritual frame or lens that is composed with marketing texts. Tourism and events marketing marks the distinction between social experience and ordinary experience, and subsequently, what may be termed the sacred and the profane. For Durkheim (1995) the conception of the sacred and profane are socially generated and underline the distinction between social and ordinary experience. In reality what this means is that in a world where people are becoming less engaged with religion, they search for other ways to define and celebrate their entry into sacred time. Thus, the purchasing of goods or services become markers of points of our lives; examples of this include the honeymoon, buying your first car or first house, all of these activities mark important transitions within consumers' lives. For Belk et al. (1989), in the absence of collectively recognised rites of passage, consumers will use their purchasing of products and services as contemporary rites of passage; consequently consumption of goods and services becomes a very important part of people's lives. Commenting on Bourdieu's conception of the sacred and profane, Genosko commented that: "He took great care to outline how the profane needs the sacred, and the regulation, through rites, of the process of consecration in the passage into the sacred from the profane." (2003:75) The sacred or extraordinary status of THEF are reinforced by their social and cultural production and consumption, but also by experiences marketing as signifying something 'extraordinary' or the 'sacred sphere of excess' (Caillois, 1988:282) within campaigns. It is within this discussion, that the sacred and profane is a useful analogy for the distinction between the sacred worlds of tourism, hospitality, events and food as represented in experiences marketing, and the profane world of everyday lived experience (see Sheldrake, 2001).

A major theme of experiences marketing is that it is not the everyday (Belk et al 1989) – it is a means of escape from our everyday lived experience of working, cooking the daily meal, utilitarian shopping and washing the dishes. By adopting Caillois' view that the sacred had shifted from celebration at the societal level to, 'individualized isolated experiences' (Genosko, 2003:76), whereby the entry into the extraordinary sacred world of experiences marketing becomes an individual quest, in which the individual consumer may find meaning and escape in their own lives. This notion of escape is identified by Berlyn who suggests that human life tries to maintain a preferred level of arousal and seeks: "…artificial sources of stimulation…to make up for the shortcomings of their environment" (1977:170). The content and structure of many THEF marketing campaigns and the experiences themselves can be examined against the ordinary workaday life; and attending an event, or family holiday or special meal become the markers of the passage of time, making up part of the consumer's memories and personal biography.

■ Time and space

The use of time and space in experiences marketing is one of the most widely used and significant conventions. Campaigns will clearly structure their advertisements to show the differences between everyday life and the sacred spaces of THEF. For example, everyday food is shown in a setting that is outside the ordinary; and the use of black and white shots reinforces the timelessness of tourism, while creating individual events that encourage you to escape. Durkheim's view was that the sacred was simply society transposed on to the spiritual level, and the distinction between the sacred and the profane is a universal social fact: "The sacred and the profane have always and everywhere been conceived by the human mind as two distinct classes" (1995:38-9). It is this idea that THEF marketing offers a different representation of time and space encompassing the sacred that makes it different from other forms of marketing. The sacred does not deny any notion of time, but rather the notion of the sacred, as represented within experiences marketing, is conceived as timeless and authentic experiences (authenticity of landscape, people, personal relationships, food, culture and experience) which transport us into a time and space that has become sacred. As Stirrat states: "To be truly at one with the sacred involves attaining an existence outside time and space, and thus to be truly sacred, religious virtuosi must attempt to live outside society." (1984:203) Experiences marketing provides an opportunity to live outside the time and space of everyday life for a limited period, and the signs and images utilised in THEF marketing create an alternative temporal and spatial dimension which becomes central to everyday life as offering a form of escape.

■ Liminality

Experiences marketing uses a notion of temporal and spatial liminality (in the form of signs and images) in which the consumer is provided with the opportunity to be released from their normal social constraints, the representations of liminality within the advert 'signposts' (Jenkins, 2003) the vicarious esoteric or metaphysical consumption of THEF. Liminality may be defined as a place or event that is out-of or in-between time, for example, we do things on holiday that we do not do at home as we are in a time that is different from our everyday life. The liminal space that exists within the marketing communication between the transmission of the marketing message, and the actual consumption of the product witnesses the blurring of the boundaries between reality and the imagined consumption of the product. This liminal period releases the consumer from the imposed norms of everyday lived experience or the social constraints and implications of overconsumption etc. It enables the virtual entrance into a world of hedonism and escape, thus experiences marketing becomes a reflexive, expressive space in which individuality is reinforced, as consumers are textually and virtually freed from the constraints of their existing social structures. Turner (1977) characterises this temporal and spatial removal from social constraints as 'antistructure', whereby the content of the social relations are no longer normative and hierarchical but egalitarian; this is a process which he hails as 'communitas'. Experiences marketing creates a form of 'communitas' where consumers can bridge their social and cultural differences by finding communitas within shared consumption patterns, and a process of harmonisation that enables them to escape and find freedom from the constraints of their normal lives. Turner states that this freedom results in a process that he classifies as 'flow' (1977:48-52) and can be characterised as:

> the non-reflective stage that is characteristic of a person who is engaged in some important activity, in which action and awareness emerge, self-awareness gives way to attention focused on a limited field in which the participant is engaged in mastering, a feeling which is a reward in itself, not a means to an external

5

end. While such feelings may characterise those engaged in religious acts, e.g., taking communion, they are also common to leisure occupations, such as hobbies, sex acts, recreation, and games. (Graburn, 1986:545)

The ritual status of THEF and the search for meaning and experiences through their consumption becomes a contemporary form of pilgrimage. Experiences marketing enables us to travel the world consuming different tastes and experiences without leaving home; THEF becomes celebrated and even worshipped. It is this hedonistic element that becomes central to so many pilgrimages (see Pfaffenberger, 1979), and that reinforces the significance of experiences marketing. At this point it is important to understand how THEF experiences gain their sacred distinction.

■ The myth of hospitality and food as sacred

The relationship between hospitality, food, the sacred and religion is clearly developed (Hely, 2002; Artbury, 2005; O'Connor, 2005; O'Gorman, 2007; Claseen, 2007). Experiences marketing utilises a particular marketing language that generates an embedded configuration of hospitality and food within the sacred domain of culture, and becomes part of the 'legitimate art of living' (Reed-Danahay, 1996). It can be seen as an example what may be termed a contemporary 'sacralisation ritual' (Belk et al., 1989). The experience of hospitality and dining is embedded with ritual and significance (Fantasia 1995, Ferry, 2003; Marshall, 2005), and the formal dining experience as represented by the formality of the table setting etc., connotes, signifies and directs interpretation by drawing upon the recognised ritualisation and formality of dining (Gvion and Trostler, 2008). This ritual of dining creates social order; the ritual acts as a script that is regulated by the order of dishes, the formality of setting and intensity of experience (Marshall, 2005). Experiences marketing offers the consumer a 'passage into the sacred' or the 'sacred sphere of excess' (Caillois, 1988:282). The embedded connotations of luxury within experiences marketing, demonstrate a social distinction that enhances social bonds in which dining and hospitality becomes a celebration of society itself (van der Veen, 2003) and in the Durkheimian tradition 'sacred'.

■ Tourism and events as sacred

Tourism and events as represented within experiences marketing fulfil a social and cultural role, and the activity itself becomes a myth (defined by expectation), whereby tourism, events and festivals become "one of the central means by which the individual makes sense of everyday life" (Lofgren, 1999:6-7). Both the activity and the promise of the activity, as represented within experiences marketing, offer various escape routes through the creation of a constructed definition or 'configuration' of time and space (Jokinen and McKie, 1997; Nelson, 2005) that is defined by hedonism, authenticity, fun and escape. This configuration of time and space, between work and play, is a recurrent theme in tourism and events marketing. It highlights the differentiation and significance of the activities and can be seen as a marketing convention to define destinations and experience (see Sturma, 1999; Pryayag, 2009). This signifies a certain binary opposition to everyday lived experience that encourages us to escape, relax or celebrate. Such an approach is clearly witnessed in events marketing, which often focuses on the heightening of experience, or carnival, of the spontaneity, exclusivity and extra-ordinariness of the event. While business events utilise a mixture of the profane business element juxtaposed with the sacred element of the reward (food, drink, excursions etc.).

■ The myth of authenticity

In addition to the above, experiences marketing often portrays tourism and events as conduits into a more mythical world, where landscape, culture, people and food are more real that the experiences we have in our own everyday life. This approach represents a time and place that is differentiated from everyday lived experience by developing marketing strategies and communications, whereby the possibility of escape is signposted for the consumer (Jenkins, 2003). As these strategies draw on the embedded significance of tourism and events they create the expected places of tourism, hospitality, events and food marketing. The timeless and spaceless landscapes free the consumer to explore their own emotions through exploring what can be termed 'existential objectivity'. The role of experiences marketing is to signify expected and available time and space in which to explore and seek authentic relations. The significance of events and tourism as an activity become heightened by creating a historical discourse and myth that draws on history, religion, ritual and cultural significance and that further embeds its significance within contemporary society. In addition to this, one of the major aspects of THEF experiences is that they are fun, are often joyful and as such, underpinned by hedonistic discourses within the surrounding marketing literature.

■ Hedonism and THEF marketing

As stated above, THEF marketing provides access into a world that is dominated by fun or hedonism, though each consumer will define fun or the search for fun in different ways. Thus in order to understand the needs of the consumer and how they consume THEF, we need to explore notions of hedonistic or ludic behaviour. Hedonistic or ludic behaviour (see Kozinets et al., 2004) has always been a central precept of THEF (Cohen, 1995) in the form of festivals and carnivals. The act of celebration has been a significant element of our lives; it makes sense of our lives and justifies our existence. Krippendorf (1999) goes as far as to state that tourism is a form of social therapy, and that its consumption revitalises and soothes us. Thus, in order to understand how consumers relate to experiences marketing, it is important that we examine the notion of hedonism and how we find pleasure, as this informs how companies or organisations theme or structure their products, services, activities and campaigns. It is also important to recognise that each of us creates our own pleasure zones, and as such we create and construct an environment that enables us to gain the maximum levels of pleasure possible.

What we find pleasurable is a direct reflection of our personalities and worldview, however experiences marking is adept at creating campaigns that create liminal spaces in which we may locate our desires, while the industry creates products and services that meet our desires. For example we can see the delivered pizza as creating an aesthetic of consumption that creates pleasure and gratification. Thus, on the one hand we can go through the process of utilitarian shopping (as opposed to hedonistic shopping) where we buy ingredients, go home, and make the pizza, which leaves us with a mess and washing up, and on top of this we have to wait to experience the meal. The alternative is to order over the phone: the pizza is made for us; we have unlimited choice as to the toppings; there are lots of extras that heighten the experience; we can choose dips, drinks, and deserts; and it is then delivered to us. This is the 'ideal pizza' – a pizza that has been made especially for us. It is bespoke, made by experts, no one else will have a pizza like ours – it is the best pizza in the world. The experience of eating, of ordering a pizza become elevated to a hedonistic aesthetic that underpins the concept of experiences marketing. However, if the consumer does not like pizza, it would not be a pleasurable experience for them. Also the notion of hedonism is formed in many ways, so people find pleasure in many differing experiences. In order to understand how the individual finds pleasure, Schiffman and Kanuk (2006) identify four forms of hedonism that are particularly significant for experiences marketing:

Psychological hedonism

This may be defined as the most dominant definition of hedonism, as it reflects the fact that we all naturally seek pleasure. This category underpins the majority of experiences marketing, whereby campaigns focus on the fun, pleasure element of the experience.

Moral or ethical hedonism

It has been recognised by marketers (O'Shaughnessy & O'Shaughnessy, 2002), for a considerable time that consumers are attracted to ethical products and campaigns. There is pleasure in knowing that we have caused no damage or are making an ethical choice, as such, many companies and organisation have invested in marketing their green or ethical credentials. Companies such as Cadburys and Starbucks have adopted a 'Fairtrade' approach through their production and purchasing strategies, as a result of this a number of their recent marketing campaigns have focussed on this rather than the product. Holiday companies such as Centre Parcs have always made their environmental policy a central premise of their promotion strategy, while events such as Glastonbury donate profits to Greenpeace. The inclusion of a moral theme adds capital to the product and removes some of the barriers to consumption by enabling consumers to obtain pleasure from their ethical behaviour.

Universal hedonism

This approach makes the assumption that there is a human right to have access to things that provide pleasure (O'Shaughnessy & O'Shaughnessy, 2002). Thus, there is a pleasure in undertaking activities as part of a group who are also finding pleasure. This very much underpins the notion of being part of a group, audience or mass all sharing and expecting the same experiences. This is experienced in the communitas which accompanies festivals, carnivals and tourism.

Rationalising hedonism

The concept of rational recreation is not a new one. The rationalisation of leisure was used in the mid 19th century to create a better educated and healthier workforce (Clarke & Critcher, 1985). There is a pleasure in feeling that you are bettering yourself through activity, and this can include gaining pleasure from educational, spiritual, cultural or physically based activities. Such activities are often removed from traditional experiences of eating, drinking and sunbathing associated with traditional holidays. The idea of abstinence or getting healthier underpins many aspects of experiences marketing, and although it may be seen to be in opposition to the more dominant definitions of hedonism, abstinence can still be seen as a hedonistic activity for some consumers (Cole, 2008).

Thus, each consumer group or individual will search for the things that give them most pleasure, and the choices they make in booking their holiday, hotel or tickets for an event reflect this choice. Kahn, Ratner and Kanemen sum up this process perfectly:

> Consider how a consumer decides which songs to play at a jukebox. If only one song is going to be played, the decision is easy: choose the song that brings the most enjoyment. (1997:85)

Thus consumer choice will reflect the experience they believe is going to give them the most pleasure for the limited amount of money and time they possess. As such, the language of THEF as discussed in Chapter 8 represents not only a semiotic language, but also a hedonic discourse of experiences marketing. Jin, Sternquist & Koh (2003) illustrate how such a hedonic discourse can inform even the simple activity of shopping, they state that there are two different types of shopping (as alluded to earlier in this chapter):

- **Utilitarian shopping** includes the majority of shopping activities such as purchasing the items we need to exist (in other words this may be seen to fall into the profane category). It is part of the ordinary, the mundane; as such it lacks the excitement of hedonic shopping and thus lacks pleasure.

- **Hedonic shopping** makes up the element of shopping that excites, the search for bargains, luxury items or those special things that we reward ourselves with. This is in direct opposition to utilitarian shopping. (This type of activity clearly falls into the sacred category of activities).

We can also use this distinction to understand how the level of pleasure or hedonism will differ according to the context and purpose of the activity. For example the degree of pleasure derived from attending an event will depend upon the motivation, the purpose of travel – for business or pleasure – eating to live, for business or celebration, will all determine individual pleasure levels. It is interesting to note that the production of marketing strategies and contexts recognise these boundaries and identify that often there is a blurring of boundaries between the utilitarian and the hedonic. A good example of this is incentivised travel whereby there is an assumption that travel will increase productivity.

The blurring of boundaries between work and pleasure is a popular convention in experiences marketing. If the business element is being marketed then the materials will also often contain links back to the facility to give you pleasure once your work is completed, for example the fine dining restaurants, the spa facilities, the nightlife of the destination. This approach attempts to reconcile the hedonistic needs of the individual consumer. Marketing can be seen to induce the need for and create expectations around hedonic consumption patterns.

■ Vicarious hedonism

The purpose of experiences marketing is to create interest or to sell our experience, however the pleasure of consumption starts not when we physically consume the product, but when we start to plan, compare, research and engage in the marketing communication process. This element builds anticipation, it enables us to begin the journey before we have left home. Solomon et al. (2010) list a number of hedonistic motivations and these can easily be adapted in the context of experiences marketing:

- **Anticipated hedonism:** Pleasure is gained from the anticipated benefits or experiences you may gain from the actual consumption of the experience. The consumption of tourism, food, hospitality and events begins with the anticipation, the thought of the experience and the pleasure this may bring. Thus, THEF marketing offers a gateway into the world of anticipated pleasure and escape.

- **Role enactment:** The consumption of experiences can be seen to change the status of the consumer and they become labelled as tourist, diner, guest etc. This change in status alters the social standing and position of the consumer, and this involves people changing their status. For example, diners in a restaurant become the people being served; there is a shift in the power relations of that individual as they are in control of the service encounter. Similarly, by attending a music event we are released from our normal social constraints, and this enables us to behave differently from usual. The adoption of the role as an experience consumer is informed by a hedonic discourse that enables us to escape from the pressures of everyday life and enter into a time and space that allows us to explore other identities.

■ **Choice optimisation:** Researching the experience and examining the offers and deals available, feeling that you have managed to track down and purchase the best buy also creates a hedonistic response. This probably explains the growth and enthusiastic response of consumers to discount voucher sites such as Wowcher and booking sites such as Laterooms.com and Lastminute.com.

■ **Negotiation:** Bartering and negotiation for goods and services is often a central experience of being a tourist; the ability to negotiate the price of the service or experience also provides pleasure and satisfaction. Supermarkets remove this bartering element and pacify the consumer interaction, thus removing a pleasurable element of the shopping process for many people.

■ **Affiliation:** One of the central aspects as defined in Chapter 6, is the idea that we are part of a crowd that is experiencing the same experience. This leads to feelings of belonging and possessing a shared cultural capital or even habitus. In the service encounter this is expressed in the feeling of communitas we find through the consumption of tourism, hospitality, events and food.

■ **Power and authority:** This is closely related to the role enactment and the persona we adopt as consumers. The feeling of controlling the service relationship, and of having power over someone, raises feelings of self-esteem and position in society, thus generating a form of pleasure underpinned by perceived superiority. It is interesting to note that much research has been undertaken (see Dann, 1996a; Tresidder, 2010a) on the representation of local people in tourism brochures and in the large majority of cases they are presented as either attractions or providing service. This convention forms a significant discourse in tourism and hospitality marketing. This theme is explored further in Chapter 8.

■ **Stimulation:** Experiences marketing utilises the concept of escape, adventure and excitement as one of its core themes, and

5

this often offers experiences that are opposite to the routine orientated structure of everyday life. What is being offered within such promotion is the opportunity to enter into an extraordinary world of experiences that remove us from everyday life; the search for new and interesting experiences is a significant element in the language of tourism, hospitality, events and food, and forms part of the hedonic discourse of experiences marketing.

All of the above form a discourse that moves away from emotions and focuses on the sensations we may encounter as tourists, guests or as a part of an audience. THEF marketing utilises marketing communications to create a sensual world that is vicariously consumed as pre-physical consumption. The pleasure element starts at the initial marketing/promotion stage and becomes elevated as we get nearer to actual consumption.

■ Imagination

This book and in particular this chapter explores the experiences that make up our understanding of THEF. It draws upon discourses and themes that include escape, authenticity, creativity, aesthetics, ambience, stimulation, fun, adventure excitement. It is interesting to examine how experiences marketing draws upon these themes and creates a stimulational world that sparks the imagination. For Schau (2000, p.50), imagination is "a fundamental everyday intellectual practice". Moreover, it is integral to both consumption practices and people's quotidian experiences in consumer society. While it is of the mind, imagination is something that is grounded in sensation and experience. That is to say, the possibilities of what can be imagined are contained and structured by what has previously been perceived by the senses. This being the case however, imagination is both reproductive and productive (Kant, 1965 in Schau, 2000). Through synthesising and reconfiguring data and information that is stored in memory, one can at once create new possibilities, enter fantasy worlds, anticipate or dream of what is to come, and recreate the past. Accordingly, it is possible to re-imagine events, holidays, meals, encounters, selves and relationships that cognitively approximate to direct experience, but also through imagination, one can construct new stories of what could have been, or who one was, or what may be yet to come. It is also possible though imagination for consumers to enter past worlds and events without having directly experienced them.

Through imagination one can transcend one's own physically bounded biological, temporal and spatial context, or in other words everyday lived experience. In this respect, imagination is integral to consumption and the consumer experience as it is a resource of significant value and variability. This variability is illustrated by Jenkins (2011) who offers a taxonomy of imagination and its relation to, and role in consumption, that encompasses six concepts and variables. These are:

1   Fanciful

2   Aspirational

3   Anticipatory

4   Nostalgic

5   Guided

6   Prospective

Jenkin's taxonomy is differentiated across a spectrum or continuum of imaginations, which commence with those that are purely fantastical and idyllic, and which are directed towards the escape from material reality, to those that are orientated towards present reality and current concerns. That is to say, that imagination is deployed and directed towards "planning, organising and decision making", resolving problems, and managing and setting expectations (Jenkins, 2011:208). This element of imagination directly links to the purchasing and consumption of THEF experiences, as we all plan, dream and overcome problems in achieving them, it is in fact one of the enjoyable elements that establish THEF as a significant activity. To elaborate on Jenkins' analysis of imagination we will outline three of these conceptual categories in more detail below.

Fanciful imagination

The function of fanciful imagination is to escape mundane or profane experiences or to compensate for felt dissatisfaction. It is fanciful in the sense that the imaginations are not perceived to be manifestly or materially possible. This could be because a consumer may not presently have, or anticipate having the material resources needed to realise a fantasy. Likewise they may not have the skills or physical capability. In other cases the world a consumer constructs may not even exist. It could be an imagined utopia for example. In many cases fanciful imagining is more pleasurable than any alternative or possible material reality, as a hyper-real world can be constructed in the mind that draws from a smorgasbord of hedonic and affective realms of experience that are tied together and sequenced in seemingly impossible ways. Despite this, 'real' consumption and consumer contexts are often central to the experience in two principle ways. First, one could be fantasising about an immersive multi-sensory experience of eating an amazing meal or vicariously consuming the risk and heightened excitement of hurtling down a snow covered mountain strapped to a snowboard. That is, you are imaging yourself engaging in a real act of consumption, whereby a consumer good or practice is in the foreground. Second, consumer products and experiences could be in the background yet still essential to a particular episode of fantasy. For example, one could be imagining the early developmental stages of a romantic relationship. This peak emotional experience could be being played out on a deserted exotic beach on an island in the Indian Ocean or in the midst of a swaying crowd at a rock festival. In this respect while fantastical this mode of imagination is often framed by our "hopes, dreams and aspirations"(2011:203).

Nostalgic imagination

Nostalgia is experienced through mentally revisiting and recollecting the past and is clearly linked to the debates surrounding authenticity. It is a recurrent theme in THEF marketing. Statements about authenticity, organic, handmade or real become a central discourse in experiences marketing, as they offer an entry into a perceived better time and space. Nostalgia is mostly bound up in material reality, as more often than not it focuses on actual events and an individual's past experiences. In this sense the degree to which one is required to engage in abstract thought is limited, however, one may be drawn deeply into nostalgia focusing greatly on the material, relational, symbolic, and affective details of past events and outcomes, but also in some cases, on the emotions and thoughts presently felt. In this sense nostalgia can be both a recounting or reflexive activity, reminiscent of critical reflection. In terms of affect it can be bitter sweet. Not only is a consumer disposed to yearning for perceived better times, or to relive or (re) construct 'the good old days'– in both mind or matter, but they may also be experiencing a protracted or recurring mourning for lost loved ones, lost irreplaceable possessions (e.g. Grayson & Schulman, 2000), or places, identities, and experiences left behind. Nostalgia can also be prone to bias and selective recollection, whereby things like emotional peaks or troughs may obfuscate other aspects and realms of experience of the time under review. Accordingly the nostalgic imagination is deployed for multiple aims and functions.

Like fanciful imagination it can be employed to escape everyday reality and situations. Daydreams in these instances will correspond with historical accounts and significant moments and experiences of one's life. These could be related to the immediate past but also the distant. Sat at their desk, a consumer could drift away into pleasurable thoughts of holidays taken or events that unfolded at a family member's wedding, so, similar to fanciful imagination, products can take a leading role or be present in the background of nostalgic imaginings. In other cases however they are expansive and take in the broad range of sites, sounds, interpersonal interactions, and emotions of that time. The nostalgic memory also plays a role in present and future consumption. Consumers use nostalgia as a resource to inform their consumer choices and practices – this is in the sense that a consumer's history becomes an itinerary for selection, but also something to be re-experienced.

The motive of recreating the past in the present, or alternatively avoiding the present through re-staging the past, is a widely acknowl-edged consumer goal and marketing trend, and is heavily utilised within the THEF sector to create experiences. In this respect, it is theo-rised as having a number of antecedents. Holbrook (1993) for example identifies life-cycle effects. Nostalgia in this case can be related to developmental cycles and specifically adolescence, which appear to be a person's formative years. These years are instrumental. During this period, attitudes, values, preferences and tastes are developed that continue into later life. Concomitant to this, the urge to re-experience these important times swells inside as a consumer ages. Holbrook goes on to quote Davis (1979:57-60)

> ...in Western society it is adolescence, and for the privileged classes early adulthood as well, that affords nostalgia its most sumptuous banquets (1979:57)

and that

> ...the tides of nostalgia which ... wash over middle-aged per-sons typically carry them back to the songs, films, styles, and fads of their late teens

There is however an interesting twist to the relationship with THEF consumption. Rather than nostalgia being the route to consumption, it is consumption that provides the link to nostalgia. In these cases products and experiences are sought to evoke memories of these people and the pleasurable moments shared with them. In this way the experience of re-consuming acts in a similar way to a memento or souvenir. Consider this extract of an interview with an 80 year old female visitor to Blists Hill Victorian Town living museum, from Goulding's (2001:557) research:

> ...it's only when you come to a place like this it makes you real-ize the sort of things you miss. I mean it takes you back. I've lost most of my family, my husband's dead and so are a lot of my friends, the ones I've known for years. So when you see things you remember it brings back happy memories ...

Similarly Russell and Levy (2011) suggest that the urge to re-consume past experiences, to revisit places where couples met or honeymooned by those who have lost loved ones, is not just about attempts at recre-ating, revisiting, or remembering the past, but is also a strategy that enables the individual to be forward-looking and future-orientated. This progressive re-consumption is based upon attempts and motiva-tions to extract new experiences from returning to old places, activi-ties and products. In these cases, there is no desire to return to the past per se; what is wanted is something new – a different encounter. Here Russell and Levy (2011) draw upon informant interviews with widowers to explain how the motivation to re-visit the places they had been with their partners. These visits were not rooted in pleasurable attempts at recreation and re-staging of what had been, rather they were about moving forward, they were therapeutic experiences. This may also explain the motivations for engaging in dark tourism or visit-ing battlefields.

5

> Nelson, now a widower, chose to re-visit Florence and Siena, towns he had visited forty years prior, with his wife and two young children. Revisiting the sites, hotels and restaurants... was 'a kind of pilgrimage, a sentimental journey' that allowed him to 'sadly mourn the loss (of his wife and son), missing them more vividly' but it was mostly a conscious attempt 'to reconcile myself to this time of my life' (Russell and Levy, 2011:136)

Progressive re-consumption therefore is a practice that is "open to the possibility of change and motivated by the desire to affirm, confirm, or dis-confirm an impression left by previous experiences" Russell and Levy (2011:138). The consumer in this case may attempt to acknowledge that they are a now a different person to the one that came before and therefore expect to find new things and meanings in an old experience. Consumption in this respect is a rite of passage and transitionary; they seek a new identity or to progressively move away from an old one.

In a similar manner to the above, Brown, Kozinets and Sherry (2003) develop Davis's (1979) work, whereby they acknowledge the role of epochal shifts and fractures in society and culture as motivat-ing consumer behaviour. Where terrorist events or natural, cultural or economic disasters pose a significant threat and risk to existential security, and threaten individual and collective identity or families or work there is a propensity to seek security in the past. Consumers attempt this through consuming brands and THEF products with heritage and history, that are simultaneously linked to former selves, communal reference points, and perceptions of more secure, communal, and innocuous times. This accounts for the rise in the number of heritage centres, historical re-enactments and claims that food is authentic or 'just like mamma makes' and the continual draw of country houses and television programmes like Downton Abbey. In these cases, in contrast to present reality, consumers are moved to romanticise the past and construct it in idealistic, authentic and utopian terms (Goulding, 2001).

In this context some authors claim that the past has become sacralised. In making this argument, Brown, Kozinets and Sherry (2003) cite the Great Depression of the 1930s, the turmoil of the 1960s, the implosion of communism and subsequent rebalancing of the world order as key transformational events and examples that share this relationship. Each of these periods, it is maintained, had a subsequent corresponding period of retrospection, nostalgia and revival. Accordingly, on a par with this reasoning, a nostalgic resurgence and boom should be presently under way given the on-going economic malaise stemming from the 2008 credit crunch, the Brexit from Europe and predicted return to recession. Indeed we do not need to look far for sector examples. In events we have school and university reunions, the revival of Pop and Indie bands, like The Beach Boys, Take That, the Stone Roses, and the Happy Mondays, who in reforming are embarking on sell-out and record-breaking tours. For food we have the return of the Wispa bar and the revival of antiquated sweet shops that both physically resemble a bygone age and sell classics like aniseed balls and rhubarb and custard boiled sweets. Hospitality, has witnessed the restaurants mining history and bringing back updated versions of classics menu items such as the ubiquitous prawn cocktail and scampi. Equally we have full concepts like 1950s diners, where not only the food is (re)created for the pleasure of diners, but the whole service-scape is theatrically staged and designed, including the fashion styles and dress codes of serving staff, décor, music and entertainment. Finally in tourism we have heritage centres, living museums (e.g. Goulding, 2001) and re-enactments like Pickering War Weekend. These, while seeking to educate, inspire and remind, offer certain consumers the opportunity to satisfy the nostalgic urge and create opportunities for new and enhanced imaginations.

■ Guided and prospective imagination

We bring together two of Jenkins' (2011) conceptual categories in this final review. Here imagination is predicated and focussed on consumption that is either very likely to occur or to take place soon. It is anticipatory in nature and in some cases akin to planning, and the imagination here is often deployed creatively. For instance, a consumer could be imagining what to cook for friends in an upcoming dinner party. They could equally put their imagination to more immediate use in working out how to make something palatable and fulfilling from food that is leftover in the fridge and kitchen cupboards. In a similar vein, a consumer could deploy the imagination in thinking through how to balance scarce material resources with creating a memorable and valuable holiday experience for the family. Relatedly, the imagination is often needed in thinking up exciting activities in which to engage the children whilst on the holiday.

In the examination of an anti-consumption festival, Kozinets (2002a) examines how participants at the Burning Man Festival (www.burningman.com) in their attempt to escape the pressures to consume, are expected to draw upon their creative imagination and other resources to produce temporary artworks or engage in practices of radical self-expression and performance art, as well as in radical self-preservation. The latter being integral to the fact that participants must be prepared to survive the harsh environment of the Black Rock Desert of Nevada, in which the festival is co-created and performed over the course of a week.

My sense of Burning Man as entertainment changes a bit as I read the ticket, which states the risks and rules of the event; "you voluntarily assume the risk of serious injury or death by attending this event. You must bring enough food, water, shelter and first aid to survive one week in a harsh desert environment. Commercial vending, firearms, fireworks, rockets and other explosives prohibited... This is not a consumer event. Leave nothing behind when you leave the site. Participants only. No spectators". (Kozinets, 2002a:20)

He further states that:

The most bizarre thing I saw at burning man was a man dressed in a three-piece business suit and carrying a briefcase, rushing through the desert one evening. He brushed by a group of us quickly, saying "excuse me gentlemen," as if he were late for a meeting. Our group burst out laughing... the source of the humour was the realization that this is a place set far apart from the logics that drive everyday business behaviour in the world of large corporations. Our mock businessman's attire, emoting, utterances and rushing were pure performance art in this desolate and distant location. (Kozinets, 2002a:31)

Such experiences guide our relationship to both experiences and their marketing. The themes and discourses that inform the communication of experience within marketing spaces is a metaphysical journey in which we engage all of our senses and we use our imagination to interpret, locate ourselves within the discourse and, most importantly, find meaning.

■ Myths and myth making in experiences marketing

It is argued that the notions of tourism (Selwyn 1996, Barthes 1997), hospitality, food (Reed-Danahay 1996) and certain events (see Belk & Costa, 1998) are underpinned and surrounded by cultural myths. Experiences marketing draws upon and reinforces these myths through the themes and experiences they communicate to the consumer and for Thompson (2004:162) "...permeate consumer culture". The notion of myth elevates the significance of the experience. Myths are integral to a consumer's knowledge base, and can essentially be summarised as cultural models and templates through which consumers (and marketers) think, feel and act (Thompson and Arsel, 2004:632). Drawing on the work of D'Andrade (1990), Miller (1998b) and Shore (1996), Thompson and Arsel (2004) go on to show that cultural models are both inter-subjectively shared and also objectified in material reality. That is, not only do these templates reside in the minds of consumers but they are also inscribed into the artefacts and practices of consumer culture. They are present in brochures, websites, novels, films, TV shows, plays and theatrical performances, brands, advertisements, and the physical design, atmospherics and communicative staging of service-scapes (Arnould, Price & Tierney, 1998; Chronis, Arnould and Hampton, 2012). Myths that surround, events, festivals, carnivals, destination, restaurants, certain foods, peoples, landscapes etc. can be conceived as marketing resources, these may:

5

1   Be presently integral to the interpretive repertoire of a consumer, having been integrated over time through everyday interaction and engagement in the world over their life-course and trajectory.

2   Be searched out, located, and assimilated during preparation for, or following, a specific mode of consumption. For example, in preparing to visit an historic site a consumer may consult historical accounts and records, or view serialised TV media to build on their stock of knowledge to enhance their experience. Likewise, on return they may engage in similar activity to augment their knowledge and experience.

3   They could have been consumed during, and through the interaction with the products and services offered by the marketplace.

Roland Barthes in his book *The Eiffel Tower and Other Mythologies*, charts how the Eiffel Tower has been defined within literature, the arts and commerce, and how as a result of these definitions it has come to represent so much more than just a tourist attraction. The Eiffel Tower is now used to represent Paris, romance and even a totem of France. This myth of the tower is then utilised by marketers to sell and communicate the idea or notion of 'Frenchness' or romance without have to describe or waste time scene-setting. This is amazing when you consider that the tower was never meant to be a permanent structure in the first place but was only constructed for the 1899 World's Fair.

Belk (1998) further explores the notion by examining the Mountain Man myth. He charts how this has been perpetuated through historical artefacts, events, festivals and texts that catalogue and provide accounts that approximate reality, and that are reinforced by folkloric interpretations and works of cultural producers such as film-makers, novelists and artists. He cites, *Gentle Ben, The Life and Times of Grizzly Adams, Spirit of the Eagle, Jermiah Johnson*, and the Mountain Men Festivals (over 50 held in the USA during 2012) as examples of the latter (Belk, 1998:221). These he argues, "implicitly or explicitly" become essential resources and cultural frameworks though which the re-enactments and experiences are constructed and mediated by "modern mountain men" (220). They are foundational to what can be experienced.

The mountain man represents a specific example of American social strata in the early to mid-1800s. Belk's (1998) account suggests that they were around 3,000 in number, mostly of white ethnicity, who lived and worked around the Rocky Mountains. They scraped out an existence in the dangerous fur trade though trapping beavers and selling and exchanging their pelts. The rendezvous was where they came together to trade. Quoting Cleland (1995:25), Belk (1998:221) describes the rendezvous accordingly. "Like a medieval fair... it... was a place of buying, selling, haggling, cheating, gambling, fighting, drinking, palavering, racing, shooting and carousing". It is this, which the rendezvous participant wishes to recreate. However, in doing this, from Belk's analysis it is possible to summarise the motive of the modern mountain man has been to temporarily reclaim mastery over one's life, and to transcend the logic that presently prescribes and constrains it. By imitating and (re)creating the lifestyles, practices and behaviours of these idealised people, one is able to momentarily reclaim the fundamental essence of human and masculine experience, which is believed to have been lost or diminished amongst the milieu and structuring effects of contemporary post-modern life. The mountain man discourse thus provides a cultural template of the rugged individual and frontier myth that is both idolised and revered in American culture, yet simultaneously mourned by a segment of US male consumers (e.g. Holt, 2006; Thompson and Holt, 2004; Hirschman, 2003). The contemporary rendezvous provides an entry point and liminal time and space in which to (re)experience, (re)create, and celebrate these ideals in contemporary marketing practice. An example of these are the famous/infamous Marlboro Man adverts. Experiences marketing draws heavily from the myths of destinations, events and history etc. It is supported by a myth making industry (Selywn 1996) that includes television, literature, marketing, culture and even postcards. Again, areas of influence such as myth and their significance within consumer society in embedding experience are what separate experiences marketing from other forms of marketing activity. Myth is located within a historical continuum that permeates the marketing of THEF. The next section charts how the significance of hospitality and food has come to be embedded within contemporary consumption practices.

5

■ Embedding the practice and myths of hospitality and food

The marketplace myths associated with hospitality and food are socially and culturally embedded within contemporary life and draw heavily from history and tradition (O,Connor, 2005; O'Gorman, 2007; Claseen, 2007). Although food and hospitality is a significant element of culture, these concepts need to be contextualised within the time in which they are being judged. For Delind (2006), both the semiotic and physical consumption of gastronomy, as contained within experiences marketing, provide a refuge from fast food culture and the instantaneous nature of postmodern society. Experiences marketing creates what may be defined as a 'pleasure zone' (Fantasia, 1995) in which we can escape into utopian food and hospitality space, and which comes to signify what Delind (2006:128) terms, a 'graceful way of living', in that it bounds our past and memory creating a sense of belonging by drawing on the embedded definitions of hospitality and gastronomy. The consumption of hospitality and food is an 'authoritative act', that 'authenticates' our identity and position within the world (Marshall, 2005:73). It also acts as a social marker of who we are (Bourdieu, 1987; Gvion and Trosler, 2008). Experiences marketing draws us into the consumption process, and particular representations of the restaurant, hotel or meal make social and cultural life real as experiences marketing is an "agency of culinary culture, lifestyle and systems" (Gvion and Trosler, 2008)

The images used in experiences marketing create what Johns and Pine (2002:127) refer to as the 'authentic environments' of hospitality: the images used are empty of humans and modernity and they offer us an empty space in which we can search for the authentic. This is a convention in experiences marketing (see Waitt & Head, 2002; Lane & Waitt, 2007) and wider cultural debates (Drolet 2004), that not only offers a reflexive space for the individual but reflects the power of the marketer to exclude and include people, culture and places. This notion of emptiness offers a mediation on taste and gastronomy which define the preparation, social character, philosophy and aesthetics of hospitality, food and the table. It identifies food and hospitality as art (Fantasia ,1995).

Hospitality and food marketing signposts various routes from everyday lived experience that facilitates a notion of escape, and the representation of hospitality and food signifies a time and space which is differentiated from everyday lived experience by its 'extraordinariness' and from the routine and often un-reflexive consumption of food as merely fuel (Marshall, 2005). Consequently, THEF marketing creates a configuration of time and space that elevates the context of the food served to that of the extraordinary. For example, in a number of adverts from Marks and Spencer, they use a collage of music, settings and dialogue to elevate what is a ready meal to that of fine dining and sophistication (see Tresidder, 2011b).

It is within these liminal places or 'pleasure zones' (Fantasia, 1995) that we find a release from our normal social constraints and enter into a state of communitas (Belk et al., 1989). The creation of these 'pleasure zones' offer a delineated space that semiotically represents a time of sophistication, in which we may hedonistically explore the experiences of food and hospitality. This liminality and release enables us to explore hospitality and food in terms of senses and the sensual, as an 'intimate frontier' (Dawkins, 2009) in which we may locate the body. In other words, the embedding of definitions of food and hospitality within experiences marketing enables the individual to explore " ... the role of the sensual, the emotional, the expressive, for maintaining layered sets of embodied relationships to food and place." (Delind, 2006:121).

Often, the images used of food in experiences marketing elevate the food and dining experience to the level of food pornography, whereby there is a breakdown between sexual and gustatory pleasures and is so removed from real life that it can only be consumed vicariously (Magee, 2007). For example, the images of finished dishes on restaurant websites, in cookbooks or on television that have been produced by celebrity chefs are so perfect they can never be replicated. This notion of sexualising food is reinforced by Ellis (1980) who states that the pornography of representation is anything that is outside of the norm; such representations promote a myth of food, and importantly for Reed-Danahay (1996) the sensual or sexual. Such approaches reinforce the images of food in marketing as the binary opposition to food as fuel, or hospitality as more than just shelter, and elevate the notion of hospitality to that of the extraordinary, or even the sacred (see Sheringham and Daruwalla, 2007) by creating marketing 'pleasure zones'. As such, everyday lived experience often means that we treat food as fuel, eating as survival or just a means to suppress hunger, but experiences marketing illustrates how hospitality, food and dining can be redefined or represented as a hedonistic practice in which we escape the mundane or profanity of everyday lived experience. The myth of food is developed through various themes that form the basis of experiences marketing.

■ Conclusion

The experience of tourism, events, hospitality and food is under-pinned by a complex historical and cultural discourse that forms the expectations and experiences of the consumer. Through the location of the practices within a different configuration of time and space, we enter into a liminal world that fuels our imagination to create a myth of experience. This is important as the historical, social, cultural and marketing definition of THEF elevates the experiences beyond the everyday and justifies the claims that experiences marketing needs to develop and be understood as a specialist field, as the definitions and values etc., utilised in other fields such as the marketing of motor cars are not applicable. As marketers we need to understand this definition as first, it enables us to identify the relationship between the product and the consumer, and second, it provides us with a set of codes, desires and expectations that should inform both marketing and com-munication strategies.

In conclusion, THEF is a significant activity in which consumers mark important aspects of their lives. This chapter has argued that as a result of this significance, THEF marketing needs to be defined and identified as a specific and specialist area of marketing. As such, this chapter furthers the central thesis of this book which seeks to show that while traditional marketing theory provides a foundation for the promotion of THEF it lacks the required contextualisation and under-standing of the experiences and cultural significance that THEF holds for the contemporary consumer.

6 Consumer Resources and THEF Experiences

■ Introduction

This chapter develops the ideas presented in Chapters 3 and 4 by further exploring how individual consumers utilise a set of resources to negotiate and form their experiences with THEF products and activities. Specifically it provides much more detail about the nature and composition of the resources that consumers bring to bear in their consumption and value creating activities. The traditional *exchange* approach of marketing normally locates the consumer at the Macro level, whereby assumptions are made that all members of a demographic, socio-economic or similar group possess the same or similar resources, and in so doing, approach the market and consumption in very similar ways. However, in following the logic and ideas of the *service and interaction* perspective, this chapter demonstrates that individual consumers possess different resources of various kinds which, when deployed, produce unique and differentiated forms of value and meanings. It is therefore important that we locate the consumer of THEF in a Micro theoretical framework of resources and practices, as only then can we truly begin to understand the consumer's relationship to marketing and THEF products more broadly, and how they create value and meaning through their consumption in particular.

■ An outline of the theory of resources

As explained in Chapter 3, the service logic of marketing is predicated on the idea that value is created through interaction as consumers integrate their own resources with those offered by the THEF marketplace (products, activities, deeds, and communications etc.). Furthermore, as illustrated in Chapter 4, this interaction based approach also mirrors the theories of the cultural perspective which maintain that marketers produce *cultural* resources that consumers incorporate into their lives through the deployment of their own resources and consumption practices. However what these chapters do not fully show or explain is the distinction between the types of resources that consumers bring to bear in their consumption, and how these in turn influence and shape consumption of products in the sector. Therefore we will commence this chapter by distinguishing between the two specific forms of consumer resources that have been theorised in the literature, and follow by describing in detail the range of resources that are integral to these concepts. Accordingly we will first draw on the seminal work of Vargo and Lusch (2004) who demonstrate that consumers essentially draw upon combinations of resources that can be situated in relation to two principal forms, which they call *operand* and *operant* resources. The differences between these are as follows:

- **Operand resources** are made up of the physical and material assets that a consumer allocates or uses to create value and would include the marketplace object or activity itself, as well as their own money, time, spaces and/or material resources (Arnould, Price & Malshe, 2006).

- **Operant resources** on the other hand, are composed of the personal cognitive assets and physical capabilities that a consumer deploys to act upon operand resources to create value (Vargo & Lusch, 2004). In this chapter these specifically include a consumer's stock of knowledge and skill (Arnould, Price & Malshe, 2006). However, we would also include a consumer's relative endowments of cultural capital resources and taste within this framework, which we discuss in depth in Chapter 7.

So for example, a consumer staging a dinner party will draw upon their ability to cook (resources of knowledge and skill) and utilise their kitchen appliances, cookbooks and utensils (material resources), alongside the kitchen and preparation area (spatial resources) to produce a meal for their friends (social resources) using items they purchased from the supermarket (marketplace resources) using their money or vouchers (financial resources). In this respect a combination of operand and operant resources are integrated alongside those offered through the marketplace during the consumption of THEF to create personalized meaning and value.

Having outlined the role and significance of consumer resources we now turn to describing the nature of each of these and their relevance in producing THEF experiences. We will begin by looking at consumer operand resources, which, to reiterate, include financial resources, time, material resources and space, and follow with an examination of the knowledge and skills that constitute the consumer's operant resources.

6

■ Financial resources

The financial resources a consumer possesses have a blunt and direct impact upon their behaviour, as the type and range of THEF experiences a consumer may engage in are broadly dependent upon how much money they have to spend in the marketplace. Money is therefore a scarce allocative resource, and consumption is both enabled and constrained simply through its availability. That is to say, a consumer either has the discretionary or disposable financial resources to allocate to THEF experiences or not. Importantly, it is discretionary spend that is of most interest to marketers of THEF experiences, because for most people, other than basic food provision, these sit outside the realm of normal everyday experience, are non-essential, and in some cases even considered luxuries.

In the first edition of this book, which we wrote subsequent to the credit crunch and in the midst of the global financial crisis, we also emphasized the important role that credit cards and other forms of borrowed financial resources played in enabling consumer access and engagement with the THEF marketplace. Following Brown et al. (2005) we argued that coupled with the economic boom between 1994 and 2004, and the relaxation of credit constraints, the Western and developed world witnessed a consumer credit explosion that was evidenced by the huge number of credit cards and loans that were available during this period, and was only momentarily derailed in the immediate aftermath of the crash. In February 2012 for example, net UK personal debt, including mortgages, stood at a staggering £1.47tn (creditaction.org), and a report by Aviva based on a randomised study of 10,000 people aged between 18 and 55 placed individual unsecured household debt at £7,944 (Papworth, 2012).

Four years on from this, it is apparent that this situation is not much improved, and recent data from the Office for Budget Responsibility (OBR) shows that consumers continue to spend more than they earn and have collectively built up £447 billion of net borrowing on unsecured credit cards and loans; a figure which is projected to rise to £662 billion by the end of the decade (Chan, 2016). As such, it seems we cannot underestimate the role that credit continues to play in the lives of THEF consumers, and a study that investigates this phenomena persuasively argues that the practice of having credit and accumulating debt has been normalised in contemporary consumer society (Peñaloza & Barhart, 2011). In relation to this, research by Bernthal, Crockett and Rose (2005) indicates that credit cards have become a primary resource for facilitating consumption orientated lifestyles, which are both quantitatively and qualitatively different from those that would be achievable without them; they enable higher levels of participation in the market, whereby people can consume more in general as well as elevate their consumption to previously unachievable experiences. Accordingly, while we do not advocate it, through leveraging these resources a consumer can take more frequent and better holidays, stage elaborate weddings at home and abroad, eat out more, or enjoy a greater range of added value foods than previously permissible, with the only constraint being their credit worthiness and ability to meet and service the resulting debt obligations.

But here lies the rub, access to credit and unmitigated use of credit cards etc., may induce the burden of debt and resultantly remove a consumer from the market altogether (Peñaloza & Barhart 2011). This may be through one or more of:

1   Reductions in discretionary spend through having to prioritise the service of loans and other forms of debt;

2   Heightened levels of perceived financial risk, and felt ontological insecurity of the financial future, due to the experienced weight of the debt; and

3   The inability to shuffle debt among financial instruments.

(Bernthal, Crockett and Rose, 2005)

■ The resource of time

Just as consumers need a surplus of cash to engage in THEF activities they also require a surplus of time. This is certainly the case for the THEF sectors in terms of the design of their marketing offer, which on aggregate can be broadly classified as high involvement services or products that are extremely time consuming. To go on holiday, attend a concert, take a romantic restaurant meal, or stay at home to cook from scratch for instance, require significant investments in this scarce resource. This is not only the case for actually undertaking or performing these activities in themselves, but also the planning and preparation that is required beforehand. In addition, consumers are also often caught up in the process of waiting to engage or experience THEF activities and products and amongst other things they:

1   Wait in line to get on the rides in theme-parks such as Disney Land or Alton Towers;

2   Queue at the tills in supermarkets, or to check in at an airport;

3   Spend countless hours on long haul flights to distant holiday resorts; and

4   Count down the time before they can escape on holiday.

Therefore, due to its scarcity, time is becoming an increasingly critical and valuable resource, which is allocated both carefully and discriminately by consumers.

What is more, consumers all possess different time equity, whereby the job they hold, the pets they own, the age of children they have all impact upon how much surplus time they have to engage in THEF experiences. Moreover, increased access to technology has not freed up this resource, but rather it has blurred the boundaries between work and home, and worked to distort consumers' perceptions of what constitutes obligated and free time. The ability to check e-mails on mobile phones or access work materials via the internet have constructed a new set of pressures that impact upon a consumer's temporal resource, as well as on how they value and think about allocating it. In many respects the market often steps in to provide consumers with time saving devices and convenience products to manage the lack of time they possess and create efficiencies. In this respect, THEF concepts such as convenience grocery stores and 'on the go' food, alongside apps designed by airlines to streamline the check-in process at airports, all alleviate the time constraints surrounding THEF experiences and help consumers to manage the burden of their time pressured lives.

Interestingly, in reaction to the temporal pressures that consumers experience in their everyday lives, a cultural movement that emphasizes slowness as its core theme has developed through the THEF marketplace, which is reflected in trends such as the slow food movement, slow travel and the revival of cooking from scratch and growing your own food. In each of these cases, consumers are actively seeking out slower lives or leisurely experiences that allow them to resist the frantic and relentless pace of the modern world. In this sense the 'slow movement' itself can be seen as a collective cultural project that seeks to resist the 'consumption ethic' and the dominant logic of the market that demands speed and efficiency, and is often facilitated through downshifting or engaging in practices of voluntary simplicity (Bekin et al., 1998). Significantly, this type of consumer experience is often overlooked in the marketing literature, which tends to mostly focus on experiences that can be classified as 'extraordinary' (Caru & Cova, 2012) or hedonic (Holbrook & Hirschman, 1982).

■ Space as a resource

Just like other operand resources, space is a significant enabler of consumer experiences in the THEF marketplace; however the most obvious application of space as a consumer resource in value creation across these sectors, is related to food. Kitchen cupboards, freezers, refrigerators, and counter tops all enable the food consumer in a very practical and obvious way. The former three examples for instance grant the consumer the capacity to store a wide range of food items under varying conditions, minimising the need to conduct frequent shopping trips and fragmented intermittent purchases. Research has also found that kitchen cupboards and pantries help consumers hide away or camouflage brands and food products that they deem to be mundane, 'not really me' or overly branded (Coupland, 2005), That is to say, these resources allow consumers to conceal products that get in the way or cause an intrusion. Ample storage space also facilitates bulk purchasing and the ubiquitous weekly or 'big' shop. Having access to a vehicle with a large storage capacity performs a similar value creation function for the consumer, as does a wine cellar for a wine collector or connoisseur. Equally, countertop space and work areas are invaluable for those who have a preference for scratch cooking or preserving produce through pickling, preserving and jam making etc.

Dining practices and the range of related consumer goals are similarly structured by allocations of space. Extending an invitation to friends or professional colleagues for dinner, or taking the opportunity to host a children's birthday party, are enabled or constrained by this resource, as is the ability to sit up to a dining table for breakfast with the family prior to leaving for work. On top of other things, space in this respect provides opportunities to meaningfully interact with the family to share experiences, build family identity and values, celebrate and play, and build networks in pursuit of career goals and aspirations.

6

Moving outside of the house, owned or rented space such as a garden or allotment, may offer further spatial resource for value creation. These resources, for example, may be used by a hard pressed and financially constrained consumer to make meaningful and valuable savings to their food budget and expenditure by allowing them to grow their own food. Equally these spaces could also be deployed in service of constructing a foodie lifestyle or may be utilised as part of a plan over the long term to down-shift to a simpler, self-sufficient and slower paced life (Bekin, Carrigan, & Szmigin, 2005).

Aside from food, we can find examples of physical space relevant to travel and events. The most obvious of these for the traveller or tourist, or indeed a festival goer, is related to luggage. Luggage delimits what can and cannot be taken on a trip, and in many cases this may have a direct relationship with a consumer's personal material resources and possessions, such as the size and quantity of their suitcases, backpack or car boot/trunk space. However in other cases it could be structured by the chosen mode and means of travel. Ryan' Air for example place significant constraints on the size and quantity of luggage that a consumer can take and store on their planes without incurring a financial penalty or having to pay a surcharge.

The potential for consumption and how and what value can be created or experienced will also often relate to the scale and scope of accommodation space. In some cases a travelling consumer may have the benefit and luxury of a suite with a super-king sized bed, desk and sofas, and in others they may be cramped into a small double room that barely has the space to store their luggage. Similarly a consumer may be taking a holiday in a large static caravan, gîte or chalet or confined to a tent, shared youth hostel dorm-room or small mobile caravan. Obviously with each of these examples there is a significant relationship to material and financial resources. Under normal conditions, the market price of suites and gîtes is greater than those for small hotel rooms or hostel accommodation of similar aesthetic and material standard, likewise the spatial resources and potential of a tent or caravan are determined by those presently owned, borrowed or rented.

■ Supporting material resources

With each of the sectors covered in this book, an experience is mobilised and only made possible through the integration of a relevant and related selection of material resources. That is to say, these resources are often, if not always, a necessary condition for value creation. What is more, material resources also perform a role in structuring the possibility and scope of value creation and meaning production more generally. In studies of tourism for example, cameras have been found to extend the boundaries of a consumer's experience, allowing it to be shared and (re)created infinitely into the future (Crouch & Desforges, 2003), while walking boots liberate consumers and enable the mastery of space and challenging environments (ibid, 2003). Cookbooks, on the other hand, while performing a rudimentary role in culinary practices by providing consumers with valuable instructions on how to cook novel dishes from scratch, have also been shown to play a significant role in structuring and shaping identity and legitimising gendered behaviours (Brownlie & Hewer, 2007). In a similar manner, clothing and other material resources allow consumers to engage in identity performances, and to seek acceptance and legitimacy in particular consumer cultures and contexts such as raving (Goulding & Shankar, 2004) and the Goth sub-culture (Goulding and Saren, 2009), while maps, GPS and mobile technology help consumers manage significant risk and uncertainty and engage in activities that would have previously proven exclusionary. In this respect it is quite possible to create an endless list of resources in relation to this concept. These could be resources that are presently owned in the stock of a consumer's possessions, or those that need to be acquired through purchase or otherwise to enable or support a consumption experience.

■ Social resources

Like the other resources covered in this chapter, *social resources* take numerous forms and are deployed and acted upon by consumers in a variety of ways. We identify three broad types here. These are:

1   People and networks from which consumers seek referral, knowledge or information about THEF product or services. In this section we focus on word of mouth marketing (WOMM) and virtual consumption communities which constitute invaluable resources in the selection process of the consumption cycle;

2   The range of people that are either integral as participants to an episode of consumption itself or those involved in delivery of a THEF experience; and

3   Individuals or groups that are needed as reference points for the personal or collective realisation of the value and meanings associated with consumer identity projects.

Word of mouth marketing (WOMM)

To begin with, there is little doubt that WOMM is the most persuasive and influential form of marketing communication (Kozinets, Valck, Wojnicki & Wilner, 2010), inasmuch as it is perceived to be relatively more trustworthy, reliable and credible than other forms (Brown, Broderick & Lee, 2007), especially when consumers defer to family, friends, work colleagues or other close acquaintances. Equally, word of mouth marketing mostly takes the form of an active dialogue so the consumer is able to extract or share information that is specifically relevant to them in terms of their motives and preferences relative to the planned consumption of a THEF product or experience. However, new forms of eWOMM (electronic word of mouth marketing) are emerging that challenge the traditional view and model of word of mouth marketing, which emphasises close ties, proximity and familiarity between the interlocutors who share their recommendations and experience with each other. On the contrary, in the case of eWOMM, it appears that immediacy is the overriding criteria through which we can now begin to understand the dynamics of this new form of communication, insofar as consumers can now access what they want, when they want.

Social media, consumption communities and eWOMM

The growth of social media which is mobilised by Web 2.0 social platforms and tools, combined with the rapid development and diffusion of mobile technology, is undoubtedly transforming the ways in which we communicate generally, and, more specifically, with whom we seek out marketing information and share our own consumption experiences and outcomes. This is clearly evident in all of our sectors where consumers have access to:

- Specific consumer social media platforms such as Tripadvisor®, foursquare or Moneysupermarket;

- Generic social tools like Instagram, Facebook, Snapchat and Twitter;

- Sector focused social apps like Foodspotting and the artofbackpacking;

- Comments sections that feature below news articles in online versions of newspapers like the *Daily Mail* and *The Guardian* (Morris et al., 2016);

- Blogs dedicated to specific THEF products and experiences such as the Burning Man Festival (http://burningman.org/culture/stories/community-blogs/) or specific consumption practices like Deliciously Ella (http://deliciouslyella.com); and

- Internet based virtual consumption communities dedicated to the discussion, devotion or disdain of particular brands, such as Nutella (Cova & Pace, 2006) or products like coffee (Kozinets, 2002b).

Intrinsically, these are providing the platform for enhanced and augmented consumption experiences, while simultaneously offering ample marketing opportunities and challenges. Kozinets (2002b, 2010, 2015) for example has modelled the numerous ways in which people interact with online consumption communities and the motives that underlay and direct their interactions and behavior, and these include:

- **Tourists,** who are consumers who have infrequent contact with the community, a low commitment to it and a very weak tie. Tourists in this context are merely people who occasionally drop in or visit a virtual community for information when it is needed for instrumental reasons, such as the lead up to a purchase. The community therefore acts as an *informational resource* that may be included in a search or assessment of a specific product, brand, activity or service. Communication in these instances is extremely didactic and unidirectional, whereas in many cases, the Tourist would merely search through and engage existing information contained in extant posts, with other interaction limited to posting specific and direct questions related to the functional attributes of a product or a consumer's experiences with them. The information gleaned from the community would normally be supplemented and evaluated alongside a range of other information sources included in a consumer's information search such as an organisation's advertisements or web pages and more traditional forms of word of mouth.

- **Minglers** on the other hand, are more active in the social aspects and life of the community. They become participants. Although drawn in, in similar ways to the Tourist, in the search for product knowledge and information, the motive branches out to be inclusive of friendly interaction, interpersonal experience and value. The Mingler will thus use the community as a resource to build virtual friendships, social capital, and relationships. Importantly, in this case, the social experience will be considered to be equally if not more valuable than the informational role and resource that the community provides. In actual fact, in most cases, the social experience will transcend the very reason why the Mingler was drawn to the community in the first place, which ultimately was to find out about, and discuss a product. Accordingly, for the Mingler the link becomes more important than the thing; whereby the product or consumption experience is simply the link and context through which social experiences and relationships are realised and developed (Cova, 1997). Under these conditions the *social resource* itself ends up providing the majority, if not all, of the value and meaning for the consumer.

- **Devotees:** We next have the devotee, whose interest and interaction with the community is fully consumption orientated and product related. These consumers will be thoroughly engaged with the endorsement and critique of products and services, as well as occupied in protracted discussions related to consumption experiences. In view of this, the devotee will typically hold the most influence over the Tourist by providing the majority of the product reviews within the community. This will be compounded by their authoritative self-positioning as 'expert' consumers which will be evident through the style of their dialogue and interactions. They will also be the most appealing and valuable to the Tourist by the fact that less consumption orientated work will be required of them in accessing desired information. As a Devotee's posts will be focussed specifically on the consumption and experience of a product, a consumer interacting with an online community for reviews and recommendations will make efficiencies and save time by not having to sift through the social chit chat that will litter the posts of Minglers and Insiders.

- **Insiders:** Finally Insiders are extremely active in both realms of experience in the community. On par with a Devotee, Insiders engage in product and consumption related dialogue, and equally, like the Mingler are similarly active in the social aspects of the community. In this respect the Insider has multiple motives attached to their engagement with the community. Value and meaning are derived in equal measure from the relational, recreational and informational modes of experience and interaction. Resultantly the Insider is an important and critical *social resource* for all of the other participants and interlocutors engaged in online consumption orientated activity and engagement, making them, along with Devotees, an important target for marketing activity. What is more, given their manifold roles, that encompass friendship, play, community maintenance, and information disseminator, they may better fit the typical and traditional model of a credible eWOMM source. In the sense that they will be perceived by others, to have expertise and be less prone to bias and in relation to this, be considered more trustworthy (Brown, Broderick & Lee, 2007).

■ Social resources integral to episodes and experiences of consumption

■ Value creation: a shared experience

We now focus on the social resources that are inclusive to the value creation process itself. Here we include the people that are either co-participants in the consumption of THEF (other customers) or those that are central to the staging or performance of the experience (the service delivery staff). With some obvious exceptions, much of what constitutes the experiences that are offered by the THEF sector can be classified as social activities and performances, and in order for these experiences to work and create value, you need the significant presence of people. This is the case whether a consumer is involved in an excursion to Glynbourne to participate in the annual opera festival, taking a week away with friends on a Club package holiday, involved in a family outing to a Nando's restaurant, or a trip to the supermarket with their children for the weekly shop. Amongst other things, these are collective experiences that may be pursued as an expression of fandom or devotion, the pursuit of hedonistic play, or merely a utilitarian ritualised practice for feeding the family. In this sense value and meaning is created within and through a social unit, and is critically dependent upon the actions and interactions of those inclusive to it. While there are exceptions to this rule, these are limited in scope. Upon leaving the home environment a consumer enters a social context that inevitably brings them into contact with others who impact upon their experience. Taking a trip to the supermarket, entering the foyer of a hotel, or walking the Great Wall of China are inherently socially mediated experiences. Even shopping online becomes a social encounter at some stage when food is delivered to a consumer's door or if they have to make an enquiry or lodge a complaint with the retailer over the telephone. What is clear is that the *interaction* that takes place between the stakeholders in THEF experiences, for example, between host and guests, air steward and passengers, or customers themselves, constitutes a resource that plays a significant role in value creation or dissipation.

■ Service delivery personnel as social resources

The people directly involved in the delivery of THEF products are undoubtedly significant social resources that are intrinsic to the experiences of consumers. Through an examination of the actions and behaviour of employees and service personnel for example, Winstead (2000) offers insight into why they must be considered important social resources for value creation and customer satisfaction. He outlines three categories of behaviour that are seemingly manifest and displayed by valued service personnel when interacting with consumers in a THEF context. These are, in no particular order, concern, civility, and congeniality. Parasuraman, Zeithaml, & Berry's (1988) research also casts light on the range of employee behaviours that shape consumer experiences and influence their perceptions of service quality during service encounters, and these include:

■ A willingness to respond to customer needs and "provide prompt service" (Responsiveness);

■ The "ability to inspire trust and confidence" and be courteous (Assurance); and

■ A propensity to care and provide individual customised attention (Empathy) (Guiry, 1992:667).

Alongside behaviours, in many cases service delivery personnel are also instrumental in presenting and bringing the THEF experience to life for consumers through communicative staging, which according to Arnould, Price & Tierney (1998:90) "involves the transmission of servicescape meanings". In their study of the wilderness servicescape and white water rafting excursions for example, these researchers demonstrate how a natural environment is commercially appropriated for the enjoyment and consumption of adventure seekers through the scripts and role performances of the raft guides (Arnould, Price & Tierney, 1998). Not only do these service delivery personnel bring the experience and the environment to life for participants through narrative framing and storytelling, they also act to make it safe and magical (Arnould and Price, 1993). In a similar way, the reps of

6

Thomas Cook's Club 18-30 are instrumental in the communicative staging of hedonistic experiences and extreme play in holiday resorts and destinations across Europe. They are simultaneously tasked with organising and leading activities, mediating between hotel suppliers and the customer, and solving consumer problems and issues. What is more, right from the moment of the first encounter with their guests through to the last, they are required to embody and perform the espoused values of the 18-30 concept and brand itself, which in their own words, is to "host the wildest party holidays".

■ Consumers as resources for consumers

Next we consider the role of customers as resources for consumers. In a similar manner to service personnel, with the majority of THEF products and activities, customers are integral to their staging and production. Ultimately customers play a decisive role in creating the experience for others. Bitner et al. (1997:195), for instance, outline a couple of significant roles that consumers play in this process, these being:

- The customer as intrinsic to experiences of quality, satisfaction and value for others. Here we can include most THEF products that bring customers together in close proximity, such as in a hotel lounge, on a tour bus, or in a supermarket aisle. In this respect customers are resources that create an atmosphere or make the consumption of a product more enjoyable; and

- The customer as competitor to the service organization. Here Bitner et al. (1997) refer to the ways in which deleterious consumer behaviours may negatively impact upon the experience of other customers who are simultaneously engaged in the consumption of a THEF product. For example, a customer publically complaining about the service or their meal in a busy restaurant, or alternatively making for an unpleasant flight by being loud and brash have the potential to de-value the experience for others. In addition, Bitner et al. (1997) go on to argue that these roles are not mutually exclusive and that a consumer can be performing each of these during their consumption. Thus *other* consumers become a resource through which valuable and meaningful experiences are created, heightened and realised or conversely through which they are impeded, or destroyed. Importantly, in relation to this, when the customer becomes an inseparable and critical resource for the firm, this creates an interesting relationship and dilemma for an organisation, which then has to focus on managing their behaviour for the benefit and experience of others (Gronroos, 2011). It is not surprising therefore that Grove and Fisk, (1992:6 italics added) made the wry observation that "consumers learn through experience that some service organizations expect their audience to arrive bathed, shaved, coiffed and dressed in formal style... and that such expectations are common for gourmet restaurants... *or...* the opera", alongside many other products that are offered through the THEF marketplace.

■ Other orientated consumption

The next social resource under review relates to what is termed 'other orientated consumption' (Holbrook, 1999). In essence, this is consumption that is orientated towards realising status or constructing a desired identity or lifestyle, and as such, requires other people to be integral to a consumer's frame of reference for value to be experienced and realised. That is to say, identity and status etc. are constructed in relation to others and the wider social milieu. To take effect the goods, services and consumption practices that are drawn upon by a consumer in these performances must, by implication, have a social meaning that is ordered and differentiated and collectively understood and shared by others. So with status play or conspicuous consumption for example, a consensus must exist amongst a social collective of how a specific hotel brand, event, or restaurant concept is different to others in relation to price, luxury, service levels and customisation. Plainly, the conspicuous consumer would choose the most expensive, luxurious and attentive in its service offer. While a status orientated consumer on the other hand, would select and consume products from the sector that would align and position them in relation to a particular and personally revered social group. Thus, this socially mediated consumer behaviour underscores most identity performances and lifestyle consumption practices, and to take effect and be meaningful a consumer must be able to make a comparison between themselves and in relation to others, as well as seek to emulate a desired groups consumption choices, tastes, behaviour and practices. This is something we return to later for more detailed examination (see Chapter 7).

■ Knowledge and skill as consumer resource

The final concepts, knowledge and skill, are both *operant resources* (Arnould, Price & Malshe, 2006) and work to grant the consumer agency and opportunity across the range of THEF consumption experiences and marketplaces. Likewise, as in the case of the *operand resources* discussed in this chapter, deficiency in these resources has the opposite effect, creating experiential redundancy across a range of dimensions and contexts. To be an independent traveller or engage in scratch cooking for example, necessitates the application and utilisation of particular knowledge and skill sets, while surviving the harsh condition of the Black Rock desert, whilst maintaining the ability to *co-create* the Burning Man festival through radical self-expression or performance art, requires a different set of specialisations (Kozinets, 2002a). In addition to this, many products in this sector can be consumed in both a generic or specialised way, dependent upon how a consumer approaches a product or experience and the type of value or meaning they aim to extract from their interactions with them. Here, amongst others, we can locate products and activities such as wine or beer, exhibitions and festivals, galleries or classical concerts, as well as restaurant meals. Within these contexts, the application of specialised knowledge and skills, integrated with specific consumer practices and goals, clearly distinguish the experiences of some from those of others. The consumption of the outdoors or a city whist on vacation are clearly two cases in point here, as these are products that can be consumed in a variety of ways dependent upon the knowledge and skills that a consumer brings to bear in their consumption. On the one hand, a climber who is equipped with the knowledge and skills to scale a rock face would have a qualitatively different experience in the Peak District than a sightseer who is only able to stand and spectate, or go for a walk. In a similar manner, the tourist who has taken the time to learn about the culture, history and architecture of a World Heritage Site such as Krakow, will arguably take more from their visit of this city than one who hasn't. In this respect, these resources afford greater opportunities for consumption in these contexts than those of the regular tourist or visitor.

The modern marketplace also demands a particular kind of knowledge and set of skills to be a competent and successful consumer in general. The ability to utilise computers and mobile devices to search out information, download and use apps, or make online bookings and reservations for air travel are but a few examples of this, as is the ability to juggle financial instruments to make the most efficient use of the marketplace and the products on offer (Bernthal, Crockett and Rose, 2005). While on the surface these seem trivial, being basic to the tacit knowledge of most contemporary consumers, we must remember that such understanding and ability are not uniformly shared across all market segments. The third age and hard pressed particularly struggle to keep pace with these changes in the structure and performance of the marketplace, and may be deficient in the necessary competencies. Accordingly in our technically mediated world, just keeping up with the rapid changes and innovation of the THEF marketplace requires a particular kind of mastery. Knowledge and skill thus frames agency and mobilises the notion of the sovereign consumer, and marketers must take great care to not purposefully exclude those who are less enabled.

■ Conclusion

This chapter has examined the role that consumer resources play in value creation and THEF consumption, and has shown that these are essential for consumers to engage the experiences offered by the THEF sectors in general. It is also clear that these resources are necessary for the realisation of individual and collective goals and projects, and that variances in consumer resources delimit what can and can't be experienced by consumers as they interact with the THEF marketplace. While the established tools, concepts and frameworks presently available to marketers for understanding their consumers are significant and valuable, namely those of market segmentation, they do not fully get to grips with how value and marketplace meanings are co-produced and created by consumers. Following Holt (1998) we agree that market segmentation often abstracts away the nuance and detail that is central to truly understanding marketplace behaviours and activity, therefore this resource based perspective offers a resolution. By really getting to grips with the resources and capabilities that mobilise and delimit consumer behaviours across a range of contexts and settings, and by understanding the consumer as a *resource integrator*, the THEF marketer will be well placed to develop and produce marketing strategies that are potentially more valuable and meaningful to their consumer's lives and projects.

In addition to the commercial applications and potential of the resource based view of the consumer, these ideas may also have an equally significant role to play in consumer protection and sustainable market practice. For example, policy makers with a stakeholder interest in the THEF sectors may be equipped to produce solutions, or to intermediate in the market where significant resource deficiencies may immobilise consumers, limit their potential or place them in harm's way (Arnould, Price & Malshe, 2006). Or alternatively, lead them into engaging in insensitive or unsustainable behaviours. Examples of this may include amongst others;

■ Deficiencies in consumer knowledge of the benefits of sunscreens and creams in protecting against skin cancer;

■ Awareness of the nutritional and ingredient constituents of food items on restaurant menus and how these may impact upon or benefit their health;

■ Knowledge of the consequences of poor hygiene or sexual practices at festivals; and

■   Contributing to the material degradation of a heritage site, through not being aware of the limits to consumptions placed on the location.

To draw this section to a close, we can thus see that this approach advocates a more microscopic and nuanced view of the consumer and consumption. Alongside the traditional approach to market segmentation, the contemporary THEF marketer, would greatly benefit from getting much closer to their customers in order to gain awareness and knowledge of the consumption practices, and consumer resources that are undoubtedly integral to the creation of customer value and their experiences in general. It also demonstrates that the THEF marketer is not the only one who is supplying the valuable *resources* that their customers interact with in forging their experiences and realising their outcomes. This perspective thus demands a closer understanding of consumption, and to reveal this insight, marketers must go much further than merely surveying their customers' experiences and satisfaction levels through questionnaires etc., and constructing segments through multivariate modelling. On the contrary, they need to be in the field with them as well, and in doing so engage a range of interpretive and interactive investigative approaches such as observation, depth interview and market orientated ethnography (see, Arnould & Price, 2006). In doing so, THEF marketers will not only achieve more for their customers by being able to offer more of the resources that are integral to their projects, but also, such insight may afford the opportunity to build deeper and more meaningful relationships with them more generally. In consequence THEF marketers will be better equipped to make more informed marketing decisions and co-produce more valuable THEF experiences in partnership with their consumers.

6

7 Marketing and Identity

■ Introduction

This book revolves around two assumptions. The first is that marketing is a cultural activity that is both informed and part of contemporary culture, and the second is that marketing needs to understand the relationship between the individual consumer and the product or experience. This chapter outlines the significance of consumption and how consumption patterns reinforce both our identity and position within society. This chapter also challenges the dominance of certain marketing practices, such as segmentation, in targeting consumers. We all think carefully before we purchase something whether it be a holiday or a meal, we go through a complex decision making process taking into account many different factors. One of the major aspects will be to think about what additional benefits may accrue from purchasing the item, what will family, friends or even strangers think. As such, we try to identify the additional benefits from purchasing the item, for example if I buy a designer coat I will get the benefit of being kept warm, but I may also get the benefit of people thinking I am affluent and on trend, and as such they may look up to me or give me respect. This process also informs the things we drink, the places where we holiday, the events we attend, the wine we choose or the restaurants we eat at. It can be argued that we go through this process every time we purchase an item or experience. Consumption identifies to the rest of the world the type of person we are and the groups, class or tribe we belong to. This chapter examines how we reinforce or create our identity through consumption and the impact this may have on contemporary marketing practices

■ The restructuring of society and the consumer

As we moved from an economy dominated by industrial production to one dominated by services and experiences, both culture and society adapted with it. The changes in working patterns, and the destruction of regionally dominant industries, such as coal mining or steel production, saw the breakdown of communities and increased migration by workers looking to access the new service industries. The upshot of this, is that the community groups that helped us form our identities and informed our view of the world disappeared and were replaced by more powerful and persuasive media that generated ways of living through cable or satellite television. What is more, the internet and mobile technology has stepped in to grant almost unrestricted access to an innumerable range of virtual communities and consumption and interest groups that allow consumers to interact with, and align with whatever lifestyle or social group they wish. What we have witnessed is a restructuring of society in which workers have become consumers and as such, a society that is dominated by consumerism and has led to a world in which:

> ...the meaning of life is to be found in buying things and repackaging experiences supplanting 'religion', work, and politics as the mechanism by which social and status distinctions may be established.

> (Izberk-Bilgin, 2010)

This is a world in which 'cultural intermediaries', specifically in advertising, the media, the fashion system, product development, broadcasting and entertainment, act as social and cultural brokers (Urry, 2001). They define the way in which consumers view the world, by defining taste, trends and fashions. This group of individuals and their organisations have replaced traditional family and kinship groups in shaping consumers' expectations and desires. However, it should not be forgotten that throughout history certain consumption patterns have always supported social class (Holt, 1998).

Magazines and television programmes that chart the lives of celebrities, by focusing on their lifestyles, their diets, their leisure time, and their holidays, supported by travel programmes, advertisements and how-to guides, create desire and demand in THEF by providing subject positions, or blueprints to live through/by, and as a result, consumers may emulate the rich and famous or aspirant others. In short, cultural intermediaries are significantly active in the definition of taste and preferences, and in creating subject positions that are made available for consumers as resources through which they can activate and express or develop their identities.

The result of this is that commodities are no longer solely defined by their function or use, or by their market price, but rather by what they signify to both the consumer and his or her peers (Izberk-Bilgin, 2010; Levy, 1959; Solomon, 1983). Experiences marketing utilises the knowledge and symbolism generated by cultural intermediaries and the manifold meanings located in the broader culturally constituted world (McCracken, 1986) to inform their own marketing practice and cultural intermediation. It enables the marketer to tailor and develop products, experiences, and mark out the boundaries of specific fields of consumption or habitus (Arsel & Thompson, 2011) that offer the maximum benefits/value to the consumer by providing them with the means and resources to generate and accumulate various forms of capital, be it cultural, social, symbolic, or even economic (Thompson and Arsel, 2004). Drawing on the myriad of symbolic and discursive resources, the language and practice of experiences marketing invites consumers into a plurality of worlds, that allows them to activate and furnish identity projects and to escape from the mundane experience of everyday life, that is, of course, if they are endowed with the required levels of financial and authoritative resources and capabilities (Arnould, 2007). Thus, experiences marketing is more than just a commercial activity, it also defines notions of taste and provides an outlet for consumers through consumption of THEF products to express their own individual taste and preferences.

7

■ Taste and consumption

The type of destination, holiday, event, food or hotel that consumers choose is a reflection of their own individual tastes, however, taste is socially and culturally conditioned whereby, consumer choice reflects a 'symbolic hierarchy' (Allen & Anderson, 1994:70) that is defined and maintained by society. This hierarchy enables groups of consumers to distance or make themselves distinct from other individuals or groups by defining trends, consumption patterns or expressions of taste. Thus, the things consumers buy, drink, eat, drive or wear, as well as the events they attend, the destinations or attractions they visit, and the broader consumption practices that they either engage in or disengage from, become social markers of who they are. Such consumption behaviours increasingly become an integral aspect of their own self-concept and additionally transform into a symbolic and social resource that has positional power within particular status hierarchies (see Levy, 1959; Belk, 2010 for review). As Allen & Anderson (1994:70) state:

> ...taste becomes a 'social weapon' that defines and marks off the high from the low, the sacred from the profane, and the 'legitimate' from the 'illegitimate'.

Consumers' consumption patterns represent who they are, and much of the meaning and symbolic authority of products is generated through the marketing process. Marketing has the ability to elevate brands and logos from the ordinary to that of the extraordinary. One of the best ways to think about this is to locate the debate within the field of designer clothes. For example, I can go to a high street store and purchase a very good quality polo shirt for £30. It is good cotton and has nice buttons. However, I can also go to a store and purchase a polo shirt of the same quality as the £30 version, but because the shirt has an embroidered man on a horse I am willing to pay £80. Thus, the symbolic value of the logo is £50. Value is generated through the sign and the symbolism of the logo, and as a consumer I am willing to pay this additional amount, as the shirt comes to represent a way of living, a view of the world that is defined by perceived notions of American sophistication, class and wealth. Thus, the shirt is not just a means to clothe myself, but also an expression of the type of person I am or at least want to be seen as. We each find meaning in the brands we purchase and there is clear evidence that consumers physically and symbolically transform branded goods as they co-produce collective, family and individual meanings (Holt, 1998:20). The marketing process is key to this, as it creates and reinforces the meaning and significance of the logo or brand etc. This process also underpins experiences marketing.

Within experiences marketing, we see knowledge and cultural awareness being continually generated; we evaluate and make judgments about people through their knowledge of food, culture, wine, geography and how they express this through their consumer behavior and consumption choices (see Morgan and Tresidder, 2015). If someone attends a classical concert we may make certain assumptions about that person, their education, cultural knowledge and social position. We make different sets of assumptions if someone attends a folk concert or 'The Ministry of Sound'. Consumers enter into the same process when they assess the leisure activities or holiday choices of others, and the activities they engage in during this time. We will make different judgments about people visiting the same destination but undertaking different activities, for example two tourists are on the same plane on route to Ibiza, one is there to visit the clubs and to see a particular DJ, the other is going to hike in the mountains and visit the churches in the hills. Although the destination may be the same both are expressing different forms of cultural capital, one is expressing their knowledge of the dance scene, the other the knowledge of ecclesiastical architecture in the Balearics. This expression of knowledge expresses who they are, which market segment they belong to, their membership to a particular class or group of people, and their position within this group.

■ Cultural capital

Our choice of food, concert or holiday generates what may be termed cultural capital, which is simply the additional social/cultural benefits we may gain from certain activities. We exchange our cultural capital with friends, family and peers, and the amount of cultural capital we are judged to have by these groups will identify where we sit within the hierarchy of the social group. Our expression of cultural capital may cement our position, or it may place us in a position that people look up to and want to emulate. There are two principal types of capital, capital that is entwined with wealth and money, and cultural capital that is defined by types and levels of knowledge. For Holt (1998), the role of cultural capital in contemporary society is to attract the respect of others, and it plays an important role in structuring consumption patterns. Simplistically, cultural capital consists of:

1 Cultural knowledge, skills, experiences, abilities

2 Linguistic competence and vocabulary

3 Modes of thought and views of the world (see Chapter 9 for discussion on this area)

We all possess particular levels of knowledge about different subjects and experiences that subsequently inform consumption patterns. This knowledge in conjunction with consumption forms our cultural capital, and this form of capital locates us within society or groups. Holt (1998:3) asserts that:

> Cultural capital exists in three primary forms: embodied as practical knowledges, skills, and dispositions; objectified in cultural objects; and institutionalized in official degrees and diplomas that certify the existence of the embodied form.

Cultural capital is not merely an expression of elitist groups, but is important in defining membership of all cultural groupings, for example people will express their knowledge of football, the intricacies of the game, their historical knowledge of players and games etc. (see Richardson & Turley, 2007 or Holt, 1997 for discussion of American baseball and knowledge). This interest or knowledge is still a form of cultural capital and it enables individuals to locate themselves within a group of people that share the same interests and worldview. Consumers, who possess similar levels of cultural capital and come together around this shared interest/knowledge, may end up in what may be termed a shared 'capital space'. As Bourdieu states, members who share 'capital space' will "...have every chance of having similar dispositions and interests, and thus producing similar practices and adopting similar stances" (1987:231). Thus, for marketers, understanding the various habitus, and the needs and desires of their members provides an effective method of segmenting and constructing communication strategies that are shaped through various cultural understandings. This is of particular significance to experiences marketing, as tourism, hospitality, events and food play a central role in how people express their levels of cultural capital and add to it.

■ Cultural capital and taste

Cultural capital, as defined by Pierre Bourdieu, represents a distinct competitive resource that people concurrently possess, embody and accumulate. As previously described, it takes the form of knowledge, skills, aptitude, and abilities that become manifested in consumer tastes and consumption practices. These in turn become resources that are deployed for both autotelic and instrumental reasons (Holt, 1997a). For example, with regard to the latter, cultural knowledge and skill could be deployed as an interpretive framework and set of associated practices to appreciate the idiosyncratic qualities of cheese or a micro brewery's beer. That is, it is activated in the service of connoisseurship and is underpinned by a search for personal pleasure and enjoyment. Alternatively, cultural capital may be explicitly accrued and deployed in pursuit of status, recognition or group membership. Objectified cultural capital that is manifest through observable or recognised consumption practices may subsequently grant a consumer access or membership to esteemed or distinct social networks or communities. Conversely deficiencies in capital could also produce the opposite effects by diminishing a consumer's relative status within a field, which in turn may exclude them from that field and from social relationships. To this end, objectified cultural capital delineates and marks out symbolic and semiotic boundaries that have significant social (and economic) significance (Holt, 1997b), or to put it another way, cultural capital translates into social capital. While this suggests

7

that a consumer may always be purposively working their cultural capital for explicit personal benefit, this is not always the case.

It is worth noting that in many cases this resource is at work socially, without it being recognised personally by a consumer. For certain consumers, their social positioning, community affiliation and group membership is just the way things are. That is, it is acting to position them within a certain social strata or group without their explicit knowledge and indirectly becomes a means of distinction and criteria for selection to esteemed or affiliate networks and groups. In this respect, in the same way that economic capital or resources can be, cultural capital can be understood as a mediator between person, experience and opportunity. That is to say, the specific quantity and quality of capital a person possesses delimits their potential as a consumer across and within the range of specific and generic 'fields' of consumption. Like Holt (1998), and Arsel and Thompson (2011), we use the Bourdieuian concept of 'field' to represent the range of consumer goods, activities and experiences that constitute consumer society and include experiences or services. In respect of this book, the field would encompass both the sectors themselves, namely the fields of THEF, and also the 'sub fields' that reside within those sectors, such as: the fine dining field; the adventure tourism field; the cultural events field; the field of coffee; the barbeque field; and so forth.

The cultural capital accrued in these fields may be later used as a means of distinction from other consumers or to reinforce membership of a group or class. This view is supported by Holt in his 1998 work on cultural capital where he identifies a number of themes, interests and activities that are closely associated with consumption, identity and cultural capital. These include *exoticism, authenticity, cosmopolitanism,* and *connoisseurship,* all of which categories are closely allied to the many 'fields' associated with THEF, and as such the consumption of experiences is a major means by which the individual may express both their identity and cultural capital; in short leisure becomes a tool for self-actualization (Holt, 1998:17). Experiences marketing often utilises a language that reinforces the cultural significance of the activity, this providing a consumption outlet for the expression of status, class and habitus.

■ Habitus as market segment

The ability to recognise how consumers construct their identity, the dynamics of particular habitus and the trends or themes that cultural intermediaries are generating are key to contemporary marketing strategy. The ability to understand the interrelationship between these various aspects of the production and consumption process provides an insight into the type of products that need to be developed. The semiotic language that should be used and the most appropriate communication channels for each group, habitus or tribe, provide the marketer with a competitive advantage as they are able to anticipate trends, the needs and desires of particular consumers and to identify types of cultural capital that needs to be exchanged with different groups. It is argued that we live in a 'classless society' and that the longstanding means of differentiating society into social groups dominated by the ruling elite, is no longer valid. This approach had been widely adopted in traditional marketing approaches and is manifested in the 'ABC1' social class demographic and a means of defining or targeting consumers. However, during the era of postmodernity, this means of differentiating society and consumers has been challenged and replaced by a more fluid egalitarian understanding of society and the consumer. Bourdieu identified that society was structured by individual cultural practices and preferences that were also shared by a group of peers, he went onto refer to these groups as forming a *habitus*. Thus:

> One's class origin is not, therefore, a structural straight jacket that determines with certainty one's actions. But on the other hand, there is a certain probability that persons exposed to similar life experiences will display similar 'lifestyles'.
>
> (Allen & Anderson, 1994:71)

Individual consumption patterns become a means to define both yourself and your position in society or within a habitus (Henry & Caldwell 2008). Habitus becomes a complex system of distinctions based on constellations of taste (or according to Baudrillard (1998:60) a "social logic of consumption") that becomes a group-distinctive framework of

7

social cognition and interpretation, and which create communities of a particular lifestyle (Izberk-Bilgin 2010). For Miles:

> ...the 'habitus' is the embodiment of the cultural dispositions and sensibilities of the group that structure group behavior, simultaneously allowing group members a mechanism for structuring their social experience (1996:152)

This position is reinforced by the consumer's 'special knowledge of things' (ibid). Within this context, any goods or activities may be used as a means of maintaining in-group solidarity and excluding status inferiors (Holt, 1998).

Cultural and consumer knowledge is generated in many ways from television, to magazines, how-to books, family and peer inter-action, and most importantly through PR and marketing activities. Consumers are surrounded by different forms and means of knowl-edge, and our engagement and interaction with these various sources enables us to develop our cultural capital (Henry & Caldwell 2008), whether that information is concerning food choices, which bands to see, which destinations to visit or which hotel to stay in. Contemporary consumption patterns enable consumers to balance the need to express their individuality while finding the comfort of being able to belong to a group or tribe, micro culture (Branch, 2007), or community of con-sumption (see Cova & Cova, 2001) that share consumption patterns, passions, emotions, values and knowledge.

■ The role of cultural capital in organising taste and consumption practices

To further explain the operative effects of cultural capital and its capac-ity as a consumer resource we can further draw upon the work of Holt (1997:1998) who has examined how quotas of cultural capital mediate the experiences and potential of American consumers. Specifically his research aimed to examine if consumption still served to reproduce social boundaries and class. His findings are instructive in terms of the ways in which cultural capital inflects the consumption of food and hospitality products and services. He constructed a measurement scale that allowed him to distinguish between consumers with High Cultural Capital resources (HCCs) and those with Low (LCCs). To identify these typologies Holt drew reference from Bourdieu, who holds that cultural capital endowments are both relative to, and accumulated through a person's formative socialization, i.e. parenting and associated experiences, informal and formal education and acculturation processes and interactions that span one's work life and leisure experiences.

Accordingly, those born to families who have highly educated parents, who have experienced a cosmopolitan lifestyle through work, leisure and habitation, and who then, themselves, proceed on similar life trajectories by attending prestigious schools and elite universities and subsequently secure careers in professions that both emphasise symbolic production and knowledge or creative work, have the opportunity to accumulate more of this resource. Such foundations position these people within a world that is replete with travel and metropolitan life and resultantly they will go on to exhibit and embody higher stocks of capital than those who do not come from such backgrounds. The logic of this argument stems from the notion that such life trajectories produce privileged consumers/citizens who will have developed through their socialisation, training, work and leisure experiences the capacity for critical abstract thought, accumulated rarefied generic and specialised knowledge and skills (for example the appreciation of art or wine), enabled by and through the associatively constructed broad and deep culturally sensitive interpretive repertoire – these are Holts HCCs.

Contrary to these, LCCs are those who have experienced relatively enclosed and situated lives within tightly bound geographic and social communities. They, and their parents before them, have at most a secondary or vocational education and typically are, or were, employed in blue collar or low skill routinised white-collar jobs. In many cases, material resources for these people are constrained, and managing the implications of this is an immediate concern and focus. Consequently, the cultural knowledge, skills and interpretive horizons, of LCCs are tied to this realm of experience and socio-historic context.

That is, relative to HCCs, the cultural capital of LCCs can be classified as limited in scope and scale.

Important to Holt's (1998) findings is that significant qualitative differences between the approaches to consumption and experiences of these two distinct categories of consumers exist. HCCs on the one hand are analytical in their consumption and deploy a range of evaluative frameworks and associated practices to extract individualised meanings and experiences from consumed products and activities. This, it is argued, is even the case with mass marketed goods and commodities. Although HCCs prefer, and selectively seek out authentic products and experiences, where unavoidable, they will deploy strategies and practices of re-appropriation, creativity or juxtaposition to cleanse commodities of their marketer implied meanings or associations, that is they personalise or customise them. For HCCs, this is arguably a significant and essential skill and practice, where increasingly it is difficult to identify an experience, object or activity that has slipped the grasp of the market or, that has not been ascribed with commercially significant meanings by marketers (Kozinets, 2002a).

What is more, the HCCs in this sample held cosmopolitan tastes, had a predisposition towards aesthetic consumption through connoisseurship and were accustomed to boundary transgression and experimentation. For instance, Holt (1998) describes how an informant (Kathryn) practiced "combinatorial inventiveness" (p.16) in her food consumption and meal preparation through drawing on these resources and dispositions:

> "[We] start with a cold soup like vichyssoise or gazpacho, my husband makes a spicy Jamaican chicken with rice, or maybe trout sauced with red wine base with Cointreau, and make a big salad with bitter greens, and a different desert such as a great big soufflé or something like that. We have wine with meals and my husband makes planter's punch". (Informant Kathryn in Holt 1998:16)

Finally the HCCs in this research sought self actualisation through their consumption and leisure experiences. In this sense much of what is consumed and experienced is a means to fulfilling a range of integrated projects. HCCs have a strong value and disposition to learn and develop through consumption. Seemingly, they would seek out and prioritise those experiences that enable this in abundance but would also be drawn to extracting the detail and nuance from apparently mundane and everyday experiences and products. They would seek to individuate them.

Taking the liberty of imposing Holt's typologies on our sectors for insight, we can outline the range of products and experiences that may engage them. In pursuing these, they would be drawn to authentic offerings or those that are not overtly commercialised. They would relish products and experiences that would encourage the deployment of skill and creativity and ones that would allow for personal development and intellectual and spiritual growth. In this respect HCCs would identify with being classified as travelers rather than tourists. Preferring to construct their own holiday itineraries and seek to encounter the new, novel, different, and interesting. They would be drawn to immersive experiences that challenged and enlarged their horizons. These consumers would achieve the goal of locating the authentic through entering "the 'world' of a different social milieu, rather than gazing at it from outside" (Holt, 1997:113). These consumption styles and tastes would be carried into the other fields of consumption covered by this book. The reference to Holt's informant Katharyn offers insight into the ways in which food is consumed. Food is selected and valorised for its authenticity, sensory characteristics, experiential and aesthetic quality and its potential to (re)connect them to nature, other cultures, and faraway lands. Combined with travel, HCCs would seek out indigenous and local cuisine to extend their eclecticism and stock of knowledge. Likewise restaurants are chosen against similar criteria. There would be a preference for the artisanal and the casual, and such consumers would not apportion much value on status orientated restaurants or celebrity chefs (Holt, 1998). Such an approach may be seen as integral to the creation of the extraordinary by these groups, and when combined with an ascetic value, it is likely that food choices and consumption would reflect sensitivities to culture, nature and the environment. In the same vein, it is possible that

7

HCCs would: be ardent supporters of local agricultural projects; value and utilise farmers' markets and local producers; and relish growing and producing their own food. This however would be balanced against the thirst to experience the novel and authentic character of distant and exotic cuisine. As such, it is the practices and experiences that offer the value to the HCC consumer, and marketing induced meanings or the conventional symbolism associated with products are often inconsequential to their consumption choices and purchases. For these consumers, the value that may be derived from interacting with the producers and their produce at farmers markets for example, is far more valuable than any particular food brand or retailer and the meanings they may hold in the marketplace.

LCCs on the other hand would be the tourists (the spectators, consumers, and the entertained). Holt (1997) reports that these consumers would be drawn to package deals and full service experiences. Disney World, cruises, beach and resort holidays and guided tours would feature heavily in their preferences and reflect their tastes. With food, given the concerns imposed by responding to the needs of everyday material reality, many LCCs would possibly be drawn to practical produce that is balanced within their financial means. Those LCC's who have achieved financial success and are not so constrained in this resource may favour premium packaged meals and branded products. This latter observation reflects Holt's (1997, 1998) contention that 'the good life' for LCCs is understood against their background and lived experience of material scarcity. Previously denied the material pleasures of life, wealthy LCCs typically counterbalance this through consuming in abundance and valuing what is conventionally understood as luxury or scarce. This logic would extend to events and hospitality, where material constraints would naturally impede and structure attendance and usage of such activities. Where this is the case local activities would predominate, such as village fayres, community and family events such as weddings, children's parties, dinner parties, and school sports days, or be restricted to weekends and special occasions, such as birthdays, anniversaries, and religious events and rituals. Restaurant preference would be familiar wholesome cuisine where the dining experience is relatively informal and unconstrained. Buffet style concepts and practices that are characterised by autonomy and 'plenty' are typical examples of this (Holt, 1998:11).

With unconstrained financial resources, tastes would be drawn to those activities and experiences that would demonstrate material abundance, luxury and entertainment. The latter value being mobilised by attempts to escape and balance the mundane reality of their everyday experience in routine and repetitive jobs. Possibly then, horse racing, attendance at major sporting events, becoming a season ticket holder of a supported football team or attending music events and gigs would now feature as exemplar activities. In a similar way, hospitality consumption would be upgraded to more frequent visits to restaurants, gastro pubs, and hotels that are marked out by some criteria or other, as those that are considered exemplary in their class. By criteria, we refer here to Michelin and AA stars, celebrity chefs, endorsement by restaurant critics, and consensus market views of a product's superiority or status.

■ Consumption as identity

As stated previously, the things and experiences we buy, drive, wear, drink, eat, or visit, as well as, the holidays we take, the restaurants we use or the events we attend all become social makers of the type of person we are or more importantly the type of person we want to be seen as. For Holt (1998:4):

> ...consumption is a particular status game that must be analyzed in isolation rather than lumped together with work, religion, education and politics...

The significance of this for the individual is identified by Cova & Cova (2002:596) who argue that:

> ...we have now entered the era of the ordinary individual, that is to say an age in which any individual can – and must – take personal action, so as to produce and show one's own existence, one's own difference.

As such, consumption becomes a source of identity (Miles 1996), and on a daily basis consumers negotiate the symbols of consumer culture choosing which elements they engage with and in. The things we consume become a means of forming our identity, thus the decision to purchase a designer suit or dress often has nothing to do with the quality of the item, but has more to do with the message it sends to our peers about our knowledge of fashion, our ambitions and our taste. It becomes a badge or code of who we are, and is read by other consumers who then make assumptions about the type of person we are. Thus, consumption is essentially a social activity that incorporates meanings within the culture in which we live, and consumers skillfully use goods to:

> ...communicate, mark and classify social relations, it is a way of communicating individual taste, status, aspiration and even protest

> (Izberk-Bilgin, 2010:307).

This reinforces Holt's view:

> ...that the pursuit of individuality through consumption is a central characteristic of advanced capitalist societies (1998:13).

What is important to re-state here is that although at first sight the relationship between consumption and identity can be seen as superficial, it provides the freedom to create and shape an identity we want rather than having one imposed upon us by society. As Miles states:

> ...the evidence suggests that consumption performs the role of *solidifying* an individual's identity. In the context of cultural ramifications of peer relations amongst you people (sic), identities in a so called 'postmodern' world might well be argued to be far more stable than many commentators would be prepared to admit. (1996:150)

The role of leisure, food, tourism and events is especially significant in the formation of identity, as the activities are often very public – attending a cultural event makes a very public statement about your cultural knowledge, desires and aspirations. Additionally we often communicate our experiences and preferences by showing our holiday photographs, using social media and blogs such as Twitter, Facebook or TripAdvisor to express our views about restaurants and hotels etc. All of these activities provide us with the opportunity to advertise our levels of cultural capital and thus they become expressions of identity.

■ Conclusion

This chapter has identified the significance of consumption in both the construction of our identity and cementing our position within particular groups, tribes or habitus. The consumption process has become one of the central elements in the formation of our identities and we are in a continual process of interaction with other consumers, whereby we exchange cultural capital with each other. Products and experiences that make us feel good are often rich in cultural capital, and this in turn becomes a significant element of the consumption process.

Tourism, events, hospitality and food are important aspects in our lives and are among the major means by which we express our identities, preferences, taste and social or cultural standing. Experiences marketing utilises the elevated significance of these activities to create a world within marketing literature that reinforces the cultural significance of the activities, and uses a language, theme and symbolism that is appropriate to differing tribes or habitus. This is a significant demarcation from traditional approaches to segmentation and communication as it privileges cultural and social movements over often quantitative oriented demographic approaches. It is also important to remind ourselves that marketing is all about people (their needs, desires wants etc.), and that understanding our relationship to consumption places the individual, the person, back in the center of the process. Additionally, by understanding how cultural intermediaries generate trends and consumer desires it becomes possible to anticipate what is going to be the next big food trend, destination, hotel style or festival, which can provide the marketer with a competitive advantage. Therefore, the next time one of your friends or colleagues is talking you through their holiday and showing you photographs, or

7

is telling you about this great little restaurant they have found, think about how they are transmitting their cultural capital and think about what group or habitus they are aligning themselves with.

8 The Semiotics of THEF Marketing

■ Introduction

This chapter examines how signs and sign systems are utilised in marketing to give meaning and award value(s) to tourism, hospitality, events and food (THEF) products, activities and experiences. It also seeks to portray the dominant semiotic codes and signifiers presently operative in each of these sectors. This chapter will draw to a close with a critical examination of the power effects of these representation systems and practices. The meaning production process, which has its roots in the structural linguistic science and philosophy of semiotics is recognised as an integral and fundamental constituent of marketing practice (e.g. McCracken, 1986; Mick et al., 2004, Mick and Oswald, 2006; Oswald, 2012). It is integral to the marketing communication process, the meaning of products and brands, the design and configuration of servicescapes and retail environments, as well as market segmentation practice and positioning more generally. By examining the semiotic structure that constitutes the various forms of marketing practice, objects and materials that are located and utilised within our sectors, it is possible to identify a semiotic language or code, that is used by marketers and which frames marketing practice. These meanings are intended to be read and understood by the consumer and other marketplace stakeholders for the purpose of achieving numerous marketing goals and ends. What is more, semiotics is also considered to be essential to the understanding of specific consumption practices within the THEF sectors and consumer behaviour generally. This is based upon the premise that consumers exist within a semiotic system of signs, they resultantly become integral nodes within this system and, are compelled into thinking and behaving symbolically. That is, they symbolically interact in the world socially and experientially – they interact with symbolic products, engage in symbolic activities and engage in symbolic experiences.

■ Semiotics and the significance of signs

Semiotics is very simply the study of signs and systems of representation. "Signs are *simply* anything that stands for something (its object/ *referent*), to somebody (interpreter), in some respect (its context, *i.e. in an advert, label, package, servicescape or retail environment*)" (Mick, 1986, p.198, italics added), therefore, as consumers or citizens we are all amateur semioticians. We are surrounded by signs from the moment we awaken in the morning until we go to bed at night. Signs essentially make the world intelligible and meaningful to us, they tell us when we can cross the road, which door to use and how we can exit a building. In the main we all understand the meaning of these sorts of signs, and this is possible because we read, interpret and comprehend them. Comprehension in this case is made possible from belonging to a shared cultural context and system of meaning that frames and directs our reading and understanding.

In the literature this context is sometimes referred to as the *code* (e.g. Alexander, 2000; McCracken & Roth, 1989; Holt & Cameron, 2010) or a *cultural template* (Thompson & Arsel, 2004). Essentially these codes or templates provide an interpretive or organising framework through which signs make sense and things in the world come to have personal and social significance. A good example of this is to think about a set of traffic lights. We all recognise and understand the function they perform: through historical convention and experience we equate the colour red with danger so we stop; Green connotes safety so when the green light shows we know to proceed. Therefore, these rule based systems or organising frameworks allow us to make sense of everyday reality and navigate our experience in the world. Codes also allow us to read into someone's communicative intentions even when drawing upon the most arbitrary of signs. For example it is only through experience and being privy to the code that: the cowboy comes to symbolise rugged individualism (Solomon, 2013; McCracken, 1993), the cafetiere becomes a representamen of the self-proclaimed British middle classes (Britain Thinks, 2011); and Hugh Fearnley Whittingstall turns into a totemic symbol of the Bourgeoisie-Bohemian (Bo-Bo) contemporary ascetic lifestyle (Holt & Cameron, 2010). With regards to the latter, on top of Holt and Cameron's insightful treatise, the interested reader should turn to McCracken (1989) for a discussion of the semiotics of celebrities and the cultural foundations of the endorsement process.

As codes are accumulated and assimilated through our lived experience and interactions with material and social realities of everyday life, they are not always universally shared. That is to say, they may vary between individual consumers and particularly across different market segments, such as age cohorts, ethnic groups or lifestyle sub cultures. In this respect, where we are unfamiliar with the rules or do not understand the code in use, we may experience discomfort, disorientation, or surprise, and struggle to interpret and make sense of what confronts us. For example while it is no surprise to find coffee being sold in branded paper cups or oversize mugs from specialised dedicated retailers in the UK, we may be uncertain of the product if confronted by coffee being served over ice in a plastic bag but, research by Denny & Sunderland (2002) and Sunderland & Denny (2007) found that this is the dominant mode of consuming this commodity in Bangkok. Equally this research also found that coffee in Bangkok has no 'clearly' identifiable place. Unlike familiar elsewheres, coffee is not found in cafés, or specialised shops, but is sold instead by street vendors from market stalls. In sum, the cultural template or code, and the semiotic chain of symbols and signs that mark it out, and which direct the production and consumption of coffee in this part of Thailand is very different to the one that frames and signposts these value creating activities in Europe and the USA and other parts of the world.

8

■ The nature of signs

In our meaning laden world pretty much anything and everything can be treated as a sign and can be seen to hold semiotic potency and value. In fact, nothing in the world is semiotically redundant; even nothing itself. In this way the world and its components, can be treated as text or narrative, just like a novel. Things in and of the world are read for meaning, they have discursive significance. Clothing for example has textual properties, and is often read in this way (McCracken & Roth 2003); the dress of service personnel (chef's whites or the black and white formal clothing of waiters and waitresses) must therefore be recognised as carrying symbolic significance and managed accordingly.

More so, THEF products and activities themselves carry and communicate meaning (Levy, 1959), as do the practices and styles of consumption deployed by consumers in their efforts to extract value and meaning from using and interacting with them (Holt, 1998). Kniazeva and Venkatesh (2007) for example have examined the meanings carried by specific food products and related consumption practices in the U.S. Their findings portray a plethora of competing meanings and associations, which include, amongst other things, romance, bonding, friendship, guilt, shame, solace, comfort, power, harmony, fun, love and hate. There are also products, activities and experiences that, because of their sign value and the way in which they are consumed, mark out time and impose a temporal social order on the world (Moisander & Valtonen, 2006). For example, products like quiche, ice-cream, Pims, and strawberries and cream, and co-production practices like growing your own food, mark out the boundaries between the seasons. While "people have a cup of coffee... when they take a break from work... or have a bottle of beer after work to create an end for the work day and to liberate themselves from work-related matters" (ibid, 2006:11). It is argued that these latter types of products, when set within and consumed in these experiential contexts, "come to embody and reproduce the Western myth of freedom" (ibid, 2006:11). In line with this argument it is possible that many of the products that constitute the THEF sectors may act in this way, when consumed to produce or mark out free time and leisurely activity. Thus, it can be argued that the meaning and significance of products and experiences semiotically structure reality and our experiences of, and in, the world. We will return to these ideas later in the chapter where we describe the specific semiotic codes and language utilised in our sectors.

Interpersonal interactions also have symbolic significance (see Solomon, 1983 for review). People search for meaning and understanding, both through verbal and non-verbal communication. We are all familiar with the lay phrase that "actions speak louder than words", and this is true in semiotic terms, as all actions have sign value. In the same way, so do expressions, utterances, and the use, display or otherwise appropriation of material objects, activities and artifacts. Therefore, service personnel involved in the staging of THEF experiences must be mindful of the meanings they are transferring through their actions and interactions, as must those who are responsible for managing their behaviour and performance.

■ The order of signs

Much of what is discussed above is reminiscent of Saussare (1983) semiotics but, from the pioneering work of Pierce (1934), it is now generally accepted that signs can be classified into a taxonomy of three general categories. These are, in no particular order, icons, indexes, and symbols. What marks these categories out from each other is the difference in the relationship between the sign (signifier) and its object (the signified).

Icons

First is the **icon**, a sign that imitates or has a resemblance or close correspondence to its object. Drawing on the multi-sensory nature and characteristic of our sectors, an iconic signifier could therefore look, sound, smell, taste, or feel like that which it signifies. Accordingly iconic signs that may be found in THEF marketing materials or contexts could include amongst others: the sound of gun shots or explosions in battlefield recreations; the smell of the everyday lived experience of our ancestors at the Jorvik Viking Centre in York, or the spritzed essence of the seashore that may accompany your fish supper at Heston Blumenthal's restaurant, The Fat Duck. They could also be:

a cartoon representation of a patriarchal Italian family in a pasta sauce advert; a performer adorned in a Roman Centurion uniform or staged as a male mine worker at an heritage centre or within an advertisement for a living museum; or the plastic lemon shaped packaging that contains Jif lemon juice.

In this respect iconic signs permeate THEF experiences. They are integral to both the *substantive* and *communicative* staging of servicescapes and retail environments, as well as being constitutive elements and component parts of advertisements, promotional materials, websites, and food packaging. *Substantive staging* refers to the physical creation of contrived environments, that is, their material configuration, while *communicative staging* includes the scripts, role performances and interactions that signpost and pattern consumer experiences in servicescape environments (Arnould & Price, Tierney, 1998:90). For example, by the use of French speaking waiting staff, stylised menus, music and décor that draws upon themes of Frenchness, a consumer can be momentarily transported semiotically to a Provençal context and setting (Arnould & Price, Tierney, 1998). Alternatively, another consumer may perceive this to be a crass attempt at mimicry of an already artificial (inauthentic) representation of reality.

Indexes

Second, the relationship between an object and an **indexical** sign is marked out by a causal relationship. Ecthner (1999), for example, explains that a suntan is an index of sun exposure, while in a similar way, drunkenness is an index of excessive drinking and, Louis Roederer Crystal Champagne is an index of the Nouveux riche and celebrity party culture. The latter, of course, requires knowledge of the cultural code that awards this particular indexical relationship with its meaning, and by the same token this underlies why a sun tan in some instances can also be an index of rugged individualism or healthiness (ibid, 1999).

Symbols

Third, a **symbol** is a sign that has an arbitrary association to its object, and works through processes of social and cultural convention. For example, one of the dominant semiotic conventions utilised within tourism brochures is the use of the deserted beach. This image not only visually approximates – the 'materiality' of the destination we may be visiting, that is, its *denotative* meaning, it also signifies various potential consumer experiences. These can range from, amongst others, notions of escape, luxury, authenticity, fun, or romance. In this way the deserted beach signifies something to each individual consumer; it is not just a beach, but in a way it defines the experience of holidaying and being a tourist – it creates desire and expectation. The image comes to hold individualised *connotative* associations and significance. These meanings are dynamic and may change over time or in different situations and contexts, based upon changes in a consumer's expectations, goals or projects, or modifications to their socio-cultural milieu and surroundings, or indeed the code currently operative.

■ The polysemic nature of objects and experiences

The latter statement of the preceding paragraph essentially implies that an object can be represented by many signifiers. In this way an object can stand for, or mean literally anything, this is down to processes involved in both the production and consumption of signs, which in themselves allow for the polysemic nature of consumption, experiences and meanings. Here lies both the power and peril of marketing: the signifier can be decoupled from its referent, and it is possible for a marketer to imbue their products, activities and experiences (social objects) with multiple meanings. Accordingly, a social object can be simultaneously positioned towards different markets or segments by using different signifiers and associations. Likewise the meaning of a social object can be adapted, tweaked or changed in accordance with marketplace trends or demands. Here lies the rub. In the same way that marketers can switch and mix the symbolic significance of their social objects, so can consumers or others who have an interest in the meaning or significance of an organisation's products or practices (or in the values, espoused or otherwise, of the organisation itself).

An evaluation of Adbuster campaigns, for example, illustrates how marketplace activists are taking on marketers and corporations at their own game by using established marketing methods and techniques.

8

Through imitating their practices, these groups are challenging the sign value and meanings of companies and brands like McDonalds though producing adverts with countervailing and oppositional meanings and associations. One particular example of a print advert targeted against McDonalds uses an image of a person lying on an operating bed who is connected to an Electrocardiography (ECG) machine and surrounded by medical practitioners performing surgery. The pattern reported on the screen of the ECG looks as if it is within a normal range until it spikes to form two large arcs. These arcs bare a striking resembles to the golden arches logo of McDonalds. Text below carries the message 'Big Mac attack'. The pattern on the ECG machine then moves to a flat line suggesting that the patient has moved into cardiac arrest.

■ Semiosis and meaning transfer

This chapter outlines a general theory for marketing that suggests that marketers use signs and sign systems to encourage and (re)produce marketplace behaviours and experiences by loading products and experiences with meaning and significance. This process is labeled *semiosis* (Bains, 2006) or *meaning transfer* (McCracken, 1986) and is critical to contemporary marketing practice and marketing success, as we inhabit a world in which consumers are said to purchase meanings rather than functional benefits (Levy, 1959), or alternatively utilise market based resources to create their own meaning laden identities and lifestyles (Arnould & Thompson, 2005).

Furthermore, the significance of marketing as a practice of semiosis is heightened with THEF experiences as the majority of customers have to be persuaded to purchase an experience before seeing it, and then if persuaded, will move into engaging in protracted consumption episodes and performances that may span several minutes, hours or weeks. In the case of the former, adverts, websites and brochures will be employed and used to communicate information and meaning but also to build anticipation, and showcase experiences. For example, due to the problem of intangibility, we will be shown images of a festival that may have been gathered the previous year, and this will seek to mitigate the risk of purchase and build anticipation by promising that type of experience. Second, these experiences often but not always unfold within the servicescape or managed context of the host organisation, and customers will need signposts to direct and narrate their experience. In these cases both the substantive and communicative staging are central to this process and should be managed not only for value but also for meaning and significance.

As marketers it is essential that we understand this semiotic language, and semiotics more generally. In order to convey specific meanings to marketplace stakeholders, and award significance to THEF experiences, we must be able to competently identify and select suitable units of meaning or signs and arrange them in meaningful and compelling ways, through understanding the range of semiotic conventions and cultural codes which support them and award them their significance. What is more we also must become adept at reading culture and accounting for changes in the semiotic codes and conventions that award signs their potency and relevance. That is to say we must strive to be conversant with, and cogent of the residual, dominant, and emergent cultural codes that animate and structure the market for experiences and award them their value (Alexander, 2000).

■ The semiotics of tourism and events

The semiotics of tourism and events is not a new subject area; it has been developed and discussed by a number of authors who have identified its significance (Uzzell, 1984; Culler, 1988; Dann, 1996a; Hopkins, 1998; Echtner, 1999; Jenkins, 2003; Berger, 2007; Thurlow and Aiello, 2007), while MacCannell (1999:3) goes as far as to state that "there is a privileged relationship between tourism and semiotics". Critically however, although a clear connection exists between tourism, events and semiotics, it has not been developed as a distinct movement in marketing literature even though it underpins the promotion process. Further, it is surprising that the area has not been developed to any great extent when you consider that Crick (1989) defined "the semiology of tourism" as being one of the three main strands of tourism research. This view is supported by Dann who states:

nowhere...is a semiotics perspective considered more appropriate than in the analysis of tourism advertising with its culture coded covert connotations, in the study of tourism imagery and in treatment of tourism communication as a discourse of myth. (1996a:6)

For Culler, "Tourism is a practice of considerable cultural and economic importance" (1988:153) and as such, tourism becomes an, "exemplary case for the perception of sign relations" within contemporary society (Culler 1988:162). Thus for Culler, the relationship between semiotics and tourism both "advances the study of tourism" and "...in turn enriches semiotics in its demonstration that salient features of the social and cultural world are articulated in the quest for experience of signs"(ibid. 165). Yet despite the recognition of the importance of semiotics within tourism and events management studies, little theoretical development has taken place in terms of developing semiotics from the purely abstract.

The application of semiotics within tourism and events has been theoretically applied as a label for the signs, images, and representations and to a certain degree the experiences of the consumer. For example, Urry (2001:139) states that:

One learns that a thatched cottage with roses around the door represents 'ye olde England', or the waves crashing on to rocks signifies 'wild, untamed nature'; or especially, that a person with a camera draped around his/her neck is clearly a tourist.

Or similarly, as Culler comments:

All over the world the unsung armies of semioticians, the tourists, are fanning out in search of the signs of Frenchness, typical Italian behaviour, exemplary Oriental scenes... (1988:158)

Such statements assume that all consumers are 'amateur semioticians' (Urry 2001), all interpreting and reading the signs and images presented by the industry within the same manner and, searching for the same types of experiences. Although both Culler and Urry refer to consumers as semioticians, the designation of visitors as semioticians is questionable as there is a difference between reading signs in practice and being a semiotician. Yet, even though the signs and images utilised by the experience industry 'signpost' experience (Jenkins, 2003), the interpretation/reading of these signs and images is an individual activity in which we draw from our own backgrounds and experiences, and this adds a complexity to the perceived relationship between tourism, events and semiotics.

It is easy to oversimplify the relationship between semiotics and events or tourism, as there is a lack of clarity within the definition of semiotics in terms of phraseology, method and definition of what a sign stands for, although Smith (2005) has undertaken a substantial semiotic analysis of Barcelona. This has gone some of the way towards clarifying terms within tourism studies by examining how Barcelona has been represented in the tourism literature and what these representations mean to tourists prior to them visiting the destination. Additionally, Jenkins (2003) in her analysis of the relationship between photographs within travel brochures and backpackers' experiences of destinations in Australia, examined how the signs and images backpackers saw before they went to the destination impacted upon where they visited and what photographs they took while there. This research found that where there was a strong or dominant image that was used in tourism marketing, such as Sidney Harbour Bridge or the Eiffel Tower in Paris, then tourists were drawn to it and they would have their photograph taken in front of it to mark that they have been there, and the photograph itself would them become a semiotic marker of this excursion. Similarly Hopkins (1998) examined the frequency of certain signs and images within a number of tourism brochures for the Lake Huron region of Canada. His findings were that marketing focused on certain myths or significant tourism attractions such as The Tower of London, The Empire State Building or the Taj Mahal and that these are elevated to almost a mythical status, but once we go there we are often disappointed as they do not live up to the images we have seen in brochures or on television. Hopkins explains this in the following way: "Imagination and desire fuel place-myths, but familiarity and dashed expectations will dissolve them" (1998:154). The significance of this is that we give places a semiotic meaning within THEF marketing.

People accept these meanings and they inform the decision to visit a place, as well as what experience they should get when they get there.

■ The semiotic language of tourism

As the interpretation process involves a certain degree of emotional involvement, we need to understand how the semiotics of tourism and events builds this relationship with the consumer. There are a number of conventions that underpin definitions of contemporary tourism and events and include certain themes and signs that construct the experience and expectations.

The first element of the language of tourism and events marketing involves the semiotic construction of a time and place in which the experience is located. Often the marketing text offers the consumer entry into a time and space that is removed from everyday lived experience or can be perceived as 'extraordinary' (Urry, 2001). This is demonstrated in the phraseology in tourism and events marketing that focuses on the use of emotive words and images that offer 'once in a lifetime experience' or 'escape', 'luxury', 'unspoilt', 'exciting' etc. By analysing tourism, events, hospitality and food marketing texts, it is possible to identify themes of words and images that construct the language of experience. Figures 8.1, 8.2 and 8.3 identify the text and image themes that underpin contemporary marketing practices, there are certain themes that run through all categories, and often revolve around, escape, authenticity and time/space.

Language of Tourism Semiotic Themes	Language of Events Semiotic Themes
Escape	Extraordinary
Luxury	A Carnival
Exciting	Unique
Freedom	Once in a Lifetime
Different notions of Time & Space	Festival
Experience	Celebration
Friendly	Fun
Untouched	Exciting
Authentic	Authentic
Play	Cannot Miss

Figure 8.1: Semiotic themes

■ The semiotics of food and hospitality

The semiotic representations of hospitality and food are socially and culturally embedded within contemporary marketing practices. This embedding forms a marketing language that draws from a long historical discourse that locates food and hospitality at the centre of nearly all cultures (O'Connor, 2005; O'Gorman, 2007; Claseen, 2007). Hospitality and food are a significant element of culture, and their marketing needs to be contextualised within the time in which they are being judged, and as such reflects trends in food, diet, cuisine and health. For example, the use of images and themes taken from the slow food movement and more organic forms of production within food marketing campaigns provides a refuge from fast food culture and the instantaneous nature of postmodern society (Delind 2007), even if they are being used to promote fast food restaurants or ready meals. The semiotic representations of food and hospitality often elevates the experience by offering links to pleasure, fun and sophistication. Fantasia (1995) defines these as 'pleasure zones'. Food and hospitality marketing creates a utopian space in which the experience or expectation of experience is elevated to a rarefied level beyond the everyday lived experience of eating food as merely food. The representation of food or restaurants in adverts, on menus or packaging as organic, authentic, luxurious or spacious, semiotically signifies a 'graceful way of living' (Delind, 2006:128), it bounds our past and memory, creating a sense of belonging by drawing on the embedded definitions of hospitality and gastronomy.

8

The semiotic consumption of hospitality and food by the consumer within advertising is an 'authoritative act' that 'authenticates' (Marshall, 2005:73) our identity and position within the world, and acts as a social marker of who we are (Gvion and Trosler, 2008). The campaign draws us into the semiotic consumption process: the represented dining experience, the available food choices, and the type of drink we are attracted to, all act as an 'agency of culinary culture, lifestyle and systems' of taste (Gvion and Trosler, 2008). For example, Bailey's Irish Cream advertising offers a lifestyle not just a drink, as do

Marks and Spencer's food marketing campaigns. The things we drink and eat, the places we stay, and the events we attend become semiotic markers to the rest of the world of what type of person we are, or who we want to be.

Just as in the marketing of tourism and events, the marketing of food and hospitality draw on certain conventions that are shared across the semiotics of experience. The marketing of food and hospitality widely utilise what Johns and Pine (200:127) refer to as the 'authentic environments' of hospitality. The images used are empty of humans and modernity, they offer us an empty space in which we can search for the authentic. For example if you examine the marketing materials of Michelin starred restaurants such as Le Manoir aux Quat' Saisons you will see that they offer a mediation on taste and gastronomy which define the preparation, social character, philosophy and aesthetics of food. They identify food and hospitality as art (Fantasia, 1995), and their meaning is heightened by the juxtaposition of the images used in relation to the nature of fast food and the homogenisation of taste in contemporary society. This is semiotically reinforced by the representation of the vegetable gardens as they represent an organic means of production and authenticity, and by empty formal restaurants with classically laid tables, again free from signs of modernity and other customers, waiting staff etc.

The marketing of food and hospitality offers escape routes from everyday lived experience by its 'extraordinariness' and is differentiated from the routine and often unreflexive consumption of food as merely fuel (Marshall, 2005). For example, Pringles 2011 campaign defines their product as 90 pieces of fun, while ice cream makers such as Haagan-Dazs or Magnum make a clear link between food and sex. Hedonistic food marketing and the semiotics of experience creates a configuration of time and space which elevates the context of the food served to that of the extraordinary. Think about how many times you have seen an advert in which someone eats something and is transported to another time or place. This is a convention that is widely used by luxury food items such as chocolate and soft drinks. This differentiation of time and space, is also a recurrent theme in hospitality marketing, the use of empty restaurants, hotels, spas or swimming pools exclude temporal markers (people, cars, computers, telephone lines), this is a semiotically constructed liminality within experience marketing that offers a "...cognitive imaginative and practical space in which everyone can access the things that mark off the social from the private" (Couldry, 2001:158). As such, food and hospitality marketing creates a certain binary opposition to everyday lived experience (Kress and van Leeuwen, 1996; Delind, 2006), whereby the consumer is guided by embedded 'analytical processes' to place themselves within the image to become a part of the experience offered by the campaign. Although the sign vehicle's (marketing texts) symbolic authority (Meyrowitz, 1992; Couldry, 2001) and representations direct the consumer towards an embedded 'signposted' definition of hospitality or food, the use of empty landscapes creates a reflexive, liminal space, in which the consumer reflexively and hermeneutically interprets and projects personal meaning onto the representations. The differentiation of time and space reinforces the significance of both the product and the experience.

The semiotic language of food and hospitality contained within marketing texts enables us to explore hospitality and food in terms of senses and the sensual, as an 'intimate frontier' (Dawkins, 2009) in which we may locate the body. In other words the embedding of definitions of food and hospitality within marketing enables the individual to explore " ...the role of the sensual, the emotional, the expressive, for maintaining layered sets of embodied relationships to food and place." (Delind, 2006:121). The images used of food in both food and hospitality marketing elevate the food and dining experience to a level whereby it is so removed from real life that it can only be consumed vicariously (Magee, 2007), and as a consequence creates a myth of food and the sensual or sexual (Reed-Danahay, 1996). The embedding of hospitality and food is more than just shelter and food as fuel. It comes to represent a significant element in our lives and often we elevate hospitality, food preparation, dining practices, and eating to that of the extraordinary or even the sacred.

Language of Hospitality Semiotic Themes	Language of Food Semiotic Themes
Escape	Extraordinary
Luxurious	Sophisticated
Service	Scientifically proven
Convenient	Sensuous
Timeless	Nutritious
Pamper	Celebration
Friendly	Fun
Timeless	Homemade/handmade
Historic	Authentic
Relax	Guilty pleasure
	Love and romance
	Passion/c arnal
	Balanced and harmonious
	Moral and ethical

Figure 8.2: Sensual themes

■ Austerity food marketing

Although the dominant discourse underpinning the semiotics of experience is defined by the notion of hedonistic food marketing, there is also another semiotic language of food that may be defined as austerity food marketing. As a reaction to the increased awareness of the relationship between food choice and bad health and the rising levels of obesity, governments and organisations have invested in the development of a number of health campaigns. These provide a marketing message to change food choices, to resist unhealthy products or to cut the intake of certain ingredients. In order to facilitate these messages, a semiotics of austerity has been developed. It creates a new language of food that is removed from the semiotics of experience, as rather than focusing on experience it focuses on consequence. It counters the semiotic language of food, ignores notions of luxury, escape and the sensual and replaces it with death, disease and threat. It places food back into the everyday, into the time and space of living and reminds us of our mortality. However, austerity food marketing faces many challenges as it draws upon a language that is not as persuasive or enticing as the others identified above. It is also a relatively new concept that is not as embedded as the other approaches outlined within this chapter, but what is significant is that it develops and utilises a language within marketing texts that attempts to challenge traditional orthodoxies and approaches to the marketing of food. Conversely, it may be argued that its impact is limited because of the embedded nature of traditional forms of food marketing and the disparity in budgets between large multi-national corporations selling fast food and those charged with promoting good health.

Language of Food Austerity Semiotic Themes
Risk
Healthy
Balance
Abstinence
Loss
Risk Disease
Exercise
Change
Less is More
Wellness
Lifestyle
Surveillance
Self-Governance
Enemy
Friend
Harmony

Figure 8.3: Austerity themes

■ Semiotics and power

8

Semiosis and the process of signification is rarely innocent, and this is especially the case when the semiotic script has a commercial base and motive. Unfortunately this is often the stark reality of commercial marketing, where the most economically beneficial meanings and signs are emphasized at the expense of those that are not. There are exceptions to this rule, and these mostly include those incidences and examples that align with the four pillars of sustainable marketing practice (see Chapter 10 for review of this conceptual normative framework) or social marketing generally. Accordingly all marketing materials and contexts can be examined for asymmetric power relations and power effects. For example in view of the latter, Schroeder and Zwick (1999:21-22), have examined the productive effects of advertising on gender and masculinity:

> Ad campaigns invoke gender identity, drawing their imagery primarily from the stereotyped iconography of masculinity and femininity. In this way, masculinity and femininity interact smoothly with the logic of the market – advertising representations and consumption practices provide a meaningful system of difference, which has established strong limits to the possibilities of male and female consumer ontologies.

Going on to say:

> Representations do not merely 'express' masculinity, rather, they play a central role in forming conceptions of masculinity and help construct market segments such as the New Man, playboys, connoisseurs, and lads, in the British vernacular

In a similar way, the marketplace for food, and particularly advertising and packaging has been examined to reveal both their persuasive effects and influence, and their relationship to social and economic problems such as childhood obesity. Schor and Ford (2007:137) for example, have argued that "the increase of marketing to children has coincided with significant deterioration in the healthfulness of children's diets, higher caloric intake and a rapid increase in rates of obesity and overweight". They particularly focus on high caloric breakfast cereals and the effectiveness of symbolic appeals in advertising and package design. They argue that the use of cartoons and other attractive signs and symbols appear to make them 'cool' and incredibly attractive to their target audience.

Academics have examined the semiotic framing of populations and cultures generally and also the relationships between consumers and those involved in the production and staging of THEF experiences. For example, Dann's (1996a) analysis of the people located within the tourism brochure illustrates the way in which local people are represented within marketing texts (see also Nelson, 2005) and provides a good example of relationships and definitions of subordination and power relations. Seemingly subordination is reinforced in marketing texts like brochures by the angle, position or size of represented participants. This process is illustrated in a *SAGA Travellers World Brochure* which locates the visitor as guest, who is being served and entertained by a number of local musicians, thus representing difference in status and economic superiority. This is representative of a number of host/ guest conventions and relationships that are continually utilised within THEF marketing practice. Those aspects of a people or culture that have the greatest attractive properties and economic value are emphasised in the foreground while those that are not remain in the background or are lost.

In a sense marketing supports and reproduces cultural myths of people, places, and populations that have the greatest commercial value, they are the things that people want to see. In the communicative staging of tourist experiences for instance, indigenous populations are often required to perform rituals and tribal acts such as dances for the pleasure of their audience. While this may have an economic return for the performer involved, an enduring consequence of this productive act is that it acts to blur fact from fiction simultaneously trivialising the history and culture of such people and places. For example, in an evaluation of cultural tourism and performances in Bali, Picard (1990) argues that a central problem for the indigenous population is integration and access into the tourism industry. For those elements of the population who are willing to engage in performance for financial exchange, it is argued that they become reliant, if not wholly dependent upon commercial intermediaries who negotiate their entry into the hotels and resorts where they perform. During negotiation freedom of expression and agency maybe sacrificed. This seems the case when elements of the population and different dance troupes or performers are pitched against each other for contracts and the right to perform. As Picard (1990, 47-48) explains "the commercial intermediaries, ... are able to manipulate the competition between the different troupes, impose their own conditions, not only financially, but also in terms of the presentation of the spectacle and even the details of its program". This implication is shared in research by Middleton (2007) who has found that the staging of indigenous cultural performance as a tourism spectacle in Ecuador has similar effects and outcomes. Here dancers are seen to perform in clothing and artefacts that have no connection to their cultural history or past such as Tiger Skins.

Arguably then, such populations are reduced to economic actors in the script of a tourist spectacle of consumption, and authenticity and heritage become lost in this process and transformation. As Kress and van Leeuwen state 'signs and images' and other representational practices such as communicative staging, (re)produce 'hierarchies of social power' (1996:83). Thus, many of the semiotic structures and material practices identified in THEF marketing, and critically in how the relationship between the host – be it the culture, population or service personnel – and the consumer is displayed, 'represent the world in hierarchical order' (1996: 85). In a way the host is often represented as a servant or a cultural attraction and the visitor is consuming this through the marketing process and their experience.

The semiotics of THEF do not often reflect real or natural classifications, but rather they imply something. Examples of this can be seen in most forms of experience marketing and are important in giving significance to the language. From a semiotic and cultural perspective, marketing is not just an economic process, but is also a significant and influential social and cultural practice. Accordingly marketers should be conscious of the social order and reality that they are imposing on the marketplace and culture generally. It is our view that marketing practitioners should hold or develop a reflexive attitude that rests upon an informed view of the general process of semiosis and the unintentional effects of meaning production practices.

■ Conclusion

This chapter introduces the semiotics of experience and more significantly the semiotic language of tourism, hospitality, food and events. It also outlines a general theory of semiotics. The semiotics of experience plays an important role in contemporary marketing practice. It underpins the marketing of experience, and raises questions as to how tourism, hospitality, food and events are presented and consumed, both within contemporary marketing texts and servicescapes. Quite often we do not take the time to understand the signs that are put in front of us, just like the traffic light example used earlier in the chapter, we merely accept that we have to stop. By taking the time to examine and analyse what images and other signifiers are being used in the staging of THEF, and what they mean and their effects, we are better equipped as experience marketers. By undertaking this we can start to make sense of what people are looking for or seeking to avoid, in the sense of what motivates them or turns them off and what fuels and frames their desires and interactions with the marketplace. How is the language of experience constructed and how can it be used? It is also important to ask the question of "what is missing?" as this is as significant as what is included. It is also important to recognise that the meanings or conventions utilised within the semiotics of experience draw from a wide range of sources, therefore in order to understand the language we need to understand the social and cultural significance of the activity. We must learn the codes. Semiotics is not an exact science as it involves interpretation, and as such, everyone is going to interpret things in different ways, however we can identify the elements that we can all agree on.

8

9 Interpreting Marketing

■ Introduction

There are certain assumptions within contemporary marketing about the consumer's behaviour, how they make decisions and how they understand marketing communications and interact with the marketplace, as a result, marketers identify groups that are clustered together in neat market segments ranging from the macro level, in which we target cultures or genders, to the micro where we target small groups of consumers that share similar backgrounds, income, education or locality etc. This approach assumes that these groups of consumers share a view of the world, a set of values and a level of knowledge that leads to a shared understanding and relationship to the product being promoted and the process of marketing. Although segmentation remains the dominant means of grouping consumers and identifying target markets, this chapter relocates the individual consumer at the centre of the marketing process by recognising that each individual consumer or customer will bring with them their own experience, knowledge etc. and that they are reflexive subjects who do not simply accept the messages propagated by marketers, but interpret, resist, negotiate and form their own perception of the marketing message.

■ The consumer as an individual

In order to gain an insight into how people understand marketing, it is important to identify some of the theoretical debates that go some of the way to explaining how individuals interpret the debates and discourses that underpin THEF marketing. Additionally, in order to understand the consumer's relationship to marketing communications and the marketplace it is important to understand how authors, organisations or professional bodies select and produce marketing texts, as the nature of the publication will also guide the final interpretation. For example the authors of this book come from differing academic traditions, one from a social science background and the other from a business tradition, however the content and structure of this book is guided by certain shared beliefs about the role of marketing in contemporary society and a dissatisfaction with the ways in which traditional marketing texts locate the consumer and the marketing process. Therefore this book reflects the knowledge base, the values and the reality of the two authors as white middle class university lecturers.

Just like the authors, each individual consumer or customer brings with them a set of knowledge, a view of their position in the world and their personal values; these are formed by their social and cultural backgrounds, their gender, their educational background, their geographical location, and their friends or families, amongst other influences. These personal influences can be categorised as three distinct areas of influence: *epistemological, ontological* and *axiological* (for a good discussion of these aspects see Bryman, 2004:21-24), it is these areas of the individual's experience or personality that define the way in which they relate to the marketing process and the product or service being sold. These three areas can be simply defined as follows:

Epistemology Knowledge base	Ontology Position in world	Axiology Value systems
Relationship with marketing informed by:	Relationship with marketing informed by:	Relationship with marketing informed by:
Knowledge Individual's perception Individual's memory Individual's consciousness Individual's reason	Individual reality Individual influences Social & cultural background Class, Education, Religion Race Geographical roots	Their values Morals Informed by epistemology & ontology

Figure 9.1: Marketing and epistemology, ontology and axiology

The implication for this is that every individual consumer, producer and marketer will come to the table with a differing set of knowledges, everyday lived experience/existence and set of values, and therefore we have to recognise that there are multiple worldviews or multiple realities. This has huge implications for the future of marketing as technological advances and the fragmentation of communication channels means that we can be more sophisticated in understanding how the consumer relates to the marketing process and ultimately how we engage and tailor approaches and communication channels for the multiple realities of segmentation.

■ The epistemology and ontology of marketing

Before we can understand how consumers interpret the marketing process, it is important that as a researcher or student you question how your own ontological and epistemological understanding of marketing has been formed, as ultimately this will direct the way in which you read and understand this book, and how you judge the contribution it makes to the field of marketing.

Burrell and Morgan (1979:4) define **epistemology** as: "Assumptions about the grounds of knowledge – about how one might begin to understand the world and communicate this as knowledge to fellow human beings." While Klein, Hirschheim and Nissen (1991:5) define epistemology as: "The nature of human knowledge and understanding that can possibly be acquired through different types of research and the appropriateness of the methods of investigation."

In comparison, **ontology** represents a particular view of reality held by the consumer or individual, and there are two main ontological possibilities that are useful in understanding how the consumer interprets THEF marketing. The first is that there is one reality and it is observable by a consumer who has little if any impact on the object being observed. The second is that reality consists of an individual's mental constructions of the objects with which they engage, and that the engagement impacts on the observer and on the situation being observed (Titscher and Meyer et al., 2000:14, Guba and Lincoln,

9

1989:23). In summary, the analysis of the interpretation process needs to be framed within the consumers' knowledge and view of the world.

Phillimore and Goodson (2004) in undertaking a survey of tourism research have recognised five distinct epistemological and ontological 'movements'.

- The First Movement is defined as the traditional period of tourism research, and is guided by a positivistic approach to tourism studies which are based upon "…predetermined rigid research agendas, studies that seek to quantify qualitative data, studies aimed at generating tourism typologies and studies that place little or no emphasis on methodological issues." (2004:10-12)

- The Second Movement they define as the 'modernist approach' in which there is "evidence of a shift to post-positivist modes of thinking, although with clear evidence that researchers continue to be convinced of the fundamental importance of maintaining positivist rigour." (2004:15)

- The Third Movement is defined as 'blurred genres'. They state that: "The Blurred Genre stage makes a distinct difference from the 'modernist' and 'traditional' phases as researchers begin to move away from natural science and recognise multiple approaches embracing a more creative, artistic approach to research." (2004:14)

- They define the Fourth Movement as a 'crisis in representation', which has led to a "profound rupture in thinking" and is reflected in the importance that: "…the personal biography of the researcher was critical in determining the way they approached research, and thus it was not possible, as had previously been argued, to simply replace one researcher with another and expect the same results, provided that the methods employed were unchanged. Instead of seeing research as a bigger process, researchers began to view all stages in the research as indistinct and overlapping. They acknowledged that there are multiple interpretations mediated by the personal biographies of researchers and their research subjects." (2004:15-16)

- ■ The final stage, which they define as the Fifth Movement, and which may be seen to have emerged from the Fourth Movement as a result of the: "rapid social change and development of new social contexts [which] make traditional approaches to research – those based on the notion that data can be interpreted objectively and then generalised to become a fact which reveals some knowledge about a singular reality – redundant." (2004:17)

However, the positivistic tradition continues to be the major influence in the construction of methodologies and THEF research (Botterill, 2001; Phillimore and Goodson, 2004). Delanty (1997) proposes five facets of positivism: scientism, naturalism, empiricism, value freedom and instrumental knowledge. In 'The epistemology of a set of tourism studies', Botterill (2001) examines these facets in relation to seven PhD projects, each utilising a positivistic approach within a multi-disciplinary study. His findings were that the adoption of a 'scientism' approach (in which the student used a social science and a physical science based methodology) led to "problematizing the interaction of people and nature in a tourism setting and preconditions the necessity of a merging of social and physical science epistemologies" (2001:203). The claim to value freedom by all the students was disputed, as all applied "a rich stock of subjective experience" (2001:205) to their studies. The correlation between positivism and the production of "technically useful knowledge" conventionally justified the approach, however, the expectation of producing useful knowledge meant that the research and the methodology were influenced by policy makers' perceptions and local state interventions. Therefore, for Botterill the adoption of a positivistic approach is fundamentally flawed.

9

The use of critical theory is almost completely absent from the study of THEF (Botterill, 2001:207; Phillimore and Goodson, 2004:15-16). The reason for this, according to Botterill, is that much tourism research focuses on a dominant industry agenda and is witnessed in the traditional approach to marketing. The best way to achieve this is by recognising the movements and approaches that construct the academic subject of marketing. The complexity of marketing as a process, as a multi-disciplinary cultural activity, as a form of communication or as the manifestation of power relations, has formed a largely unrecognised and certainly unspoken ontological and epistemological tradition. The majority of marketing texts and journals are located within the fields of business management or applied marketing; this has created a significant body of empirically orientated data that has been underpinned by the positivistic tradition. Yet it is possible to question the viability of positivism as an appropriate and encompassing form of epistemology and ontology, as it may be seen to limit the ability of the researcher to adequately investigate the social and cultural world in which marketing is located.

■ The interactive consumer

An interesting way of conceptualising the contemporary consumer is to think of the consumer not as a passive participant within the marketing process, but to define them as an 'interactive participant' (see Kress and van Leeuwen, 2001). This allows us to think of marketing as an interactive dynamic cultural activity, in which all the stakeholders or participants in the process, from the commissioning company, to the marketers, students or consumer all engage in dynamic cultural interaction. It is within this interaction/mediation that consumers draw from their epistemological, ontological and personal biographies (Guba and Lincoln, 1989) to interpret, or negotiate the meaning and purpose of the text, whether it is in the form of a brochure, flyer, radio/ television advertisement or website etc. As stated previously in this book, the marketing of THEF often involves the semiotic construction of a language that is embedded with social, cultural and individual meaning, and is underpinned by a ludic/hedonistic or celebratory discourse, and by interacting with marketing communications the consumer forms an emotional attachment to the experience by becoming an interactive participant in the marketing process. This interactivity relies on how the individual applies their epistemological (knowledges), ontological (being in the world) and axiological (values) foundations to the process. The impact of this reflexivity or interaction is to create multiple individual and personal readings and interpretations.

Much human activity (including our relationship to experiences, products and marketing texts) is devoted to ordering processes through the organisational patterning of experience by means of tacit, emotional meaning-making processes. We emotionally invest in products and services and marketing plays a significant role in this as it guides how we should interpret representations of THEF. Such a process identifies the consumer as an axis of experience and selfhood, in which we cannot be understood apart from our 'embeddedness' (Kress & van Leeuwen, 1996) in the social and symbolic systems of the culture or society in which we live. This 'embeddedness' is personally reinforced and expressed by our consumption patterns, for example, there are a number of recent television adverts that sell a lifestyle that is lived out through the consumption of tourism. In the case of the recent SAGA cruise commercials (2011) this locates the two lucky guests within a privileged formal environment of chauffer-driven, formally dressed guests, all socialising within a particular elitist grouping. The consumption of such an experience demonstrates a view of the world and a set of individual values that become reinforced by the consumption of joining the club. In the same way this also reflects residual cultural templates of deferred gratification, where you have earned the right during your working life to live out your twilight years in this pleasurable or hedonic environment. This aligns with the marketing segments known by the acronym SKIER (spending the kids inheritance in early retirement) (Willetts, 2011).

The consumer then becomes central to the marketing/consumer dichotomy in which producers and consumers interact. However, in order to understand how the individual interprets experiences marketing, we need to understand how the symbolic authority of the text directs and influences the consumer's understanding and subsequent behaviour. As stated previously, the intangible nature of the tourism, hospitality, events and food product produced a reliance on the production of effective marketing materials that has become the recognised means of promoting the sector. As such, the consumer forms a particular relationship with the text, in which it guides and signposts experience, adding to their personal biography and informing the

9

consumer's 'being in the world' (Maloney, 1993). Therefore there is an interrelationship between marketing materials and the individual consumer that leads to multiple interpretations, even though the text may be generic for the producer.

■ Interpretation and marketing

All marketing materials, whether in the form of a radio advertisement, product, logo or a simple flyer, may be seen as vehicles for carrying the marketing message – they transfer the message from the marketer to the consumer. However, the nature of the sign vehicle (advert, sponsorship or sales promotion), where it is placed (newspaper, radio station or pavement), as well as the context through which it is communicated (time of year, reputation of sender, country or region) will impact upon how a consumer reads and interprets the communication, as will the consumers political, economic and socio-cultural positioning etc. The impact of this on marketing practice is to inform our understanding of the elements that inform the consumer's interpretation of marketing texts, and in order to develop an effective marketing strategy it is necessary to adopt a holistic and critical approach to marketing, and this includes at the basic level understanding your customer.

As stated in Chapter 8, the contemporary consumer is an amateur semiotician, as they negotiate the commercial world that surrounds everyday lived experience. It is argued that we negotiate somewhere in the region of marketing communications advertisements every day. As we walk around we read the images and words that are contained within these messages, we interpret them, find meaning, reject them or get excited and change our behaviour or buy the product. As consumers we understand the language of contemporary marketing practice, and this is particularly significant in the context of experiences marketing as it is located in a particularly strong historical, social and cultural discourse (see Chapter 5) that surrounds THEF.

The reading and interpretation of marketing communications becomes a very personal and reflexive activity in which, as consumers we find our own meanings and understandings. Therefore, what we can say is that marketing communications signpost experience, they direct us, attempt to influence our perceptions and ultimately try to inform our purchasing behaviour in favour of the product or experience that is being marketed. The signposting of experience leads us on a journey in which we negotiate the marketing materials, drawing from our depository of experiences and feelings that construct our worldview, and the role of the marketer is to influence the way in which we negotiate these, to accept and privilege their message by following the message in the marketing communication, whether it be to change our eating habits, to escape on holiday or to celebrate through attending an event. Although the marketer can influence, signpost or guide interpretation it is important to recognise that the consumer is a free thinking reflexive individual who will draw on their experiences, values etc. to form an opinion and develop their own individual relationship to and with the product or experience. In order to understand the consumer's relationship to marketing communications we need to understand how the relationship is defined by the consumer's value system.

■ The axiology of marketing: Values

When we examine the axiology of marketing, we need to understand that brands, experiences and products will often be underpinned by a value system, what the product stands for, and what it means to consumers. For example, many food companies such as Cadbury's and Starbucks are adopting a 'Fairtrade' approach to their production, (see Chapter 10 for further information) whereby they are ensuring that their ingredients are ethically sourced; many restaurants will advertise that their products are locally sourced and organic; while destinations make claims about how sustainable their tourism product is. When organisations do this they are developing values that underpin the ethos of their company or add an ethical value to their brand. However, when examining how consumers relate to or interpret products and experiences, they draw on their axiological foundations, or in other words their value systems.

The consumer's value system can be seen as a cognitive or mental construct or interpretive framework that comes into play when judgments are made about the products and experiences on offer in the THEF marketplace. In most cases consumers seek out products that align with their values or avoid those that don't. For example an 18-30 holiday brochure may be offensive to an older tourist as representations of scantily clad men and women, and the text which explores the more hedonistic tendencies of contemporary tourism may offend the values of the older tourist. On the other hand, a food consumer with a strong concern for the environment would seek out and purchase products that are organic or packaged in biodegradeable materials etc. Because each of us possesses a complex value system that we draw upon every time we evaluate products and marketing materials, it is crucial for THEF marketers to understand how consumers relate to their specific marketing offer. Our axiology, or value system, is developed from the various experiences and knowledge that we have collected over our lifetime, from sources such as our social and cultural location/background, and is reflected in our inherent and learnt behaviour. Thus our value systems will vary according to where we live, our religion, ethnic background, schooling and education, as well as what books we have read, what television programmes we have seen, the values of our parents, friends and family, and as such we will all make different value judgments as part of the interpretation and consumption process.

■ Conclusion

We often take for granted that consumers will understand and interpret generated meanings contained within products, communications or brands. Although marketing can significantly influence the interpretation process, the consumer is still a free-thinking reflexive individual who will use their world view and value system to find meaning. It is important that we recognise this, as it is easy to treat a consumer as part of one large market segment or demographic grouping. Although we can guide interpretation we must recognise that every individual will find their own meaning, will negotiate and often resist the marketing of experiences and products. Often the adoption of an overly prescriptive communication will deter the consumer as it does not provide room for the individual to find their own meaning, and as a result they may not purchase the product. The marketing of THEF requires a careful signposting of experience that leads the consumer, but at the same time provides a space in which they can find individual meaning and significance and may express their epistemological, ontological and axiological preferences.

9

10 Ethics, Sustainable Marketing and the Green Consumer

■ Introduction

There is a growing trend within marketing to work towards a more sustainable agenda, in which the ethics of both the production, dissemination and consumption of marketing materials is becoming increasingly questioned. Sustainability has been a significant theme in THEF for a number of years. There is a long traditional of sustainable tourism experiences that range from trekking in undeveloped areas to visiting Centre Parcs, while food production has developed clear links with the 'Fairtrade', organic and slow food movements. Organisations such as Marriott Hotels have invested heavily in their green credentials and large events such as Glastonbury Music Festival have their foundations in raising money for charities. As such the notion of sustainability has become one of the central themes of experiences marketing and has seen the emergence of the green consumer.

The theme of sustainability within experiences marketing can be seen to fulfill a number of objectives that can be broadly divided into three elements. The first is where sustainability is used as a means of product differentiation, adds to the brand value, reinforces the credentials of the organisation, and impacts on buyer choice – in other words it adds an economic value to the company's or organisation's product. The second element is the impact the notion of sustainability has on the consumer's perception of products, how it makes us feel and ultimately how it makes us behave. Finally, is the view that organisations pursue these agendas as ends in themselves; simply for altruistic reasons and a belief that it is the right thing to do. This chapter will examine the greening of marketing has on THEF marketing.

■ The greening of experiences marketing

It is argued that current marketing practices have failed the sustainability agenda (Mitchel & Saren, 2008). This failure may be seen to be the direct result of the paradox that exists between marketing and the concept of sustainability. Marketing is fundamentally a commercial activity that encourages people to buy products, to purchase things they do not need or require. As Kotler states, marketing is:

> ...a social and managerial process by which individuals and groups obtain what they need and want through creating and exchanging products and value with others. (2008:7)

As stated previously, experiences marketing needs to be understood as being different from other forms of marketing and as such, the above quote needs to also reflect the social and cultural practices that underpin the production and consumption of food, tourism, events and hospitality, and the impacts that occur as society and culture is shaped and consumed in relation to their production. Parsons & Maclaran (2009:14) summarises the criticism of marketing as "fueling consumption and encouraging materialism by stimulating wants as a means of satisfying human needs". Whereas, sustainability is underpinned by notions of anti-consumerism, sensitive development and not encouraging waste etc. *Our Common Future* (The Brundtland Report, 1987) provides one of the most useful and widely used definitions of what is meant by sustainability. The report defines sustainability as "meeting the needs of the present without depleting resources or harming natural cycles for future generations". As marketers we have to reconcile this paradox and question our role within the global economy. As Mitchell & Saren (2008:399) state:

> The philosophy of marketing speaks the language of mate-

rial possession, individuality, and newness, and works on the assumption of unlimited growth and the accumulation of waste"

Thus, every time we promote a form of food, destination, event etc. we need to understand that our behaviour and actions have an impact upon communities, individuals, hosts and the environment. Sometimes this is positive and sometimes it is negative. Nevertheless, all of this makes the assumption that notions of morality and rationality are a given, and that all organisations and consumers are concerned about their ethical footprint (Moisander & Pesonen, 2002).

However there has been a growing movement by companies to adopt, or to be seen to adopt, more sustainable practices, and for many companies these form the basis of their campaigns (Mitchel & Saren, 2008). For example, Starbucks and Cadbury's have used their association with 'Fairtrade' as the core message of the campaign, while McDonalds have focused on the zero additives approach to their products. These strategies not only enable them to attempt to maintain their market position, but also to develop the brand value of their companies. This approach is reflected in the Chartered Institute of Marketing's Ethics and Social Responsibility framework which states that:

> The role of the marketer these days could be seen in terms of connecting with stakeholders not only in terms of value, but in terms of values. In a world where intangible assets and corporate reputation are centre stage, the marketing team needs to focus on ethical issues more than ever before. (CIM, 2010)

This movement within the marketing industry is not purely motivated by philanthropic actions, but has its foundation in maximising profit or protecting the market position, or in marketing speak the 'Triple Bottom Line'. The CIM (2010) declare that the Triple Bottom Line:

10

> ...creates a framework for companies to become sustainable without ignoring the importance of the financial bottom line and other concerns that are vital to a company's survival, growth and economic success.

This raises the question as to what is exactly meant by the phrase or concept of sustainability in marketing. Is the sustainability movement just an aspect of marketing that has provided a new dimension to the formulation of marketing strategies? (Mitchel & Saren, 2008) or is it a social and cultural movement that has infiltrated contemporary marketing practices. It is clear however that experiences marketing utilises and has developed a relationship to the sustainable movement that differs from other areas of marketing.

Experiences marketing utilises the notion of sustainability and ethical marketing differently from social marketing. In most cases social marketing utilises marketing and advertising to reduce consumption, waste etc. (see Peattie and Peattie, 2009), and can often be seen as de-marketing the product and encouraging anti-consumption, for example the campaigns that are used to encourage healthy eating, reduction in salt intake, or anti-smoking. However, representations of the sustainability or ethical within experiences marketing incorporates the ethical or green element into the product. It may be argued that it is encouraging consumption, but consumption in a more sympathetic or informed manner, and that sustainability is core to the tourism, food, hospitality or event experience. It becomes the experience and 'enculturates' (Kozinets, Handelman & Lee, 2010) the experience with cultural capital and confirms its cultural credentials as a form of consumption. This is quite a significant distinction as the motivation, consequences and significance of a marketing campaign will depend upon how we contextualise the product. For example, in the case of the social marketing campaigns that encourage us to eat five pieces of fresh fruit and vegetables in order improve our health, it can be argued that to a degree they are motivated by an anti-marketing sentiment that attempts to moderate or stop the consumption of processed or fast food. It is selling an ideal, thus it is not commoditising the food, but attempting to change behaviour. However, if we see a vegetarian dish that forms part of an advert for a Michelin starred restaurant and is essentially healthy, as it contains part of our 'five a day' vegetable and fruit intake, even the healthy becomes elevated to that of the sacred or hedonistic, as the humble vegetable is elevated to the level of the extraordinary. There has been a growing agenda of integrating the natural environment into business agendas and practices and a common corporate objective has developed around sustainability (see Mitchel & Saren, 2008 for interesting discussion on sustainable marketing). In short, THEF marketing is a commercial process that uses sustainable or green consumption as an element of the experience. Experiences marketing thus commodifies the notion of ethical consumption, sustainability and greening – in short it encourages consumption. On the other hand, social marketing does not encourage consumption, but encourages austerity and denial of excess. Thus, sustainable or green tourism is not anti-marketing, but it is selling consumers the experience of being considerate or ethical, thus sustainability becomes the product that is aimed at a particular market segment and subsequently generates income or profit. However, we cannot ignore the significance of sustainable or green marketing as a driving force in contemporary THEF marketing, and as such, it is important that we understand the debates that surround sustainability that inform contemporary THEF marketing practices.

■ Defining sustainability

Sustainability in its purest form may be seen as an ideological and idealistic concept in which exploitation of people, landscapes, countries, cultures and peoples is eradicated. In social marketing literature, green consumer behaviour has been viewed as a form of ethically orientated consumer behaviour that is motivated not only by personal needs, but also by concern of the welfare of society and the environment (see Mosiander & Pesonen, 2002). However as we live in a society that is dominated by commerce, the best we can hope to create is a definition that offers some form of workable compromise. The best way of understanding sustainability is to think of it as the roof that straddles a building and is held up by four pillars (see Figure 10.1). When we are assessing or making judgments about the values of a brand or the sustainability of the product or experience, we need to consider how sustainable it is in terms of its social, cultural, economic or environmental credentials. It is these four pillars upon which sustainability

10

sits. In the truest sense, if we ignore one or two of these pillars then the whole concept of sustainability collapses. When analysing the way in which experiences marketing approaches sustainability we often find that it concentrates on only one of the pillars, rather than all four, with economic sustainability driving the company at the cost of overlooking the other elements.

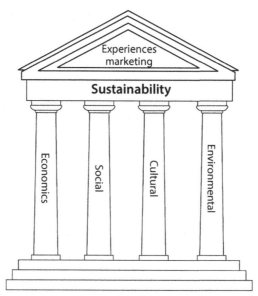

Figure 10.1: The four pillars of sustainable marketing

In order to analyse sustainable marketing, it is important that we understand how experiences marketing is related to and influences our relationship with THEF experiences, and the debates that underpin the marketing and promotion of experiences and destinations, as this determines what we mean by sustainability and how we utilise the concept in contemporary marketing practices. There is increasing pressure on companies and marketers to adopt a more ethical or sustainable approach to their marketing practices. Traditionally these issues have been located within the discussion surrounding the ability of the sovereign consumer to filter information and to make judgments utilising their own value systems, rather than being persuaded by marketing to consume unethical or non-sustainable products. Thus marketers are not responsible for consumption patterns or consumer behaviour as it is the consumer than has made their own informed choice. This approach in normative marketing has traditionally let the sector off the hook, as they distance themselves from the actual act of production and consumption. As such it can be argued that experiences marketing is complicit in promoting the consumption of experiences that may in turn lead to negative social or cultural impacts, and that, without the effective marketing or commodification of experiences that impact may not have occurred. Ultimately, marketers are central to the process and as such need to accept and take responsibility for their actions.

As can be seen from Figure 10.1, sustainability sits upon four different pillars. Each of these pillars can be seen to be underpinned by certain debates and ideas, it is to these that we now turn.

■ Social sustainability

Social inclusion and exclusion

Marketing is both inclusive and exclusive – some people are invited into the consumption experience while others become excluded because of their social position, demographic status or the fact that they make up part of the society that is being marketed in experience marketing texts. For example, if you examine how local people are represented in tourism brochures, they are seen as either providing service or are represented as an attraction (Dann, 1996a). This simple distinction identifies power relations in respect of who has the economic superiority within societies – in many cases the local or host society becomes excluded from the marketing experience. Thus, experiences marketing define social relationships and come to represent contemporary power relations between the First and the Third world, the North or the South or even the Provincial and the Urban. Marketing comes to represent the world in which we live in hierarchical order.

10

Marketing defines social relationships

The use of identified language, images and referents are determined by positioning, and segmentation within experiences marketing texts. However, this process makes assumption about the social and cultural position and knowledge of the consumer. It includes and excludes consumers according to their social knowledge/position and represents the power relations that surround contemporary consumer relations by distributing and awarding power.

■ Cultural sustainability

Cultural commodification

The use of cultural images, forms of cultural production or cultural events often form the basis of experiences marketing campaigns. The consumption of culture, whether in the form of an event or activity, is often one of the major motivating factors in the consumer's decision making process, and as such culture becomes a commodity to be bought, sold and consumed as part of the touristic or leisure process. However, any form of culture represents its generating culture – the very essence of who we are. People have fought and died to protect and defend their cultural autonomy and freedom to produce elements of their own culture. Therefore, the representation or commodification of culture within experiences marketing needs to be treated in a sensitive and sustainable manner. Often there is little concern about protecting or representing culture in a manner that reduces it to its lowest common denominator, in which images and text remove the activity from its cultural context and which communicate that culture to the rest of the world.

Marketing and cultural representation

The images and words that form marketing campaigns and adverts create a story that makes up our understanding of the world, and in particular it makes up part of a historical discourse that informs how we define people, places and their culture. Thus, there is a significant amount of power in the ability to define and make judgements about culture. This power becomes elevated in experiences marketing as tourism brochures, food advertisements and the like commodify culture by selecting and promoting only the themes and attributes that are seen to attract consumers who are searching for escape, authenticity or something extraordinary that cannot be found in their own culture. For example, think about how we define countries such as Australia. Often our first thoughts are the outback, Aboriginal people or Aboriginal art, and many of these images are defined by our relationship to brochures, adverts or travel programmes. It is an idealistic view of Australia that removes culture from the realities of the everyday, or the struggles that Aboriginal people face living in a modern world. As a consequence, as marketers we have a responsibility to think about the impact marketing has on the cultures we are representing, what it says about those cultures, and how the consumer may interpret these. This responsibility forms one of the significant elements of the notion of sustainability put forward in this chapter.

■ Economic sustainability

Marketing in a capitalist world

The debates that surround the notion of sustainability within normative marketing often focus on the financial or economic impact, or of how to sustain market share or turnover, and this is not surprising as one of the fundamental purposes of marketing is to create wealth, and economic value is omnipotent (Firat and Dholakia, 2000). However, as part of the sustainability/ethics debate we need to own up to the reality of the marketing process and to recognise that as an economic activity, there has to be an exchange of goods and services, and that surplus is made by utilising the resources of others. What this does is to locate marketing in the debate that recognises the essential asymmetries that exist within both the production and consumption of experiences, but also in the economic system in which it is located. The global nature of tourism and hospitality and food production often relies on the relationship between developed and less developed countries and that developed economies utilise the resources (cheap labour, minerals, coffee, cocoa, culture, food, landscapes, rivers, beaches etc.) of less developed countries, and that by processing or utilising the resource a profit or surplus can be made. This can clearly be demonstrated by analysing the relationship between globalisation debates and the hospitality industry.

10

The economy of THEF

THEF is part of a large globalised industry and can be used to illustrate how globalisation creates an economic inequality between developed and less developed countries or economies. For example, a hotel may be developed in Kenya. Cheap labour is used to build it; it is then furnished by importing beds and carpets from a central depot that may be in the UK, leading to negative exports for the receiving country; the larders are then stocked with European or American beer and liquor; and the managerial staff are usually expatriates. All of this leads to the income not entering Kenya. The impact of this is that the country needs to generate foreign exchange in order to bring wealth into the country. However, as goods are imported, the income generated by tourists leaves the country and impacts upon the country's balance of payments. So although the solution may be financially sustainable for the hotel, this may not be the case for the country whose resources are supporting the enterprise. The marketing of food, events, hospitality and tourism reinforces the global relations between host country and guest organisations, and this creates a formal duty of care that for many years was ignored. However many large companies have recognised that they have a social responsibility, and merely exploiting a developing country's resources, whether this be extracting minerals for mobile phones or using poorly paid labour to produce footballs and football kits is at odds with this, thus they are working hard to make amends through developing policies and business practices that positively impact upon the countries in which they do business. This approach to corporate responsibility can be seen to make good business sense and can directly shape positive consumer behaviour by informing choice or reinforcing consumer loyalty. Thus, to act sustainably and ethically can make good business sense as it builds a relationship between the producer and consumer.

■ Environmental: The green consumer

There appears to have been the emergence of a new category of consumers whose purchasing behaviour is motivated by how ethical or sustainable the product they are buying is. This concern can be seen as a direct result of the excesses of globalisation and mass production and consumption, and perhaps fulfills a need for something that is more authentic and simple. Over the past decade there has been a huge increase in the number of products that fall into this category, whether it is organic food, sustainable or green tourism or ethically sourced coffee or chocolate.

Moisander recognises that "environment-friendly consumption may be characterized as a highly complex form of consumer behaviour, both intellectually and morally as well as in practice" (2007:1). Significantly, our awareness of sustainable approaches to consumption and our purchasing habits is endowed with high levels of cultural capital. This cultural capital is used by THEF consumers to distinguish themselves from other consumers by using the moral dimensions of green consumerism as an "aesthetic of existence" or "art of existence" (Moisander & Pesonen, 2002:330). Sustainable or eco are reflected in certain forms of consumer behaviour that are informed by the moral discourses of "making a difference, voluntary simplicity and radical environmentalism" (ibid).

There is a great deal of evidence that if we have the choice of two similar products at a similar price but one is organic, sustainable or green we would be more likely to choose that product. Thus, adopting a sustainable approach to production and management practices, will often promote positive buying practices by consumer. Therefore, being green makes good business sense and is becoming increasingly significant in underpinning brand values and brand equity. In addition to this the consumption of sustainable or ethically based products often elicits a hedonistic response, as individuals we find joy in doing something good. Thus our hedonistic pleasure from eating an organic or 'Fair Trade' chocolate bar becomes heighted as we enjoy it at the gustatory level and at the philosophical level. Consumers are also becoming more militant in their consumer behaviour, and take direct action by boycotting products that have been shown to be unethical or damaging to the environment. For example, Nike came under a great deal of criticism for their production methods and utilising cheap or child labour in developing countries, and this led directly to a boycott

10

of their products (Eckhardt, Belk & Devinney, 2010). The result of this consumer behaviour forced Nike and many of their competitors to change their production practices (see Kozinets, Handelman & Lee, 2010 for discussion on anti-consumption). Similar concerns have been raised about Nestlés use of palm oil in Kit Kats and Sainsbury's sourcing of GM-reared cows in their products and butchery. It is also interesting to look at the work of pressure groups such as Tourism Concern (www.tourismconcern.org.uk) which encourages and organises direct action to counteract the pressures of globalisation on less developed countries and fragile habitats. Consequently, companies are increasingly changing their stance and relationship to sustainable or ethical sourcing of materials and management approaches. This approach often forms a significant element in the retention of customers strategy and in turn protecting market share. Companies such as Starbucks, Cadburys and Marriott (Euro RSG, 2010) have used their green credentials as a central element in their current marketing campaigns.

It can be argued that consumers' relationship to sustainably or ethically produced products is more than a trend or fashion, but rather it has come to represent the foundations of a cultural movement and an identifiable demographic whose lives are informed by the green and sustainable movement. The uncertainties of the post-industrial society coupled with the search for simplicity and authenticity of experience that is presented in television shows such as *River Cottage* and *Jamie at Home* informs the consumers' search for the sustainable and ethical practices that become part of everyday lived experiences. Experiences marketing again utilises the theme to create and promise an experience that will make you feel good in a hedonistic way and good in a value driven/philosophical way. Yet in normative marketing terms the green consumer forms an identifiable target market, that is generally well educated and relatively affluent and most important is searching for the 'good life' within contemporary consumerism. However, for some authors such as Eckhardt, Belk & Devinney (2010), the ethical or green consumer may be seen as merely a myth. In identifying the consumer's relationship and understanding of ethical consumption patterns they state:

Economic rationalization focuses on consumers wanting to get the most value for their money, regardless of their ethical beliefs. Institutional dependency refers to the belief that institutions such as the government are responsible to ethically regulate what products can be sold [and].... that some unethical behaviours on the part of corporations must exist in order for macro level economic development to occur. (2010:426)

As such, although consumers may have ambitions to change their purchasing patterns by purchasing more green or ethically sourced products they are "ultimately blinded by the seduction of consumer goods" (Devinney, 2010) and that although they may wish to be seen as caring, they ignore social and environmental issues as they purchase the products, brands and services they are loyal to (Eckhardt, Belk & Devinney, 2010). Nevertheless, marketing continues to utilise the green and ethical discourse to underpin marketing campaigns and attribute the desire to consume ethically as part of the characteristics of various identified segment groups.

■ Sustainable approaches to tourism

The analysis of the impacts of tourism has a long and rich tradition (Swarbrook, 1998; Inskeep, 1991; Neto, 2002), and this has resulted in a complex debate over both the analysis of the sector and the identification of a niche that can be discussed in some depth. For example, Euro RSG (2010:3) identifies the following categories of green tourism experiences:

- **Flashpacking:** Backpacking with flash or style; travel that combines modest accommodation with free spending on activities and other indulgences; budget backpacking that incorporates high-end technology.

- **Geotourism:** Tourism that sustains or enhances the character of a place – its environment, heritage, aesthetics, culture – and the well-being of its residents.

10

- **Rough lux:** Luxury experiences that incorporate time for reflection and personal encounters with people, nature, and architecture, as well as food and social and cultural experiences linked to geographic locations.

- **Slow travel:** Travel that provides an opportunity to become part of local life and to connect to a place, its people, and its culture.

- **Staycation:** A vacation spent at home or nearby.

- **Voluntourism:** Voluntary service experiences that include travel to a destination in order to realize one's service intentions; the conscious, seamlessly integrated combination of voluntary service to a destination with the traditional elements of travel and tourism (arts, culture, geography, history, and recreation).

What this recognises is that there are various categories and levels of greenness. This follows through into food, events, hospitality and tourism, and as consumers we position ourselves within experiences that meet our definitions of authenticity and the simplistic. As such, although the green consumer may be categorised as an identifiable habitus or consumption group, it is particularly sophisticated and may be segmented in a number of additional ways.

■ Green marketing and the process of greenwashing

The inclusion of a company's green credentials within both their marketing campaigns, their mission and values statements is becoming increasingly common and often forms the unique selling point of a product. The marketing of food and tourism in particular often utilize green discourses to underpin marketing campaigns, with banner claims about the ethical, sustainable or organic nature of their products. Often these claims are not investigated, or there is little proof provided to substantiate the green statements, yet we are willing to accept them without question as it eases our conscience about being a consumer. For Alves (2009:3), "Green marketing is the tactical instrument by which companies derive value from Corporate Social Responsibility (CSR): hyping their green credentials in a poorly regulated environment where most claims cannot be corroborated." However, claims of being green or ethical are often overstated and in certain cases just untrue. Greenpeace define *greenwashing* as:

> ...the act of misleading consumers regarding the environmental practices of a company or the environmental benefits of a product or service.
>
> (Gallicano, 2011:1)

The concept of greenwashing appeared as pressure groups and individuals began to identify inconsistencies between companies' claims and their actual behaviour. For example, Romero (2008) analyses the work of Jay Westeveld who in the 1980s recognised the trend for hotels to encourage customers to reuse towels and bedding, yet they did not have recycling policies, and as such, the policy for reuse was motivated by cost cutting rather than environmental concerns or ethical behaviour. It is clear that consumers are motivated and influenced by the green debate, yet often this desire to engage in ethical or sustainable consumption has been adopted by marketers as an effective strategy to sell their products more successfully.

Alves (2009:5) identifies that there are six common sins of greenwashing and green marketing that inform contemporary marketing practices, these include the sins of:

■   **The Hidden Trade-off:** Whereby a product is deemed green as the result of one attribute, for example where the packaging is recyclable, but the contents are not, or in the terms of tourism, the holiday may be sustainable but not the flight to the destination.

■   **No Proof:** Companies will make green claims without them being substantiated by a third party. For example, there are many companies claiming their foods are produced in an ethical manner, but unless they are accredited by organizations such as Fairtrade or the Soil Association there is little proof.

■   **Vagueness:** The messages contained within advertisements are often very vague or obscure, for example, packaging maybe labelled as recyclable, but this may only relate to 10% of the entire packaging. Phrases such as 'ethically sourced', 'free range' or 'benefits the local community' also fit into this category of sin.

10

■   **Irrelevance:** Companies will claim attributes such as the product being biodegradable, yet it may never have been harmful in the first place. A similar claim is that the packaging is CFC-free, yet it has been illegal to produce such packaging since the 1970s.

■   **Lesser of Two Evils:** This involves offering the consumer a product that is harmful to the planet but appears to be less so than alternative versions. For example, hybrid cars which still produce carbon emissions when they are being built and driven, but are marketed as environmentally friendly. There is also a strong trend in food to make claims about levels of fat being reduced, but often this is compensated with higher levels of salt or sugar to give taste. Or chips/crisps that have no 'transfats' or 'MSGs' but are still bad for your health.

■   **Fibbing:** Some companies just lie about their green credentials.

Alves also quotes that in research undertaken by TerraChoice Environmental Marketing in 2007, 1,017 out of 1,018 green-marketed products committed at least one of these sins, with over 50% of the products committing the sin of hidden trade off.

As stated previously, there is still a concern that green practices as CSR policies are motivated by saving money (Bivins, 2009; Gallicano, 2011), or are for its branding, public relations, and legal value (Alves, 2009) rather than the planet. However, through marketing practices, organisations have been able to promote themselves as 'environmental stewards' as they provide very little in-depth information or transparency regarding their operations and business practices (Lyon & Maxwell, 2006), and that in reality, little is being done to protect the environment despite the claims they make in their marketing (Bivins, 2009). This raises questions as to the obligations and responsibilities of companies to be transparent. Rawlins (2009) provides guidelines:

1   Companies must present accurate, substantial and relevant information.

2   Companies should liaise with stakeholders to discover what type of information they require.

3   Companies must provide objective and balanced data about policies and activities.

Rawlins defines these guidelines as providing "substantial completeness" whereby "a reasonable person's requirements for information are satisfied" (2009:74). If we are to adopt a sustainable or ethical approach to marketing, it is important that the industry adopts an approach to green marketing that is truthful and transparent. The debate surrounding the 'sovereign consumer' rests on the precept that the consumer is provided with all the information and they reflexively make the purchase or behavioural decision as a result of interpreting and analysing the provided data. If the information is not clear, transparent, appropriate or true, then the defence of the sovereign consumer is negated and as marketers we become culpable for some of the inequalities, health problems and environmental damage that exists in the world in which we inhabit.

■ Conclusion

The relationship between sustainable and ethical practices and marketing is a complex one that is tied up in many of the debates such as consumer behaviour, choice and power put forward in this book. The use of sustainability and the ethical approaches or themes within THEF marketing provide us with an interesting paradox, which is different from the traditional definition of sustainability within normative marketing theory and practices. Sustainable and ethical marketing is becoming an increasingly popular element of experiences marketing and can be seen to present two very different messages which are "sustainability as product" and "sustainability as non-consumption". Both are part of experiences marketing, but each offer very different experiences. The green consumer as presented in this chapter is also a complicated construct who is motivated by various experiences and products. Each consumer is driven by their own motivations, whether those be to increase cultural capital, to belong to a particular habitus or to behave in the most ethical and sustainable way possible. To be truly sustainable is not to consume at all, however in the consumer

10

orientated world in which we live and the continual search for hedonistic experiences, the best we can hope to achieve is some form of light green consumption patterns.

This chapter also encourages us as marketers, and as consumers, to think about the role of marketing in commoditising and promoting societies, cultures, history, heritage, products and environment as part of the economic system, rather than adopting cynical greenwashing tactics to hide or mask the nature or impact of our product upon both individuals and the environment. Marketing fuels desires, and creates wants which when exercised through consumption generate wealth. It is no good to merely argue that governments or the sovereign consumer is ultimately responsible for any impacts through their freedom of choice. Marketing needs to be accountable and ultimately ethical. Is this possible in a consumerist capitalist society? The answer is highly debatable and is ultimately the product of your own and the marketing industry's conscience and behaviour.

11 Conclusion

◼ Introduction

This book has built on the first edition by further developing the critical approach to marketing in THEF. As stated previously, the work developed here should be used to complement traditional approaches that will be found in most general marketing texts. This book is motivated by the recognition that although there is a growing body of work that takes a critical approach to THEF experiences, there is no text that brings together these debates into a coherent work. This concluding chapter provides an overview of the book and what may be seen as a manifesto for the critical marketing movement in THEF.

◼ A journey into critical marketing

Like the first edition of this book, the order of the chapters was intended to introduce and develop the reader's knowledge of the debates that underpin critical marketing in the THEF sectors. The adoption of a multi-disciplinary approach enables the analysis of marketing as a management, social, cultural, economic and individual process and practice. The chapter structure and content was constructed in a manner so as to develop a progression in the understanding and knowledge of marketing in the THEF arena. It is possible to organise the chapters into four distinct but overlapping debates:

Marketing, exchange and co-creation of experiences (Chapters 2-3)

These chapters add to the approach presented in the first edition of this book by further developing the idea of THEF marketing to encompass wider established marketing debates. Chapter 2 explores how the exchange perspective still remains the dominant discourse within contemporary marketing studies and how the construction of the marketing offer is used to produce or reduce value. It is important to undertake this process as it enables the idea of THEF marketing presented within this book to be both located in and to contribute to more traditional understanding of the marketing process. Chapter 3 introduces a perspective for marketing that is profoundly different from that which was described in the previous chapter, yet is critical to both the process of marketing and our understanding of the role of the consumer. Essentially this perspective moves marketing on from a discipline underscored by exchange of value towards one that can be better explained by the concepts of interaction and the exchange of service, whereby it is possible to recognise that both experience and value is co-created. In making this conceptual shift we demonstrate that many of the foundational constructs and assumptions underlying the exchange paradigm have been recast, and follow by arguing that as a result so should the way in which we think about marketing. The impact of this is that it challenges and reformulates practice across our sectors which must also align with this re-orientation and shift in logic. Importantly to aid this shift, the language of marketing needs to be changed to accommodate the essence and underlying characteristics and features of these changes.

Marketing, culture, experience and resources (Chapters 4-6)

Chapters 4 and 5 form important parts of this book as they recognise that marketing cannot be separated from the society and culture in which they are located and additionally that THEF marketing is underpinned by a set of understandings and practices that make it a distinctive and unique area of marketing activity. Chapter 4 builds upon the preceding two chapters by introducing the important idea that both marketing and consumption are fundamentally cultural activities. By this we mean that the marketing and consumption of THEF products and services not only create value but also mediate and (re)produce socio-cultural meaning and values. Additionally, this chapter further locates the consumer by examining their motivations and more fully explains the reasons for interacting with the THEF marketplace as well as the outcomes of their consumption; which when taken together, form a culturally orientated definition and view of the marketing audience. In adding to our understanding of the cultural practices that underpin the marketing process, Chapter 5 outlines the social, cultural and historical practices that contribute to THEF being a significant part of everyone's lives. The purpose of this is to enable readers to locate and identify how the experiences that surround THEF become central to the idea of experiences marketing presented within this book. Although both marketing and THEF can be seen as social and cultural activities, access to both marketing and THEF experiences are mediated by the resources consumers' possess; as such Chapter 6 attempts to explore the wide ranging definitions of consumer resources and how this impacts upon their engagement with THEF marketing.

The consumer as individual (Chapters 7-9)

This section explores the individual's relationship with the product, the consumption process and how they negotiate marketing practices. Just as the first section located the THEF product or experience, this section locates the consumer at the centre of marketing practice. Chapter 7 explores how the individual's knowledge of products, experiences and their consumption patterns are used by others and themselves to locate and identify them with a particular group or habitus. Thus the way in which the consumer engages with THEF becomes a marker of their identity and membership of a particular class of consumer. The remaining two chapters in this section (8 and 9) are concerned with understanding how the individual consumer interprets, negotiates, resists and finds meaning within THEF marketing. Within this context, Chapter 9 explores how as individuals we all interpret the world in which we live, and that as a result of this, many influencing factors such as our value systems or life experiences will result in each consumer interpreting marketing practices and communication in individual and creative ways. The result of this is that, as marketers we cannot make the assumption that every consumer will find meaning in products in the same way. This theme of interpretation is initially

11

developed in Chapter 8 by exploring the semiotics of marketing, and how meaning is transferred from the marketer to the consumer through the use of signs and semiotic conventions. This chapter draws on the previous chapters as all of the information about products and the individual become manifested in what may be termed a semiotic language of THEF.

This section is of particular importance as it enables marketers to understand how the individual finds meaning, and importantly how to communicate with them in an efficient and creative manner while recognising that each consumer is a free thinking, reflexive individual.

The marketer as moral guardian (Chapters 10-11)

The final two chapters in this book develop the theme of ethical and sustainable marketing in the THEF sector. If you break down the THEF product, although we are apparently selling experiences to the consumer, what we are in fact selling is other people's culture, society, traditions, environment and natural resources. All of these are very fragile and once damaged or destroyed are very difficult to repair or replace. As marketers we have a responsibility to behave and operate in an ethical and sustainable manner. However, as marketing is located within a competitive and commercial context, it is often at odds with this assertion. Chapter 10 explores the notion of ethics and sustainability within the THEF sector, while this last chapter presents a manifesto for THEF practices that responds to some of the concerns highlighted in the previous chapter.

The purpose of this book has been to create a critical framework in which the marketing of THEF experiences may be located. As this is one of the first texts that attempts to do this, the authors feel that it is important that we present what may be seen as a manifesto for the marketing of THEF. This manifesto lays out an agenda and philosophical discourse that should both influence traditional marketing practice and stimulate debate in the THEF marketing community.

■ A Manifesto for THEF Marketing: The five precepts of critical marketing

Precept 1

Marketing needs to be understood as a social and cultural activity that surrounds the world of commerce and which frames the needs, wants, desires and goals of consumers in the THEF sector. The result of this is to place the consumer at the centre of the marketing process. Consequently this is to move away from an over reliance on economic and psychological theory and notions of exchange that are expressed in the positivistic marketing tradition, and to adopt an approach which effectively utilises both positivistic and interpretivistic modes of enquiry.

Precept 2

As expressed in Chapters 4 and 5, it must be recognised that THEF marketing needs to be located in a particular and specific context as the experiences that form THEF and their subsequent marketing is significant at the social and cultural levels, as well as at the level of the individual consumer. It cannot be ignored that THEF is used as markers of consumers' lives and expressions of their social identity. The upshot of this for marketers is that they must take a multi-disciplinary approach so that they can truly understand the significance of their sector. It is only once that this has been achieved that we can engage effectively in the practice and process of marketing THEF experiences.

Precept 3

In recognising the multi-disciplinary nature of marketing within the THEF sector, marketers should be equipped with a broadened view of this practice and process. Specifically, they should develop a commercially significant repertoire that not only includes the exchange perspective of marketing, but also incorporates the service and interaction perspective that acknowledges the significance of marketing as a cultural process and practice. This will allow marketers to appreciate the significance and influence of what they presently do, which

11

is arguably framed within the exchange perspective. They also need to understand the significant agentic properties and nature of their consumers and marketing audience. Consumers are not merely the target of marketing activities, but they are incredibly adept at shaping the meanings and values that are provided by THEF products, activities and services. Marketers should therefore widen their viewpoint and practices to allow for the cultural expressions and projects of their consumers and target markets. This view is expressed in Chapter 7, whereby we accept and develop the notion that consumers cannot merely by seen as part of a homogeneous segment but that we need to recognise each individual's motivations, values and ambitions. Additionally, it is important to accept that there has been a restructuring of society in which society and group membership is not defined by class or income but rather by cultural and consumer knowledge, practices and experience. The result of this is that we cannot simplistically place individuals in one market segment as they are dynamic and reflexive. What is more we also must appreciate that people can and do belong to more than one consumer group and can and will happily flit between them without experiencing any disorientation or discomfort. In fact this juxtaposition of styles and patterns of consumption will arguably be celebrated and embraced (Firat & Dholakia, 2006).

Precept 4

There has been a long tradition in marketing that carries an assumption that the consumer does not resist or question marketing authority (see Holt, 2002 for review) and that, we as marketers, do not question how the consumer finds meaning or relates to marketing communication or practices. As such there has been an assumption of a singular worldview or consumer reality. In contrast to this, by accepting that the consumer interprets and negotiates marketing, and to understand how and why they do this, the THEF marketer is better able to reflect the worldview and reality of consumers in their design of products and experiences. This reinforces the need to adopt more qualitative methods and techniques when developing marketing strategies and approaches. Not only do we need to account for a consumer's worldview or ontology when trying to understand our marketing audiences, we also need to consider the elements that support or constrain their choices and which frame the outcomes of their consumption. Consumers come to the market equipped with their own unique range and quota of resources. Whilst marketing has always recognised the significance of a consumer's socio-economic status and its relationship to a segment's propensity to consume, it has previously neglected the range of other allocative resources which consumers deploy when consuming goods, services and activities. Accordingly, THEF marketers should seek to get closer to their consumers on what can be described as a micro level to try to understand how material objects and other resources such as time and space, create opportunities both for consumers and marketers to create valuable and meaningful experiences. Equally, on a more critical level, we must recognise how apparent deficiencies in these resources may subject consumers to significant disadvantages or place them in harm's way.

Precept 5

It is no longer acceptable to use the 'sovereign consumer' clause as an excuse for the excesses of marketing. As global citizens, marketers should and must take responsibility for their actions and approaches. The adoption of ethical and sustainable approaches should be at the core of all of our activities, and subsequently should be an essential part of any marketing activity. Sustainable marketing should not be a bolt-on to the traditional approach to marketing; instead it should be an overarching value that feeds into all marketing strategies and approaches. This is of particular significance within the THEF sectors as we are promoting and selling the environment, people's cultures, their history and their natural and physical resources. What is more, in many cases we are also promoting, producing and staging ludic and hedonic pleasures that if taken to the excess can lead to personal, social and economic harm. Sustainability should be there to protect and preserve, not as a marketing commodity to be packaged and sold.

11

◼ Conclusion

This second edition provides an introduction to critical marketing in THEF, and should only be seen as a starting point for the reader. Although critical marketing is often criticised for its lack of empirical data or its purely theoretical foundations or approaches, it can be argued that adopting such an approach can enhance practice. If engaging in the debates that surround critical marketing result in the reader or practitioner understanding the significance of their sector and what they are selling, and understanding what wants, needs, desires and motivations their target consumers have, then surely this must make the marketer more efficient in their everyday professional lives. Additionally, the adoption of a more sensitive approach to marketing does not only attract consumers but also ensures that marketers have a product to promote and sell in the future. In short, while traditional marketing approaches are demonstrably important and successfully engage customers, this book argues that a critical approach will serve to enhance this by making marketing more creative, reflexive, and effective.

R References

Alexander, A. (2000) Codes and contexts: practical semiotics for the qualitative researcher, *Market Research Society Annual Conference*, London MRS, pp 139-46.

Allen, D. and Anderson, F. (1994) Consumption and social stratification: Bourdieu's distinction, *Advances in Consumer Research* 21, 70–74.

Alves, I. (2009) Green spin everywhere: how greenwashing reveals the limits of the CSR paradigm, *Journal of Global Change and Governance* II (I), winter/spring.

Armstrong, G. and Kotler, P. (2012). *Principles of Marketing, 14th Edition,* Pearson Prentice-Hall, London.

Arnold, M. J., & Reynolds, K. E. (2003). Hedonic shopping motivations. *Journal of Retailing,* 79(2), 77-95.

Arnould, E. J. (2007). Service-dominant logic and consumer culture theory: Natural allies in an emerging paradigm. *Research in consumer behavior, 11,* 57-76.

Arnould, E.J. and Price, L.L. (1993) River magic: extraordinary experience and the extended service encounter, *Journal of Consumer Research* 20 (1), 24–45.

Arnould, E.J. Price, L.L. and Malshe, A. (2006) Toward a cultural resource-based theory of the consumer, in R.F. Lusch and S.L. Vargo (eds) *The Service-dominant Logic of Marketing: Dialog, Debate and Directions,* pp. 91–104

Arnould, E.J., Price, L.L. and Otnes, C. (1999) Making magic consumption, *Journal of Contemporary Ethnography* 28 (1), 33–68.

Arnould, E., Price, L. and Tierney, P. (1998) Communicative staging of the wilderness servicescape, *Services Industries Journal* 18 (3), 90–115.

Arnould, E.J. and Thompson, C.J. (2005) Consumer culture theory (CCT): twenty years of research, *Journal of Consumer Research* 31 (4), 868–882.

Arsel, Z. and Thompson, C.J. (2011) Demythologizing consumption practices: how consumers protect their field-dependent identity investments from devaluing marketplace myths, *Journal of Consumer Research* 37 (5), 791–806.

Artbury, A. (2005) *Entertaining Angels,* Sheffield: Sheffield Phoenix Press.

Arvidsson, A. (2005). Brands: a critical perspective. *Journal of Consumer Culture*, **5**(2), 235-258.

Askegaard, S., & Linnet, J. T. (2011). Towards an epistemology of consumer culture theory: Phenomenology and the context of context. *Marketing Theory*, **11**(4), 381-404.

Bagozzi, R.P. (1975) Marketing as exchange, *Journal of Marketing* **39** (4), 32.

Bains, P. (2006) *The Primacy of Semiosis: an Ontology of Relations*, Toronto: University of Toronto Press.

Barak, B. and Gould, S. (1985) Alternative age measures: a research agenda, *Advances in Consumer Research* **12** (1), 53–58.

Bathes, R. (1997) *The Eiffel Tower and other Mythologies*, trans. R. Howard, University of California Press.

Baudrillard, J. (1993) *Simulacra and Simulation*, trans. S. Farine-Glaser, University of Michigan Press.

Bauman, Z. (1999) *Culture as Praxis: Theory, Culture and Society*, London: Sage.

Beane, T. P., & Ennis, D. M. (1987). Market segmentation: a review. *European Journal of Marketing*, **21**(5), 20-42.

Bekin, C., Carrigan, M. & Szmigin, I. (2005) Defying marketing sovereignty: Voluntary simplicity at new consumption communities, *Qualitative Market Research*, **8**(4), 413-429.

Belk, R.W. (2010) Benign Envy, Key note speech, Academy of Marketing Conference, Available: http://www.youtube.com/watch?v=IZwgznJwGno [21/11/2011].

Belk, R. W. (2013). Extended self in a digital world. *Journal of Consumer Research*, **40**(3), 477-500.

Belk, R. W. and Costa, J.A. (1998) The mountain man myth: a contemporary consuming fantasy, *Journal of Consumer Research* **25** (3), 218–240.

Belk, R.W., Wallendorf, M. and Sherry, J. (1989) The sacred and the profane in consumer behaviour: theodicy on the Odyssey, *Journal of Consumer Research* **16** (June), 1–38.

Beresford, P. (2016). A cultural branding analysis of discount grocer success (Unpublished doctoral thesis). Sheffield Hallam University, Sheffield, UK.

Berger, A.A. (2007) *Thailand Tourism*, Haworth Press.

Bernthal, M., Crockett, D. & Rose, R. (2005) Credit cards as lifestyle facilitators, *Journal of Consumer Research*, **32**(1) 130-145.

Bitner, M.J. (1992) Servicescapes: the impact of physical surroundings on customers and employees, *Journal of Marketing* **56** (2), 57–71.

Bitner, M., Faranda, W., Hubbert, A. and Zeithaml, V. (1997) Customer contributions and roles in service delivery, *International Journal of Service Industry Management* **8** (3), 193–205.

Bivins, T. (2009) *Mixed Media: Moral Distinctions in Advertising, Public Relations and Journalism*, 2nd edn, New York: Routledge.

Booms, B.H. and Bitner, M.J. (1981) Marketing strategies and organization structures for service firms, in J.H. Donnelly and W.R. George (eds), *Marketing of Services*, American Marketing Association, .

Borden, N.H. (1964) The concept of the marketing mix, *Journal of Advertising Research* **4** (2), 7–12.

Botterill, D. (2001) The epistemology of a set of tourism studies, *Leisure Studies* **20** (1999), 199–214

Bourdieu, P. (1987) *Distinction: a Social Critique of the Judgement of Taste*, trans. R. Nice, Cambridge, MA: Harvard University Press.

Britain Thinks (2011) *A Study of the Middle Classes* available: http://britainthinks.com/sites/default/files/reports/SpeakingMiddleEngish_Report.pdf

Branch, J, (2007) Postmodern consumption and the high-fidelity audio microculture, consumer culture theory, *Research in Consumer Behaviour*, **11**, 79-99

Brown, J., Broderick, A.J. & Lee, N (2007) Word of mouth communication within online communities: Conceptualizing the online social network, *Journal of Interactive Marketing*, **21**(3) 2.

Brown, S., Garino, G., Taylor, K. & Price, S.W. (2005), Debt and financial expectations: an individual- and household-level analysis, *Economic inquiry*, **43** (1) 100-120.

Brown, S., Kozinets, R.V. and Sherry, J. (2003) Teaching old brands new tricks: retro branding and the revival of brand meaning, *Journal of Marketing* **67** (3), 19–33.

Brownlie, D. and Hewer, P. (2007) Prime beef cuts: culinary images for thinking 'men', *Consumption Markets and Culture* **10** (3), 229–250.

Bryman, A. (2004) *Social Research Methods*, Oxford: OUP.

Burrell, G. and Morgan, G. (1979) *Sociological Paradigms and Organizational Analysis*, Heinemann.

Buttle, F. (1996) SERVQUAL: review, critique, research agenda, *European Journal of Marketing* **30** (1), 8–31.

Caillois, R. (1988) *Man and the Sacred*, Glencoe : Free Press.

Carù, A. and Cova, B. (2003) Revisiting consumption experience: a more humble but complete view of the concept, *Marketing Theory* **3** (June), 267–286.

Caruana, R., Crane, A., & Fitchett, J. A. (2008). Paradoxes of consumer independence: A critical discourse analysis of the independent traveller. *Marketing Theory*, *8*(3), 253-272.

Chan, S.P. (2016) Household debt binge has no end in sight, says OBR, *The Telegraph*, [online] 17 March. Available at http://www.telegraph.co.uk/business/2016/03/17/household-debt-binge-has-no-end-in-sight-says-obr/ [Accessed 10 July 2016]

Cherrier, H. (2009), Disposal and simple living: exploring the circulation of goods and the development of sacred consumption, *Journal of Consumer Behaviour*, **8** (6) 327-339.

Christopher, M. (1969). Cluster analysis and market segmentation. *European Journal of Marketing*, **3**(2), 99-102.

Chronis, A. (2008). Co-constructing the narrative experience: staging and consuming the American Civil War at Gettysburg. *Journal of Marketing Management*, **24**(1-2), 5-27.

Chronis, A., Arnould, E.J. and Hampton, R.D. (2012) Gettysburg re-imagined: the role of narrative imagination in consumption experience, *Consumption Markets and Culture*, **15**(3). http://www.tandfonline.com/doi/abs/10.1080/10253866.2011.652823

CIM (2010). *Ethics and Social Responsibility* [Homepage of the Chartered Institute of Marketing], [Online]. Available: http://www.cim.co.uk/resources/ethics/home.aspx [2010, May 10th].

Clark, J. and Critcher, C. (1989) *The Devil Makes Work: Leisure in Capitalist Britain*; London: Macmillan.

Claseen, A. (2007) The symbolic function of food as iconic representation of culture and spirituality in Wolfram von Eschenbach' Parzival (ca. 1205), *Orbis Litteratum* **62** (2), 315–335.

Cockerham, W.C. (2005) Health lifestyle theory and the convergence of agency and structure, *Journal of Health and Social Behavior* **46** (1), 51–67.

Cohen, C.B. (1995) Marketing paradise, making nation. *Annals of Tourism Research*, 22(2): 404–421.

Cohen, S. and Taylor, L. (1992) *Escape Attempts: the Theory and Practice of Resistance to Everyday Life*, London: Routledge.

Cole, M. (2008) Asceticism and hedonism in research discourses of veganism, *British Food Journal*, **110 (7)**, 706 - 716

Cooper, T. (2010) *Longer Lasting Products: Alternatives to the Throwaway Society*, Farnham: Gower.

Couldry, N. (2001) *Inside Culture: Re-imagining the Method of Cultural Studies*. London: Sage.

Coupland, J. C. (2005). Invisible brands: An ethnography of households and the brands in their kitchen pantries. *Journal of consumer research*, **32**(1), 106-118.

Cova, B. (1997) Community and consumption: towards a definition of the linking value of product of services, *European Journal of Marketing* **31** (3/4), 297–316.

Cova, B. and Cova, V. (2001) Tribal aspects of postmodern consumption: the case of French in-line roller skaters, *Journal of Consumer Behavior*, **1** (1), 67-76

Cova, B. and Cova, V. (2002) Tribal marketing: the tribalisation of society and its impact on the conduct of marketing, *European Journal of Marketing* **36** (/6), 595–620.

Cova, B. and Pace, S. (2006) Brand community of convenience products: new forms of customer empowerment – the case "my Nutella The Community", *European Journal of Marketing* **40** (9), 1087–1105.

Cova, B., Kozinets, R.V. and Shankar, A. (eds) (2007) *Consumer Tribes*, Oxford: Butterworth-Heinemann.

Crick, M. (1989) Representations of sun, sex, sights, savings and servility, *International Tourism in the Social Sciences, Annual Review of Anthropology* **18**, 307–344.

Crouch, D. and Desforges, L. (2003) The sensuous in the tourist encounter, *Tourist Studies* **3** (1), 5–22.

Culler, J. (1981) Semiotics of tourism, *American Journal of Semiotics* **1**, 127–140.

Culler, J. (1988) *Framing the Sign: Criticism and its Institutions*, Oxford: Basil Blackwell.

Dahl, S. (2014). *Social Media Marketing: Theories and Applications.* Sage.

Dann, G. (1996a) The people of tourist brochures, in T. Selwyn (ed.), *The Tourist Image: Myths and Myth Making in Tourism*, Chichester: Wiley, pp. 61–82.

Davis, F. (1979) *Yearning for Yesterday: a Sociology of Nostalgia*, Glencoe: Free Press.

Dawkins, N. (2009) The hunger for home: Nostalgic affect, embodied memories and the sensual politics of transnational foodways. *UG Journal of Anthropology* **1**, 33–42.

De Langhe, B., Fernbach, P. M., & Lichtenstein, D. R. (2016). Star Wars: Response to Simonson, Winer/Fader, and Kozinets. *Journal of Consumer Research*, **42**(6), 850-857.

Delanty, G. (1997) *Social Science: Beyond Constructivism and Realism*, Buckingham: Open University Press.

Delind, L. (2006) Of bodies, places and culture: re-situating local food, *Journal of Agricultural and Environmental Ethics* **19**, 121–146.

Denny, R.M. and Sunderland, P.L. (2002) What is coffee in Bangkok?, *Research Magazine*, Nov., available at http://www.practicagroup.com/pdfs/Denny_and_Sunderland_What_is_Coffee.pdf

Devinney, T., (2010) Using market segmentation approaches to understand the green consumer, in *Oxford Handbook of Business and the Environment*, Bansel, P & Hoffman, A (eds) Oxford, 2010.

Dickson, P. R., & Ginter, J. L. (1987). Market segmentation, product differentiation, and marketing strategy. *The Journal of Marketing*, 1-10.

Drolet, M. (2004) *The Postmodernism Reader: Foundation Texts*, New York: Routledge.

Durkheim, E. (1995) *The Elementary Forms of Religious Life*, London: George Allen and Unwin.

Echtner, C.M. (1999) The semiotic paradigm: implications for tourism research, *Tourism Management* **20** (1), 47–57.

Eckhardt. G. Belk. B. & Devinney. M. (2010) Why don't consumers consume ethically; *Journal of Consumer Behaviour*, **9**, 462-436.

Eco, U. (1990) *Travels in Hyperreality*, trans. W. Weaver, Harcourt Brace & Co.

Edensor, T., and Richards, S. (2007). Snowboarders vs skiers: Contested choreographies of the slopes.*Leisure studies,26*(1), 97-114.

Eigler, P. and Langeard, E. (1975) Une approche novelle pour le marketing des services, *Revue Française de Gestion* **2** (spring), 97–114.

Ellis, J. (1980) Photography/pornography/art/pornography, *Screen*, **21**, 81–108.

Euro RSG. (2010), *Know: The Furure of Travel*, Euro RSCG Worldwide Network.

Fantasia, R. (1995) Fast food in France, *Theory and Society* **24**, 201–243.

Ferry, J. (2003) *Food in Film: A Culinary Performance of Communication*, London: Routledge.

Firat, A.F. & Dholakia, N. (2006) Theoretical and philosophical implications of postmodern debates: some challenges to modern marketing, *Marketing Theory*, **6**(2), 123–162.

Fiske, J. (1990) *Introduction to Communication Studies*, 2nd edn, London: Routledge.

Foucault, M. (1980) *Power/Knowledge: Selected Writings and Other Interviews*, New York: Pantheon.

Franklin, A. and Crang, M. (2001) The trouble with tourism and travel theory, *Tourist Studies* **1** (1), 1–12.

Gabriel. S. (1993) *The Barbarian Temperament: Towards a Postmodern Critical Theory*, London: Routledge.

Gallicano, T. (2011) A critical analysis of greenwashing claims, *Public Relations Journal* **5** (3)

Garlick, S. (2002) Revealing the unseen: Tourism, art and photography, *Cultural Studies* **16** (2), 289–305.

Genosko, G. (2003) The bureaucratic beyond: Roger Caillois and the negation of the sacred in Hollywood cinema, *Economy and Society*, **32** (1), 74-89.

Getz, D., Robinson, R., Andersson, T., & Vujicic, S. (2014). *Foodies and Food Tourism*. Goodfellow Publishers.

Getz, D. and Sailor, M. (1993) Design of destination and attraction specific brochures, in U. Musaffer and D. Feisenmainer (eds), *Communication Channel Systems in Tourism Marketing*, New York: Hayworth Press, pp. 191–215.

Giesler, M. (2006) Consumer gift systems, *Journal of Consumer Research*, **33**(2) 283-290.

Goldsmith, R.E. and Heiens, R.A. (1992) Subjective age: A test of five hypotheses, *The Gerontologist* **32** (3), 312–317.

Goulding, C. (1999) Heritage, nostalgia, and the grey consumer, *Journal of Marketing Practice: Applied Marketing Science*, **5**(6/7/8), 177-199.

Goulding, C. (2001) Romancing the past: Heritage visiting and the nostalgic consumer, *Psychology and Marketing* **18** (6), 565–592.

Goulding, G. and Saren, M. (2009) Performing identity: An analysis of gender expression at the Whitby Goth festival, *Consumption Markets and Culture* **12** (1), 27–46.

Goulding, C. and Shankar, A. (2004) Age is just a number: Rave culture and the cognitively young thirty something, *European Journal of Marketing* **38** (5/6), 641–658.

Goulding, C., Shankar, A., Elliott, R. and Canniford, R. (2009) The marketplace management of illicit pleasure, *Journal of Consumer Research* **35** (5), 759–771.

Graburn, N.H. (1986) The anthropology of tourism, *Annals of Tourism Research*, **10**, 530-563.

Grayson, K. and Shulman, D. (2000) Indexicality and the verification function of irreplaceable possessions: A semiotic analysis, *Journal of Consumer Research* **27**(1), 17–30.

Grier, S., & Bryant, C. A. (2005). Social marketing in public health. *Annual Review of Public Health*, **26**, 319-339.

Grönroos, C. (2008) Service logic revisited: Who creates value? And who co-creates?, *European Business Review* **20** (4), 298–314.

Grönroos, C. (2011) Value co-creation in service logic: A critical analysis, *Marketing Theory* **11** (3), 279–301.

Grove, S. and Fisk, R. (1992) The service experience as theater, *Advances in Consumer Research* **19**, 455–461.

Guiry, M. (1992). Consumer and employee roles in service encounters, in *Advances in Consumer Research Volume 19*.

Guba, E. and Lincoln, Y. (1989) *Fourth Generation Analysis*, London; Sage.

Gvion, L. and Trostler, N. (2008) From spaghetti and meatballs through Hawaiian pizza to sushi: The changing nature of ethnicity in American restaurants, *Journal of Popular Culture* **41** (6), 950–974.

Hall, S. (1997) *Representation: Cultural representations and Signifying Practices*, Sage.

Hanna, J. (2009), 18th November-last update, *Customer Feedback Not on elBulli's Menu*. Available: http://hbswk.hbs.edu/item/6105.html [2011, May, 10th].

Harvey, D. (1989). *The Condition of Postmodernity* (Vol. 14). Oxford: Blackwell.

Harvey, D. (1993) From space to place and back again: Reflections on the condition of postmodernity, in J. Bird, B. Curtis, T. Putnam, G. Robertson and L. Tickner (eds), *Mapping the Futures: Local Cultures, Global Change*, London: Routledge, 3–39.

Hawkes, C. (2009) Sales promotions and food consumption, *Nutrition Reviews* **67** (6), 333–342.

Hely, J. (2002) Hospitality as sign and sacrament, *Journal of Religion, Disability and Health* **64** (4), 462–482.

Henry, P. and Caldwell, M. (2008) Spinning the proverbial wheel? Social class and marketing, *Marketing Theory* **8** (4), 387–405.

Herbert, D. (1995) Heritage as a literary place, in D. Herbert (ed.), *Heritage, Tourism and Society*, London: Mansell, pp. 212–221.

Hirschman, E.C. (2003) Men, dogs, guns, and cars: the semiotics of rugged individualism, *Journal of Advertising* **32** (1), 9–22.

Ho, M., & O'Donohoe, S. (2014). Volunteer stereotypes, stigma, and relational identity projects. *European Journal of Marketing*, **48**(5/6), 854-877.

Hodge, R. and Kress, G. (1979) *The Ideology of Language*, Cambridge: Polity Press.

Hodge, R. and Kress, G. (1995) *Social Semiotics*, Cambridge: Polity Press.

Holbrook, M.B. (1993) Nostalgia and consumption preferences: Some emerging patterns of consumer tastes, *Journal of Consumer Research* **20** (2), 245–256.

Holbrook, M.B. (1996) Special session summary: customer value a framework for analysis and research, in K.P. Corfman and J.G. Lynch Jr. (eds) *Advances in Consumer Research*, vol. 23.

Holbrook, M.B. (1999) *Consumer Value: a Framework for Analysis and Research*, London: Routledge.

Holbrook, M. B., & Hirschman, E. C. (1982). The experiential aspects of consumption: Consumer fantasies, feelings, and fun. *Journal of Consumer Research*, **9**(2), 132-140.

Holt, D.B. (1995) How consumers consume: A typology of consumption practices, *Journal of Consumer Research* **22** (1), 1–16.

Holt, D.B. (1997) Distinction in America? Recovering Bourdieu's theory of tastes from its critics, *Poetics* **25** (2–3), 93–120.

Holt, D.B. (1998) Does cultural capital structure American Consumption, *Journal of Consumer Research* **25** (1), 1–25.

Holt, D.B. (2002) Why do brands cause trouble? A dialectical theory of consumer culture and branding, *Journal of Consumer Research* **29** (1), 70–90.

Holt, D.B. (2004a) Consumers' cultural differences as local systems of tasters: a critique of the personality/values approach and an alternative framework, in J.A. Cote and

S.M. Leong (eds), *Asia Pacific Advances in Consumer Research*, vol. 1, Association for Consumer Research, pp. 178–184.

Holt, D.B. (2004b) *How Brands Become Icons: the Principles of Cultural Branding*, Cambridge, MA: Harvard Business Press.

Holt, D.B. (2006) Jack Daniel's America: Iconic brands as ideological parasites and proselytizers, *Journal of Consumer Culture* **6** (3), 355–377.

Holt, D.B. and Cameron, D. (2010) *Cultural Strategy: Using Innovative Ideologies to Build Breakthrough Brands*, Oxford: Oxford University Press.

Holt, D.B. and Sternthal, B. (1997) Post-structuralist lifestyle analysis: Conceptualizing the social pattering of consumption, *Journal of Consumer Research* **23** (4), 326–350.

Holt, D.B. and Thompson, C. (2004), Man-of-action heroes: The pursuit of heroic masculinity in everyday consumption, *Journal of Consumer Research,* **31** (2), 425-440.

Hopkins, J. (1998) Signs of the post-rural: Marketing myths of a symbolic countryside, *Geografiska Annaler* **80** B (2), 65–81.

Houston, F.S. and Gassenheimer, J.B. (1987) Marketing and exchange, *Journal of Marketing* **51** (4), 3–18.

Humphreys, A., and Thompson, C. J. (2014). Branding disaster: Re-establishing trust through the ideological containment of systemic risk anxieties. *Journal of Consumer Research,* **41**(4), 877-910.

Inskeep, E. (1991) *Tourism Planning: an Integrated Approach*, New York: Van Nostrand Reinhold.

Ireland, M. (1998) What is Cornishness? The implications for tourism, *Tourism, Culture and Communication* **1** (1), 17–26.

Izberk-Bilgin, E. (2010) An interdisciplinary review of resistance to consumption, some marketing implications, and future research suggestions, *Consumption Market and Culture* **13** (3), 299–323.

Jameson. F. (1985) Postmodernism and consumer society; in Foster. H. (Ed) *Postmodern Culture*, London: Pluto.

Jameson, F. (1991) *Postmodernism or the Cultural Logic of Late Capitalism*, London: Verso.

Jenkins, O. (2003) Photography and travel brochures: The circle of representation, *Tourism Geographies* **5** (3), 305–328.

Jenkins, R. (2011) Consumption in the everyday imagination: how culture gives shape to everyday thinking, PhD thesis, Bournemouth University.

Jin, B., Sternquist, B. and Koh, A. (2003), 'Price as hedonic shopping', *Family and Consumer Sciences Research Journal,* **31**, 378–402

Johns, N. and Pine, R. (2002) Consumer behaviour in the food service industry: a review, *Hospitality Management* **21**, 119–134.

Jokinen, E. and McKie, D. (1997) The disorientated tourist: The figuration of the tourist in contemporary cultural critique, in C. Rojek and J. Urry (eds), *Touring Cultures*, London: Routledge.

Kahn, B., Ratner, R., & Kahneman., (1997) Patterns of hedonic consumption over time, *Marketing Letters*, **8** (1), 85-96

Kates, S. M., & Belk, R. W. (2001). The meanings of lesbian and gay pride day resistance through consumption and resistance to consumption. *Journal of Contemporary Ethnography*, **30**(4), 392-429.

Klein, H., Hirschheim, R. and Nissen, H. (1991) A pluralist perspective of the information research arena, in H. Klein and R. Hirscheim (eds), *Information Research: Contemporary Approaches and Emergent Traditions*, Amsterdam: North Holland.

Klein, J. G., Smith, N. C., & John, A. (2004). Why we boycott: Consumer motivations for boycott participation. *Journal of Marketing*, **68**(3), 92-109.

Kniazeva, M. and Vekatesh, A. (2007) Food for thought: A study of food consumption in postmodern US culture, *Journal of Consumer Behaviour* **6** (6), 419–435.

Kotler, P. (1972) A generic concept of marketing, *Journal of Marketing* **36** (2), 46–54.

Kotler, P. (2008) *Principles of Marketing*, Harlow: Pearson Education.

Kotler, P. and Levy, S.J. (1969) Broadening the concept of marketing, *Journal of Marketing* **33** (1), 10–15.

Kotler, P. and Levy, S.J. (1971) Demarketing, yes, demarketing, *Harvard Business Review* **79** (6), 74–80.

Kozinets, R.V. (1997) I want to believe: a netnography of the X-philes' subculture of consumption, *Advances in Consumer Research* **24** (1), 470n475.

Kozinets, R.V. (1999) E-tribalized marketing?: The strategic implications of virtual communities of consumption, *European Management Journal* **17** (3), 252–264.

Kozinets, R.V. (2001) Utopian enterprise: articulating the meanings of Star Trek's culture of consumption, *Journal of Consumer Research* **28** (1), 67–88.

Kozinets, R.V. (2002a) Can consumers escape the market? Emancipatory illuminations from Burning Man, *Journal of Consumer Research* **29** (1), 20–38.

Kozinets, R.V. (2002b) The field behind the screen: Using netnography for marketing research in online communities, *Journal of Marketing Research* **39** (1), 61–72.

Kozinets, R.V.(2007) Inno-tribes: Star Trek as Wikimedia, in B. Cova, R.V. Kozinets and A. Shankar (eds), *Consumer Tribes*, Butterworth-Heinemann, pp. 194–211.

Kozinets, R.V. (2010) *Netnography: Doing Ethnographic Research Online*, London: Sage.

Kozinets. R.V. (2015). *Netnography: Redefined*. Sage.

Kozinets, R. V. (2016). Amazonian forests and trees: Multiplicity and objectivity in studies of online consumer-generated ratings and reviews, a commentary on de Langhe, Fernbach, and Lichtenstein. *Journal of Consumer Research*, **42**(6), 834-839.

Kozinets, R. V., Sherry, J. F., Storm, D., Duhachek, A., Nuttavuthisit, K. & DeBerry-Spence,B. (2004) Ludic agency and retail spectacle. *Journal of Consumer Research* **31**(3): 658-672.

Kozinets, R., de Valck, K., Wojnicki, A. & Wilner, S. (2010) Network narratives: understanding word-of-mouth marketing in online communities, *Journal of Marketing* **74** (2), 71–89.

Kozinets, R.V., Handelman, J.M., & Lee, M.S.W., (2010) 'Don't read this; or, who cares what the hell anti-consumption is, anyways?'. *Consumption Markets & Culture* **13** (3), 225-233.

Kozinets, R.V., Iacobucci, D., Mick, D.G., Arnould, E., Sherry, J., John F., Storm, D., Duhachek, A., Nuttavuthisit, K. & DeBerry-Spence, B. (2004) Ludic Agency and Retail Spectacle, *Journal of Consumer Research* **31** (3), 658-672.

Kress, G. and van Leeuwen, T. (1996) *Reading Images: the Grammar of Visual Design*, London: Routledge.

Kress, G. and van Leeuwen, T. (2001) *Multimodal Discourse: the Modes and Media of Contemporary Communication*, London: Arnold.

Krippendorf, J. (1999) *The Holiday Makers*, Oxford: Heinemann.

Kupfermann, J. (2014) Bawdiness, booze and the women who have turned my beloved Ascot into... CHAVSCOT, by a traditional lady race fan, *Mail Online*, 19th June, viewed, 22nd August 2014. Available at: http://www.dailymail.co.uk/femail/article-2663179/Bawdiness-booze-women-turned-beloved-Ascot-CHAVSCOT.html#ixzz3B8XIyTg5

Lages, L. and Fernandes, J. (2005) The SERPVAL scale: a multi-item instrument for measuring service personal values, *Journal of Business Research* **58** (11), 1562–1572.

Laing, J.F. (2006) Extraordinary journeys: motivations behind frontier travel experiences and implications for tourism, PhD thesis, La Trobe University, Victoria, Australia.

Lane, R. and Waitt, G. (2001) Authenticity in tourism and native title: place, time and spatial politics in the East Kimberley, *Social and Cultural Geography* **2** (4), 381- 405.

Lane, R. and Waitt, G. (2007) Inalienable places, *Annals of Tourism Research* **34**(1), 105–121.

Lash, S. and Urry, J. (1994) *Economies of Signs and Space*, London: Sage.

Lauterborn, R. (1990) New marketing litany: Four Ps Passé: C-Words Take Over.' *Advertising Age* **61**(41), 26.

Levy, S.J. (1959) Symbols for sale, *Harvard Business Review* **37** (4), 117–124.

Levy, S.J. (2006) How new, how dominant? in R.F. Lusch,. and S.L. Vargo (Eds.), *The Service-dominant Logic of Marketing: Dialog, Debate and Directions*. pp. 57-65. Armonk, N.Y, M.E. Sharpe.

Lofgren, O. (1999) *On Holiday: a History of Vacationing*, London/Berkeley: University of California Press.

Lusch, R.F. and Vargo, S..L. (2006) *The Service-dominant Logic of Marketing: Dialog, Debate and Directions*, Armonk, NY: M.E. Sharpe.

Lyon, T. and Maxwell, J. (2006) Greenwash: corporate environmental disclosure under threat of audit, Ross School of Business Working Paper Series.

MacCannell, D. (1999) *The Tourist: A New Theory of the Leisure Class*, Los Angeles: University of California Press.

Magee, R. (2007) Food Puritanism and food pornography: The gourmet semiotics of Martha and Nigella, *American Journal of American Popular Culture*, **6** (2)

Maloney, M (1993) A personal exploration of critical action research and critical ethnography, Conference Proceedings, Nursing Research Geelong 8th-9th July 1993, Institute of Nursing Research, Deakin University

Marshall, D. (2005) Food as ritual, routine or convention, *Consumption, Markets and Culture*, **8** (1),69–85.

McAlexander, J.H., Schouten, J.W. & Koenig, H.F. (2002) Building brand community. *Journal of Marketing*, **66** (1), 38-54.

McAlexander, J. H., & Schouten, J. W. (1998). Brandfests: Servicescapes for the cultivation of brand equity. in: Sherry, J. F. (Ed.) *Servicescapes: The Concept of Place in Contemporary Markets*, Lincolnwood, IL, pp. 377-401

McCabe, D., Rosenbaum, M. and Yurchisin, J. (2007) Perceived service quality and shopping motivations: A dynamic relationship, *Services Marketing Quarterly*, **29** (1), 1n21.

McCarthy, J. (1964) *Basic Marketing: A Managerial Approach*, Richard D. Irwin.

McCracken, G. (1986) Culture and consumption: A theoretical account of the structure and movement of the cultural meaning of consumer goods, *Journal of Consumer Research* **13** (1), 71–84.

McCracken, G. (1989) Who is the celebrity endorser? Cultural foundations of the endorsement process, *Journal of Consumer Research*, **16** (3), 310–321.

McCracken, G. (1993) The value of the brand: An anthropological perspective, in D.A. Aaker and A.L. Biel (eds), *Brand Equity and Advertising*, Hillside, NJ: Lawrence Erlbaum Associates, pp. 125–139.

McCracken, G.D. and Roth, V.J. (1989) Does clothing have a code? Empirical findings and theoretical implications in the study of clothing as a means of communication, *International Journal of Research in Marketing* **6** (1), 13–33.

McDonald, M. and Dunbar, I. (2010) *Market Segmentation: How to Do It, How to Profit from It*, Oxford: Goodfellow Publishers.

Meyrowitz, J. (1992) *No Sense of Place*, New York: Routledge.

Mick, D.G. (1986) Consumer Research and semiotics: Exploring the morphology of sign, symbols and significance, *Journal of Consumer Research* **13** (2),196–213.

Mick, D.G., Burroughs, J.E., Hetzel, P. and Brannen, M.Y. (2004) Pursuing the meaning of meaning in the commercial world: an international review of marketing and consumer research founded on semiotics, *Semiotica* **152** (1–4), 1–74.

Mick. D.G. and Oswald, L.R. (2006) The semiotic paradigm on meaning in the marketplace, in R.W. Belk (ed.) *Handbook of Qualitative Research Methods in Marketing*, Cheltenham: Edward Elgar, pp. 31–45.

Middleton, A. (2007) Trivialising culture, social conflict and heritage tourism in Quito, *International Seminar of Heritage Tourism*, CEDLA, Amsterdam, 14–16 June.

Miles, S. (1996) The cultural capital of consumption: Understanding "postmodern" identities in a cultural context, *Culture and Psychology* **2**, 139–158.

Mintz, S. and Du Bois, C. (2002) The anthropology of food and eating, *Annual Review of Anthropology* **31**, 99–119.

Mitchell, I. and Saren, M. (2008) The living product – using the creative nature of metaphors in the search for sustainable marketing, *Business Strategy and the Environment* **17**, 398–410.

Moisander, J. (2007) Motivational complexity of green consumerism, *International Journal of Consumer Studies* **31**, 404–409

Moisander, J. and Pesonen, S. (2002) Narratives of sustainable ways of living: Constructing the self and other as a green consumer, *Management Decision* **40** (4), 329–342.

Moisander, J. and Valtonen, A. (2006) *Qualitative Marketing Research: A Cultural Approach*, London: Sage.

Moisio, R., Arnould, E. J., & Gentry, J. W. (2013). Productive consumption in the class-mediated construction of domestic masculinity: Do-It-Yourself (DIY) home improvement in men's identity work. *Journal of Consumer Research*, **40**(2), 298-316.

Moore, H. L., & Hussey, G. (1965). Economic implications of market orientation. *Journal of Farm Economics*, **47**(2), 421-427.

Morgan. G. & Tresidder. R. (2015) *Dancing with Bacchus: A Contemporary Approach to Wine Studies*, Routledge, Oxford.

Morris, C., De La Fuente, G. A. Z., Williams, C. E., & Hirst, C. (2016). UK Views toward breastfeeding in public: an analysis of the public's response to the Claridge's incident. *Journal of Human Lactation*, (accepted 16/04/2016)

Muñiz Jr., O'Guinn & Thomas, (2001). Brand community. *Journal Of Consumer Research*, **27**(4), 412-432.

Neilson, L. A. (2010). Boycott or buycott? Understanding political consumerism. *Journal of Consumer Behaviour*, **9**(3), 214-227.

Nelson, V. (2005) Representation and images of people, place and nature in Grenada's tourism, *Geografiska Annaler B* **87** (2), 131–143.

Neto, F. (2002) *Sustainable Tourism, Environmental Protection and Natural Resource Management*, Cancun: UN.

O'Connor, D. (2005) Towards a new interpretation of hospitality, *International Journal of Hospitality Management* **17** (3), 267–271.

O'Gorman, K. (2007) Dimensions of hospitality: exploring ancient origins, in C. Lashley, P.A. Lynch and a. Morrison (eds), *Hospitality: A Social Lens*, Oxford: Elsevier.

O'Shaughnessy, J. and O'Shaughnessy, N.J. (2002) Marketing, the consumer society and hedonism, *European Journal of Marketing* **36** (5/6), 524–547.

Oswald, L.R. (2012) *Marketing Semiotics: Signs, Strategies and Brand Value*, Oxford: Oxford University Press.

Panzarella, R. (1980) The phenomenology of aesthetic peak experiences, *Journal of Humanistic Psychology* **20** (January), 69–85.

Papworth, J. (2012) Money: debt soars as families use plastic to pay bills: borrowing: we owe 48% more than last year as savings drop, *The Guardian*

Parasuraman, A., Zeithaml, V.A. and Berry, L.L. (1988) SERVQUAL: a multiple-item scale for measuring consumer perceptions of service quality, *Journal of Retailing* **64** (1), 12–40.

Parsons, E., & Maclaran, P. (2009). *Contemporary Issues in Marketing and Consumer Behaviour*. Routledge.

Peattie, K. & Peattie, S. (2009), Social marketing: A pathway to consumption reduction?, *Journal of Business Research,* **62** (2), 260-268.

Peirce, C.S. (1934) *Collected Chapters: Vols 1, 2, and 5*, eds C. Hartshorne and P. Weiss, Boston, MA: Harvard University Press.

Peñaloza, L. (2000) The commodification of the American West: Marketers' production of cultural meanings at the trade show, *Journal of Marketing* **64** (4), 82–109.

Peñaloza, L. and Barnhart, M. (2011) Living U.S. capitalism, the normalization of credit/debt, *Journal of Consumer Research* **38** (4), 743–762.

Pfaffenberger. B. (1979) The Kataragama Pilgrimage: Hindu Buddhist interaction and its significance in Sri Lanka's polyethnic social system, in *Journal of Asian Studies*, **38** (2), 253-70.

Phillimore, J. and Goodson, L. (2004) *Qualitative Research in Tourism: Ontologies, Epistemologies and Methodologies*, London: Routledge.

Picard, M. (1990) Cultural tourism in Bali: cultural performances as tourist attraction, *Indonesia* **49** (April), 37–74.

Porter, M.E. (1980) *Competitive Strategy: Techniques for Analyzing Industries and Competitors*, Glencoe: Free Press.

Prahalad, C.K. & Hamel, G. (1990), The core competence of the corporation, *Harvard Business Review*, **68** (3), 79-91.

Prayag, G. (2009) Tourists' evaluations of destination image, satisfaction and behavioural intentions – the case of Mauritius, *Journal of Travel & Tourism Marketing*, **26** (8), 836-85.3

Price, L.L., Arnould, E.J. and Tierney, P. (1995) Going to extremes: managing service encounters and assessing provider performance, *Journal of Marketing* **59** (2), 83

Rawlins, B. (2009) Give the emperor a mirror: toward developing a stakeholder measurement of organizational transparency, *Journal of Public Relations Research* **21** (1), 71–99.

Reed-Danahay, D. (1996) Champagne and chocolate: taste and inversion in a French wedding ritual, *American Anthropologist* **98** (4),750–761.

Richardson, B. and Turley, D. (2007) It's far more important than that: football fandom and cultural capital, *European Advances in Consumer Research* **8**, 33–38.

Ritzer, G., Dean, P. and Jurgenson, N. (2012) The coming of age of the prosumer, *American Behavioral Scientist* **56** (4), 379–398.

Rojek, C. (1995) *Decentring Leisure: Rethinking Leisure Theory*, London: Sage

Romero, P. (2008) Beware of green marketing, warns Greenpeace exec, ABS-CBN News, available at https://abs-cbnnews.com/special-report/09/16/08/beware-green-marketing-warns-greenpeace-exec

Russell, C.A. and Levy, S.J. (2011) The temporal and focal dynamics of volitional reconsumption: a phenomenological investigation of repeated hedonic experiences, *Journal of Consumer Research*, **39**(2), 341-359

Said, E. (1995) *Orientalism: Western Conceptions of the Orient*, London: Penguin History.

Saussure, F. (1983) *Courses in General Linguistics*, trans. W. Baskin, London: Duckworth.

Schau, H.J. (2000) Consumer imagination, identity and self expression, in S.J. Hoch and R.J. Meyer (eds), *Advances in Consumer Research*, vol. 27, Provo, UT: Association for Consumer Research, pp. 50–56.

Schau, H. J., Muniz Jr, A. M., & Arnould, E. J. (2009). How brand community practices create value. *Journal of Marketing, 73*(5), 30-51.

Schor, J.B. and Ford, M. (2007) From tastes great to cool: children's food marketing and the rise of the symbolic, *Journal of Law, Medicine and Ethics* **35** (1), 10–21

Schroeder, J.E. and Zwick, D. (2004) Mirrors of masculinity: representation and identity in advertising images, *Consumption Markets and Culture* **7** (1), 21–52.

Schwartz, R., & Halegoua, G. R. (2015). The spatial self: Location-based identity performance on social media. *New Media & Society,* **17**(10), 1643-1660.

Sheldrake, P. (2001) *Spaces for the Sacred: Place, Memory and Identity,* Cambridge: SCM Press.

Sheth, J. N., and Solomon, M. R. (2014). Extending the extended self in a digital world. *Journal of Marketing Theory and Practice,* **22**(2), 123-132.

Sheringham, C. and Daruwalla, P. (2007) Transgressing hospitality: polarities and disordered relationships?, in C. Lashley, P.A. Lynch and A. Morrison (eds), *Hospitality: A Social Lens,* Oxford: Elsevier.

Sherry, J.F. Jr. (1983) Gift giving in anthropological perspective, *Journal of Consumer Research* **10** (2), 157–168.

Sherry, J.F. Jr. (1990) Dealers and dealing in a periodic market: informal retailing in ethnographic perspective, *Journal of Retailing* **66** (2), 174–200.

Shostack, G. L. (1977). Breaking free from product marketing. *The Journal of Marketing,* **41**, 73-80.

Silverstone, R. (1988) Television, myth and culture, in J. Carey (ed.) *Media, Myths and Narratives,* Newbury Park, CA: Sage.

Smith, A. (2005) Conceptualizing city image change: the "re-imaging" of Barcelona, *Tourism Geographies* **7** (4), 398–423.

Smith, P. (1999) Food truck's party hat, *Qualitative Inquiry* **5** (2), 244–261

Smith, W. R. (1956). Product differentiation and market segmentation as alternative marketing strategies. *Journal of Marketing,* **21**(1), 3-8.

Solomon, M.R. (1983) The role of products as social stimuli: a symbolic interactionism perspective, *Journal of Consumer Research* **10** (3), 319–329.

Solomon, M.R. (2006) *Consumer Behaviour: A European Perspective,* Harlow: Financial Times Prentice Hall.

Solomon, M.R. (2013) *Consumer Behaviour: Buying, Having and Being,* 10th edn, Pearson.

Solomon, M. R., Surprenant, C., Czepiel, J. A., & Gutman, E. G. (1985). A role theory perspective on dyadic interactions: the service encounter. *The Journal of Marketing,* **49**(1), 99-111.

Solomon, M., Bamossy, G., Askegaard, S., & Hogg, M. (2010). *Consumer Behavior: Buying: A European Perspective*. FT Prentice Hall

Sturma, M. (1999), Packaging Polynesia's image, *Annals of Tourism Research,* **26** (3), 712-715.

Sunderland, P.L. and Denny, R.M.T. (2007) *Doing Anthropology in Consumer Research*, Walnut Creek, CA: Left Coast.

Swarbrook, J. (1998) *Sustainable Tourism Management*, Wallingford: CAB International.

Thomas, T. C., Price, L. L., & Schau, H. J. (2013). When differences unite: Resource dependence in heterogeneous consumption communities. *Journal of Consumer Research*, **39**(5), 1010-1033.

Thompson, C.J. (1996) Caring consumers: Gendered consumption meanings and the juggling lifestyle, *Journal of Consumer Research* **22**(4) 388-407.

Thompson, C.J. (2004) Marketplace mythology and discourses of power, *Journal of Consumer Research* **31** (1), 162–180.

Thompson, C. J., Arnould, E., & Giesler, M. (2013). Discursivity, difference, and disruption: Genealogical reflections on the consumer culture theory heteroglossia. *Marketing Theory*, **13**(2), 149-174.

Thompson, C.J. and Arsel, Z. (2004), The Starbucks brandscape and consumers' (anticorporate) experiences of glocalization, *Journal of Consumer Research,* **31** (3), 631-642.

Thompson, C.J. and Hayto, D. (1997) Speaking of fashion: Consumers' uses of fashion discourses and the appropriation of countervailing cultural meanings, *Journal of Consumer Research*. **24** (1).

Thompson, C.J. and Holt, D.B. (2004) How do men grab the phallus? Gender tourism in everyday consumption, *Journal of Consumer Culture* **4**(3) 313-338.

Thompson, C.J. and Troester, M. (2002) Consumer value systems in the age of postmodern fragmentation: the case of the natural health microculture, *Journal of Consumer Research* **28** (4), 550–571.

Thompson, C., & Tian, K. (2008). Reconstructing the south: how commercial myths compete for identity value through the ideological shaping of popular memories and countermemories. *Journal of Consumer Research*, **34**(5), 595-613.

Thurlow, C. and Aiello, G. (2007) National pride, global capital: a social semiotic analysis of transnational visual branding in the airline industry, *Visual Communication* **6** (3), 305–344.

Titscher, S. Meyer, M. *et al.* (2000) *Methods of Text and Discourse Analysis*, London: Sage.

Tresidder, R. (1999) Sacred spaces, in D. Crouch (ed.) *Leisure Tourism Geographies: Practices and Geographical Knowledge*, London: Routledge.

Tresidder, R. (2001) The representations of sacred spaces in a post-industrial society, in M. Cotter, W. Boyds and J. Gardiner (eds), *Heritage Landscapes: Understanding Place and Communities*, Southern Cross University, pp. 65–76.

Tresidder, R. (2010a) What no pasties!? Reading the Cornish tourism brochure, *Journal of Travel and Tourism Marketing* **27** (6), 596–611.

Tresider, R. (2010b) Reading food marketing: the semiotics of Marks and Spencer, *International Journal of Sociology and Social Policy* **30** (9/10), 472–485.

Tresidder, R. (2011a) Reading hospitality: the semiotics of Le Manoir aux Quat' Saisons, *Hospitality and Society* **1** (1), 67–84.

Tresidder, R. (2011b) Health and medical tourism, in P. Robinson, S. Heitmann and P. Dieke (eds), *Research Themes in Tourism*, London: CAB International,

Tumbat, G. and Belk, R.W. (2011) Marketplace tensions in extraordinary experiences, *Journal of Consumer Research* **38** (1), 42–61.

Turner, V. (1977) Process, performance and pilgrimage: a study, in L.P. Vidyarthi (ed.), *Comparative Symbology*, New Delhi: Concept.

Urry, J. (2001) *The Tourist Gaze: Leisure and Travel in Contemporary Society*, London: TCS.

Uzzell, D. (1984) An alternative structuralist approach to the psychology of tourism marketing, *Annals of Tourism Research* **11**, 87–99.

van der Veen, M. (2003) When food is a luxury?, *World Archaeology* **34** (3), 405–427

Vargo, S.L. & Lusch, R.F. (2004), Evolving to a new dominant logic for marketing, *Journal of Marketing*, **68** (1), 1-17.

Vargo, S.L. and Lusch, R.F. (2008a) Service-dominant logic: continuing the evolution, *Journal of the Academy of Marketing Science* **36** (1), 1–10.

Vargo, S.L. and Lusch, R.F. (2008b) Why service, *Journal of the Academy of Marketing Science* **36** (1), 25–38.

Waitt, G. and Head, L. (2002) Postcards and frontier mythologies: sustaining views of the Kimberley as timeless, *Environment and Planning: Society and Space* **20** (3), 319–344.

Wallendorf, M., & Arnould, E. J. (1991). "We gather together": consumption rituals of Thanksgiving Day. *Journal of Consumer Research*, (1), 13-31

Wang, Yu & Fesenmaier, 2001 CHAP 4

Willets, D. (2011) *The Pinch: How The Baby Boomers Took Their Children's Future - And Why They Should Give It Back*, Atlantic Books

Winstead, K.F. (2000) Service behaviors that lead to satisfied customers, *European Journal of Marketing* **34** (3/4), 399–417.

Index

Printed in the United States
By Bookmasters